LETTERS IN GOLD

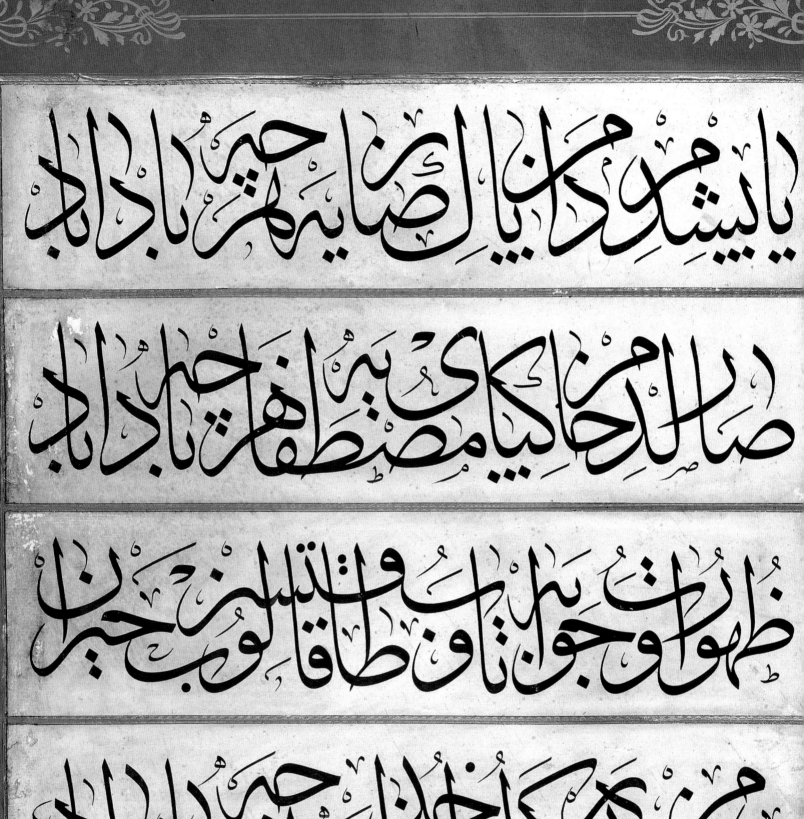

LETTERS IN GOLD

OTTOMAN CALLIGRAPHY
FROM THE
SAKIP SABANCI COLLECTION,
ISTANBUL

M. UĞUR DERMAN

THE METROPOLITAN MUSEUM OF ART, NEW YORK

Distributed by Harry N. Abrams, Inc., New York

This publication is issued in conjunction with the exhibition "Letters in Gold: Ottoman Calligraphy from the Sakıp Sabancı Collection, Istanbul, held at The Metropolitan Museum of Art, New York, September 11, 1998– December 13, 1998; at the Los Angeles County Museum of Art, February 25, 1999– May 17, 1999; and at the Arthur M. Sackler Museum, Harvard University Art Museums, Cambridge, Massachusetts, October 9, 1999– January 2, 2000.

The exhibition is made possible by
SABANCI HOLDING / AKBANK
Istanbul, Turkey.

The exhibition was organized by The Metropolitan Museum of Art and the Los Angeles County Museum of Art.

Published by The Metropolitan Museum of Art, New York

John P. O'Neill, Editor in Chief
Jane Bobko, Editor
Patrick Seymour, Designer
Gwen Roginsky, Production Manager

The Turkish text was translated by Mohamed Zakariya, with assistance from Dr. Esin Atıl, Elif Gökçiğdem, İbrahim Kalın, Heath Lowry, and Cinuçen Tanrıkorur.

Some of the text in this catalogue previously appeared, in somewhat different form, in M. Uğur Derman's essay "Calligraphy," translated by Priscilla Mary Işın, in *The Sabancı Collection* (Istanbul, 1995). Işın's translation served as a helpful source for this translation.

Photography by Bruce White

Kıt'a and *hilye* drawings based on originals by Ersu Pekin; *tuğra* drawing from original in the Derman Collection, Istanbul

Printed on 135 gsm Leykam Magnomatt
Color separations by Mas Matbaacılık A.Ş., Istanbul
Printed and bound by Mas Matbaacılık A.Ş., Istanbul

Jacket/Cover illustration: *Tuğra* from *berat* of Murad III, 983/1575. Sakıp Sabancı Collection, Istanbul (cat. no. 65, detail)

Frontispiece: Çırçırlı Ali Efendi (d. 1320/1902), *Levha*, 1297/1880. Sakıp Sabancı Collection, Istanbul (cat. no. 44, detail)

Library of Congress Cataloging-in-Publication Data

Derman, M. Uğur.
    Letters in gold : Ottoman calligraphy from the Sakıp Sabancı collection, Istanbul / M. Uğur Derman.
        p.   cm.
    Catalog of an exhibition held at The Metropolitan Museum of Art, Sept. 11– Dec. 13, 1998, the Los Angeles County Museum of Art, Feb. 25–May 17, 1999, the Harvard University Art Museums, Oct. 9, 1999–Jan. 2, 2000.
    Includes bibliographical references and index.
        ISBN 0–87099–873–0 (hc). —
    ISBN 0–87099–874–9 (pbk. : alk. paper). —
    ISBN 0–8109–6526–7 (Abrams)
        1. Calligraphy, Ottoman—Exhibitions. 2. Calligraphy, Islamic—Turkey—Exhibitions. 3. Sabancı, Sakıp, 1933– —Art collections— Exhibitions. 4. Calligraphy—Private collections—Turkey—Istanbul—Exhibitions. I. Metropolitan Museum of Art (New York, N.Y.). II. Los Angeles County Museum of Art. III. Harvard University. Art Museums. IV. Title.
NK3636.5.A2D47 1998
745.6'19927'0956—dc 21   98-21945
                                                    CIP

Contents

Collector's Foreword

I would like to express my gratitude for the opportunity to exhibit a selection of Ottoman calligraphy from the Sakıp Sabancı Collection at such prestigious, world-renowned institutions as The Metropolitan Museum of Art, New York, and the Los Angeles County Museum of Art. The Sakıp Sabancı Collection of Ottoman Calligraphy includes works dating from the fifteenth through the mid-twentieth century and is the largest such private collection in Turkey. It is particularly satisfying for me to be able to share with an American audience this remarkable art that is so emblematic of my own national heritage, but which is still little known in the West.

Among the many glorious arts of the Ottoman period, pride of place was given to calligraphy, which was regarded as the most prestigious form of art. The Ottoman sultans, some of whom were themselves accomplished in the art of writing, supported calligraphers in much the same way as princes and wealthy patrons in the West sponsored painters. As did Western painters through the nineteenth century, Turkish calligraphers shaped their art through study and emulation of the works of earlier masters. Apart from the obvious beauty of Ottoman calligraphy, what most appeals to me is the important relationship between master and apprentice, and the infinite capacity of this art to renew itself from one generation to the next. This notion of respect for and veneration of earlier generations has special resonance for me.

My father, Hacı Ömer Sabancı, was born in the village of Akçakaya in central Anatolia—the son of a poor family of farmers. He did not have the opportunity to go to school; he did not learn to read and write. At the age of twenty, he left home in search of work, walking 125 miles to the city of Adana, where he began working as a laborer in the cotton fields. He took advantage of the opportunities offered to him and finally became the owner of a cotton yarn and textile factory. In time, his business grew, and he moved to Istanbul. Although Istanbul's cosmopolitan environment gave my father a healthy appetite for art and culture and he began to collect antiques, he never forgot his roots.

My father instilled in his children a pride in our heritage; we are as closely linked to our past as we are to one another. He also inculcated in us a deep appreciation of education and a love of art.

As part of the modernization movement initiated by Mustafa Kemal Atatürk, the founder of the Turkish Republic, the Latin alphabet was introduced in 1928 and the Arabic alphabet was virtually abandoned. I belong to the generation that learned to read and write modern Turkish. Although I do not know the Arabic alphabet, Ottoman calligraphy has become my main focus as a collector. Initially, I was attracted by the beauty and majesty of this art form; later on, I came to understand the importance of protecting and preserving Ottoman calligraphy so that it might be appreciated by a new generation in Turkey and elsewhere.

I am enormously pleased to offer the first exhibition in the New World dedicated exclusively to Ottoman calligraphy and to introduce to an American audience the rich culture exemplified by these works of art.

Sakıp Sabancı

Directors' Foreword

The exhibition "Letters in Gold: Ottoman Calligraphy from the Sakıp Sabancı Collection, Istanbul" brings to The Metropolitan Museum of Art and the Los Angeles County Museum of Art seventy-one rare and beautiful calligraphies and illuminated manuscripts from the magnificent collection assembled by the prominent Turkish businessman and philanthropist Sakıp Sabancı. It is thanks to his generosity and enlightened initiative that these treasures are being shared for the first time with an international public. These remarkable pieces are usually housed in his private residence overlooking the Bosphorus.

Almost every major Ottoman calligrapher working in the fifteenth to the early twentieth century is represented in the Sabancı Collection by important examples of calligraphy. The manuscripts include exquisitely illuminated Qur'ans and prayer handbooks, elegant albums or *murakkaalar* composed of calligraphic exercises and often decorated with sumptuous marbled paper called *ebrû,* and spectacular, large-scale lettered compositions, called *levhalar,* which were framed and hung in mosques and homes. In addition, the exhibition displays eleven royal edicts, beautifully crafted scrolls topped by the *tuğra,* a sultan's imperial monogram. Fine, rich gold letters and delicate blue-and-gold illuminations demonstrate how the written word can be transformed into a work of art.

Sakıp Sabancı is justifiably proud of his Anatolian origins and of his father's modest beginnings in Adana, Turkey. He has devoted some of the profits of his company—now one of Turkey's largest industrial groups—toward building numerous schools and hospitals throughout the country.

Because Mr. Sabancı considers the Ottoman Empire's aesthetic traditions important and feels it imperative that they be preserved, he has assembled his extraordinary collection with a view toward sharing it with as large a public as possible. Toward that end The Metropolitan Museum of Art and the Los Angeles County Museum of Art are privileged to show to their visitors these high exemplars of Ottoman civilization.

Throughout the planning and realization of this exhibition, the Metropolitan Museum enjoyed the support of the government of the Republic of Turkey, and we are especially grateful to the Minister of

Foreign Affairs, İsmail Cem; the Minister of Culture, Mustafa Istemihan Talay; Tekin Aybaş, Undersecretary, Ministry of Culture; and the Turkish Ambassador to the United States, Nuzhet Kandemir, for their indispensable cooperation.

The primary mover, aside from Mr. Sabancı, in bringing these magnificent treasures to the American museum-going public is Mahrukh Tarapor, Associate Director for Exhibitions, at the Metropolitan Museum. Curatorial guidance and expertise for the exhibition and catalogue were provided by Linda Komaroff, Associate Curator of Islamic Art, Los Angeles County Museum of Art, and at the Metropolitan by Stefano Carboni, Associate Curator, Department of Islamic Art. Staff members from both institutions were privileged in Istanbul to work closely with Mr. Sabancı's knowledgeable representatives, Ali Haydar Taşlı, private executive officer; Arzu Çekirge Paksoy, advertising and public relations manager; and Orhan Kural, Akbank representative. We also extend special thanks to Raffi Portakal for his guidance, hospitality, and ready assistance at all times, and to Hülya Karadeniz who efficiently and effectively coordinated various aspects of the exhibition with both our institutions.

The richly illustrated catalogue accompanying the exhibition is published by The Metropolitan Museum of Art under the direction of John P. O'Neill, Editor in Chief and General Manager of Publications, in close collaboration with the Los Angeles County Museum of Art, especially Linda Komaroff. Its authoritative text was written by the foremost expert on the subject, M. Uğur Derman, a professor at Mimar Sinan University, Istanbul, and a trained calligrapher.

The Metropolitan Museum of Art and the Los Angeles County Museum of Art are honored to be the only American venues for this distinguished collection, and we offer sincere thanks to Sakıp Sabancı and Sabancı Holding/Akbank Istanbul for making the exhibition and catalogue possible.

Philippe de Montebello
Director
The Metropolitan Museum of Art

Graham W. J. Beal
Director
Los Angeles County
Museum of Art

Acknowledgments

Sakıp Sabancı has managed to bridge the past and the future with this exhibition of magnificent works of art from his collection—testaments to a great cultural heritage. Through the initiative of Mahrukh Tarapor of The Metropolitan Museum of Art, these works are being exhibited to the American public for the first time, and the stage has been set for a renewed appreciation of Ottoman arts. This book is not just a catalogue; it has become a handbook of Turkish calligraphy thanks to the guidance and encouragement of Hülya Karadeniz in Istanbul and Linda Komaroff of the Los Angeles County Museum of Art.

My primary obligation is to acknowledge my debt to Necmeddin Okyay (1883–1976), Mâhir İz (1895–1974), Dr. Süheyl Ünver (1898–1986), Mâcid Ayral (1891–1961), Mustafa Halim Özyazıcı (1898–1964), and Nihad M. Çetin (1924–1991). These friends and mentors were crucial figures in my education in the art of calligraphy and other arts of the book.

The computer specialists Ersu Pekin and Nejla Somalı worked closely with me. I received generous advice from Dr. Çiçek Derman on the illumination and decorative aspects of the works in the catalogue, and from Professor Mehmed İpşirli of the University of Istanbul on the historical and technical aspects of the *beratlar, fermanlar,* and *menşûrlar.* Dr. Halil Sahillioğlu, professor emeritus at the University of Istanbul, helped me calculate the value today, in American dollars, of Ottoman currency.

My old American friend Mohamed Zakariya, a knowledgeable calligrapher himself, translated my text into English accurately and on a tight schedule; Jane Bobko carefully edited the result. Professor Zikri Altun of Marmara University, Istanbul, assisted with the translation of some fine points in the text. John P. O'Neill and his staff at the Metropolitan Museum; Bruce White, who photographed the works with such artistry; and Mas Matbaacılık A.Ş., Istanbul, also contributed their expertise to this undertaking.

Here I offer my deepest thanks to all those who shared in making *Letters in Gold* a reality.

And if you, the reader, should admire the contents of this book, you, too, are included in my thanks.

M. Uğur Derman

Note to the Reader

The Prophet Muhammad (A.D. ca. 570–632) fled from Mecca, and from persecution by the city's pagan establishment, to Medina to preach his religion in the year A.D. 622. Muslims take the date of this flight (*hijra*) as the beginning of their calendar. The Islamic calendar is a lunar calendar consisting of twelve months, each 29.5 days long, for a total of 354 days. Thus the Islamic year is eleven days shorter than the solar year, which is the basis for the Western calendar. As a result, for every 33 Western years, there are 34 Islamic years; for every 100 solar years, there are 103 lunar ones. Islamic calligraphers used the lunar *hijra* calendar to date their works.

In this text, dates are given Western-style. The dates of calligraphic works and of calligraphers' lives, however, are given according to both the lunar and the solar calendars, with the *hijra* date supplied first.

This book deals with an Ottoman subject. At the request of the author, the names of the chapters of the Qur'an, and all other Qur'anic terminology, are given in Turkish transliteration. Thus the Qur'anic invocation of Allah, commonly transliterated as the *basmala*, is given here as the *besmele*. All technical terms, even those of Arabic origin, are given their Turkish spellings. These terms, which include the names of scripts, represent original, unique, and distinct categories of artistic style and content that have no specific analogues in English. Each term is defined or described at its first mention in the text. Turkish plurals, most of which are formed by the addition of *-ler* or *-lar*, are also employed.

Turkish orthography—in 1928, the Arabic alphabet that had been used to write Turkish was replaced by a modified version of the Latin one—includes a number of letters and symbols that will be unfamiliar to the general reader. Here is a list, along with pronunciation:

c	*j, as in jar*	j	*s, as in pleasure*
ç	*ch, as in cheese*	ö	*the German ö*
ğ	*usually a silent letter*	ş	*sh, as in ship*
ı	*a, as in cereal*	ü	*the German ü*
i	*i, as in pit*		

A circumflex, or *şapka* (hat), placed over a vowel lengthens it.

During Ottoman times, Muslim children were usually given a single name at birth. To distinguish themselves further, they would often take on names that identified their fathers or referred to their occupation or place of origin. A young man could take on a *künye*, or patronymic, using the Persian suffix *-zâde* (son of), as in Yesârîzâde, or the Arabic word for "son," *ibn* or *bin*, as in İbni'ş Şeyh or Hasan bin Mustafa.

A place name could also be added to a person's name, using either the Arabic ending *-î* or the Turkish ending *-li* (or *-lı*). Thus, Mustafa Kütâhî and Kütahyalı Mustafa both describe Mustafa of Kütahya. A word signifying a person's occupation, rank, or title could also be applied as a name. For example, the calligrapher Mustafa Râkım, named Mustafa at birth, acquired the appellation Râkım, which means "Writer" or "Calligrapher," when he became an accomplished artist. Other examples include Kâdıasker (Supreme Judge) Mustafa İzzet Efendi, Çömez (Apprentice) Mustafa Efendi, and Şeyh (Sheikh) Hamdullah. Nicknames were also possible, as in Deli (Crazy) Osman.

Honorifics such as Efendi (Master, Gentleman) or Hanım (Lady) were used by members of literate or clerical society. A person who had made the pilgrimage to Mecca was called Hacı (Pilgrim). The title Bey (Sir, Mister) has a less religious connotation and was more closely associated with civil authorities.

Over the course of their lives, people might acquire more than one such appellation. Repeating the entire multipart name can be unwieldy and repetitous, and for that reason, the names can be shortened in various ways. Yesârî Mehmed Es'ad Efendi, for example, can properly be referred to as Yesârî Mehmed Efendi, Yesârî Efendi, Mehmed Es'ad Efendi, or Es'ad Efendi—often within the same paragraph. This usage is reflected in this book for the sake of simplicity and readability, and as an example of Turkish style.

The works in this catalogue were measured in centimeters. Dimensions are given in centimeters followed by inches, which have been rounded off to the nearest eighth of an inch. Height precedes width. Folios are identified as *r* (recto) or *v* (verso). In Ottoman books, the recto is the left-hand page; the verso is the right-hand page.

LETTERS IN GOLD

*Figure 1. Mustafa Halim Özyazıcı
(1315/1898–1384/1964), Besmele,
1379/1959. Ink on paper, celî sülüs,
8.8 × 30.4 cm (3⅛ × 11⅞ in.).
Sakıp Sabancı Collection,
Istanbul (238)*

The Art of Turkish Calligraphy

Art is not the monopoly of any society. Only when a society stamps its character on an art can the art be claimed, and recognized, as an expression of that society's identity.

The Ottoman Turks had such an art: calligraphy. This art was not Turkish in origin. But having adopted it with religious fervor and inspiration, the Ottomans created marvels. Turkish calligraphy is a unique artistic creation.

When we speak of "Turkish calligraphy," we refer to writing of aesthetic value based on the letters of the Arabic alphabet, which the Turks had adopted after their conversion to Islam. The process by which the Arabic alphabet acquired its aesthetic characteristics was slow at first, but from the mid-eighth century that process began to accelerate. By the time the Turks joined the Islamic world in the tenth century, calligraphy was already an important art form. It is necessary, therefore, to review briefly the structure of the original Arabic alphabet and its development during the early centuries of Islam.

FROM ALPHABET TO ART

"Calligraphy is a spiritual geometry produced by a material instrument." This succinct aesthetic dictum, found in early Islamic sources, has guided the development of calligraphy.

Before the advent of Islam, the North Arabian tribe called the Nabataeans lived in what is today Jordan and Syria. Their main cities were Hijr, Petra, and Bostra, and their writing system was called *nabatī*. The Arabic alphabet originated with *nabatī*, which itself originated with Phoenician. In its early form, the Arabic script consisted only of rudimentary shapes, giving no indication of its future potential as a powerful artistic medium. With the emergence of Islam, however, and especially after the *hijra*—that is, Muhammad's flight from Mecca to Medina in 622 to escape persecution and preach the new religion—Arabic writing was ennobled, becoming Islam's primary means of visual expression.

Calligraphy had its origins in religion, as Muslims searched for the

3

Figure 2. Calligraphy exercises. Top sheet: nineteenth-century Ottoman sülüs. *Middle and bottom sheets:* meşkler *written by Suud Yavsi (1299/1882–1367/1948) for his teacher Hattat Kâmil Akdik (1278/1861–1360/1941). In the middle* meşk, *the first line* (sülüs) *and the third line* (nesih) *are the student's; the second and fourth lines show the teacher's corrections. The bottom* meşk *is in* celî dîvânî, *the top line by the student, the line below it by the teacher. Derman Collection, Istanbul*

most suitable way to make the sacred book of Islam, the Qur'an, a volume or codex (*mushaf*) whose physical beauty would reflect its spiritual beauty. In the Arabic writing system, most letters undergo a change of form according to their position at the beginning, middle, or end of a word, or when they stand alone. As this basic writing system was transformed into an art, the letters acquired highly supple shapes. A rich visual effect was achieved by writing the letters in strategic relationship to one another; the top sheet in figure 2 demonstrates many combinations, in nineteenth-century Ottoman *sülüs*, of the letter *bâ* (B) with the letter *mim* (M). It was possible to write the same word or phrase in many ways, opening the door to an endless search for new styles and novel approaches. The letters varied to an astonishing degree, depending on which of various scripts was used and by which calligrapher.

The Arabic alphabet was adopted, primarily as a token of religious allegiance, by virtually all of the peoples who converted to Islam. Within a few centuries after the *hijra*, the alphabet had become the shared property of the entire Muslim world. "Arabic calligraphy," a term appropriate to the early period when Islam was limited to the Arab lands, grew over time into what more accurately might be described as "Islamic calligraphy."

The number of people literate in Arabic multiplied rapidly, and in time the script was perfected into a vehicle suitable for recording the Qur'an—and hence the Arabic language itself, in which the sacred book was revealed—with precision. Vowel signs known as *hareke* were invented to accompany the all-consonantal alphabet (three of the consonants, however, can double as vowels). Letters identical in form but different in sound were distinguished by variously placed dots and groups of dots. As time passed, the use of these diacritics to differentiate letters became universal. Both the diacritics and the vowel signs, as well as the symbol indicating undotted letters (*hurûf-ı mühmele*), acquired decorative forms, which played a major role in the development of writing as an art. Meanwhile, the frequently used Arabic definite article, consisting of the letters *alif* and *lām* (*al-*), became an aesthetic balancing element.

In the pre-Islamic era, depending on the cultural center at the time, Arabic writing was known variously as *anbârî*, *hîrî*, and *mekkî* (Meccan). After the *hijra*, it was known as *medenî* (Medinan). Artistic considerations were not a concern for the original Qur'an copyists. The first Islamic text compiled in book form, the Qur'an was initially written in the *mekkî/medenî* script, in black or dark brown ink on animal-skin parchment, without vowel signs or diacritics. In time, this early writing evolved into two forms. One was a sharply angled form reserved for the Qur'an and important correspondence; this form became known as *kûfî* (Kufic), after the city of Kufa, in Iraq, where it was most often used.

The other form, which was more rounded and flexible and could be written more quickly, was used for day-to-day purposes. Under the Ummayad caliphate (661–750), this form of writing spread and evolved rapidly in Damascus, the capital of the Arab empire. Following the development, in the eighth century, of pens whose nibs were cut to different widths, this style of writing gave rise to new scripts, named for the pens with which they were written. Among the earliest of these scripts were *celîl*, reserved for large-scale lettering, and *tûmâr* (a very large script, and pen, for use on scrolls), which was the standard in official correspondence. Some of the new scripts were based on *tûmâr* (Turkish *tomar*) and written with pens whose nibs were in specific proportion to the *tûmâr* pen. Pens with nibs two-thirds as wide as the nib of the *tûmâr* pen were known as *sülüseyn* (two-thirds), and those with nibs one-third as wide were known as *sülüs* (one-third). As the pens were scaled down, the scripts took on specific features of their own. Other new scripts that emerged, only to fall later into disuse, included *riyâsî*, *kalemü'n-nısf*, *hafîfü'n-nısf*, and *hafîfü's-sülüs*.

At the same time, the word *kalem*, or pen, which referred to the writing instrument, came to be used for the writing itself. For example, the script *kalemü'n-nısf* literally means "half-size pen," because the nib employed is half as wide as the *tûmâr* nib. The term *hat*, or calligraphy, was used for scripts such as *kısas* and *muâmerat*, which were devised for special uses and did not involve the proportional scaling down of the pen.

Under the ʿAbbasid caliphate (750–1258), learning and the arts flourished, leading to a swelling demand for books in Baghdad, the main capital, and in other major cities. To meet this demand, the number of copyists and stationers, called *verrâklar*, also rose; the script they used for copying was variously known as *verrâkî*, *muhakkak* (no relation to the modern *muhakkak*), *neshî*, and *irâkî*.

From the end of the eighth century, the practice of writing letters in accordance with specific proportions and symmetries became known as *aslî hat*, or fundamental calligraphy, and *mevzûn hat*, or balanced calligraphy. The outstanding calligrapher of this period was Ibn Muqla (d. 328/940), who composed rules for proportioning and ordering writing. Writing done according to these principles was called *mensûb hattı*, or proportioned writing.

While these developments were taking place, the *kûfî* script was flourishing, especially for copying Qur'ans. Within *kûfî* there were regional variations, especially in Andalusia and North Africa, where the script took on a more rounded form called *magrıbî*. In Persia and the East, meanwhile, a *kûfî* variant called *meşrık kûfîsi* (Eastern *kûfî*) was used until it was superseded by the *aklâm-ı sitte*, or six scripts, discussed below. The large-scale form of *kûfî* known as *iri kûfî*, which is mainly used on monuments, was primarily decorative.

The form of *mensûb hattı* known as *verrâkî* was generally reserved for copying books and was therefore referred to as *neshî*, from the verb *istinsâh*, to copy. This script was the prototype for the *muhakkak*, *reyhânî*, and *nesih* scripts that emerged in the eleventh century. The finest calligrapher of this period, Ibn al-Bawwāb (d. 413/1024), amended the rules promulgated by Ibn Muqla, establishing a method that was widely used until the mid-thirteenth century. The calligrapher Ibn al-Khāzin (d. 518/1124) contributed to the development of the *tevkî'* and *rıkâ'* scripts. Finally, Yāqūt al-Mustaʿsimī (or Yāqūt; d. 698/1298), working in Baghdad, further developed the method elaborated by Ibn al-Bawwāb and wrote the finest thirteenth-century examples of *sülüs*, *nesih*, *muhakkak*, *reyhânî*, *tevkî'*, and *rıkâ'*, which are together known as the *aklâm-ı sitte*, or six scripts. The idea of cutting the nib of the reed pen at an angle instead of straight across was his, and it was an innovation that brought a great deal of elegance to calligraphy. Once the six scripts, with all their rules, had taken their place in the art of calligraphy, other scripts were abandoned. Today no trace remains of

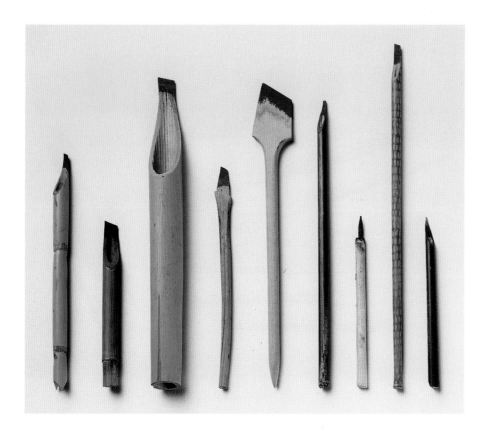

Figure 3. Calligraphy pens. From the left: three kargı kalemler, *made of reed or bamboo, for* celî *script; two wooden* ağaç kalemler, *for* celî *script; seasoned reed pen;* cava kalemi; menevişli kalem *(decorated pen) with a "tiger-skin" pattern; seasoned reed pen. Derman Collection, Istanbul*

these lost scripts except their names, among them, *sicillât, dîbâc, zenbûr, mufattah, harem, lûlûî, muallak,* and *mürsel.*

After Yāqūt's death, the master scribes who had studied under him carried his method of writing the six scripts from Baghdad to Anatolia, Egypt, Syria, Iran, and Transoxiana in Central Asia, where the art continued to attract interest. New generations of calligraphers in these lands dedicated themselves to Yāqūt's method. But as time passed, that method lost its originality. It remained for the Ottoman Turks to rescue the six scripts and develop them to their fullest, a story we shall continue after a brief look at the tools and materials used in the art of calligraphy.

TOOLS AND MATERIALS

The primary requisites for the tools employed in calligraphy are soundness and usability. But in the Ottoman period, artisans lavished more care and attention on these tools than on the tools of other trades, creating objects of great beauty. Many are of museum quality.

Used as both musical instrument (the *ney,* or flute) and pen, the reed evokes the mystical atmosphere of the Oriental Islamic world. Yellowish white reeds are harvested from the marshy banks of lakes and rivers in warm regions. They are not usable as pens in their natural state but first must be seasoned by burial (traditionally, for a period of four years) in horse manure, which maintains a constant moist warmth. During burial, the reeds harden and change color, becoming

Figure 4. Calligraphy tools. Clockwise from the top: çakmak mühre; makta *and* tashih kalemtıraşı; *penknives; scissors.* Türkpetrol Foundation, Istanbul

reddish brown, light or dark brown, or even black, depending on the type of reed (fig. 3).

When the reed is seasoned, the end is cut into an angled nib, which must be recut regularly as it wears. Even the slightest deviation in the width of the nib after recutting noticeably alters the appearance of the writing. This is considered a serious artistic flaw, especially in the case of *nesih* and other fine scripts. Therefore, in the case of long texts, such as the Qur'an, calligraphers use pens made from the hard, straight, slender thorn of a palm tree native to Indonesia and Malaysia. (Ottoman calligraphers discovered these pens in the early nineteenth century among Javanese Muslims who carried them on pilgrimages to Mecca.) These pens, which are called *cava kalemliri,* are extremely durable and require little recutting. For ease of use, the *cava kalemi* is affixed to a normal reed pen, which serves as a handle (fig. 3).

As the thickness of the writing increases, correspondingly thicker reeds are required. These are called *kargı kalemler,* or spear pens (fig. 3). Hard bamboo may be used. Even these pens, however, cannot accommodate some of the *celî* (large) scripts; in such cases, calligraphers use pens carved from wood, called *ağaç kalemler* or *tahta kalemler* (wooden pens; fig. 3). Extremely large *celî* inscriptions cannot be written directly by hand at all, as a pen big enough to produce the letters would be too heavy to hold. Such inscriptions are written first on a smaller scale and then enlarged by means of squaring.

To make the nib, the reed is laid on the palm of the left hand (if the calligrapher is right-handed), with the tip extending toward the wrist. The tip is cut away with a penknife called the *kalemtıraş,* held at a slant. The blade, known as the *tîg,* is mounted in a handle that is often

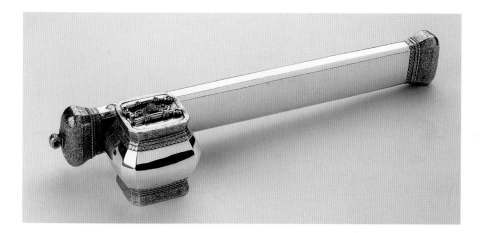

made of valuable materials, such as gold-inlaid steel, enameled gold, ivory, coral, mother-of-pearl, or ebony. The bolster that connects the blade to the handle is known as the *parazvana*. The penknife is commonly between four and eight inches in length. The master knife maker generally embosses his name on the blade; the makers' stamps are visible on the blades of the penknives in figure 4.

The pen is cut until the cavity of the hollow reed appears almond-shaped. The projecting tip that results is called the *kalem dili* (pen's tongue). The edges of the tongue are cut to obtain a nib of the desired width. The nib is then split to a depth of one-half to one and one-half inches. It is essential that the split (*çatlak*) be exactly parallel to the pen shaft. The opening thus formed becomes a reservoir that contains a small store of ink, which flows down to the nib as the calligrapher writes.

The nib is cut against the cutting surface of the *makta*, a small, flat piece of wood, ivory, tortoiseshell, or mother-of-pearl. These materials

Figure 7. Tools and materials. Clockwise from the top: rıhdan *(container for* rıh *powder), from disassembled* kubur; *rıh powder;* karalama, *in* nesih *script;* hokka, *from the* kubur; *lika; cylindrical brass* kubur *and pens. Derman Collection, Istanbul*

are hard enough to cut against but will not damage the edge of the penknife. (Figure 4 shows an engraved *makta*, made of silver and black polyester resin, with an inlaid ivory cutting pad, by the contemporary artist Salih Balakbabalar [b. 1950].) At one end of the *makta* is a small grooved protrusion. In cutting or recutting the nib, the calligrapher rests the pen in this groove, holds the handle of the pen securely, and brings the sharp blade of the penknife down to snip off the end of the nib. In cutting the *çatlak*, the calligrapher holds the knife parallel to the pen and presses down against it.

The angled nib results in writing that slants toward the calligrapher, who holds the pen so that the edge of the nib rests fully on the paper. Moving the pen from top to bottom, the calligrapher produces a fine perpendicular line. Moving the pen from right to left results in a thick line. Sometimes the calligrapher alters the angle of the pen to the work, to achieve a subtle effect. The proper size of the letters in each script is measured in dots, and the size of the dot depends on the width of the nib. Thus the pen is the most vital element in the aesthetic quality of calligraphy.

Pens are sometimes kept in a case containing an inkwell at one end, known as a *divit* (fig. 5), and sometimes in cylindrical or rectangular boxes called *kalemdanlar*, which may be plain or decorated. The cylindrical *kalemdan* is also called a *kubur* (fig. 7).

In the past, paper was not ready to be used as soon as it was procured from the factory. Because this raw paper was normally white and tired the eyes, it was first dyed. Then it was sized with a substance called *âhâr*, and finally burnished with a tool called a *çakmak mühre* to smooth the surface and stabilize the *âhâr* coating. This process, still used by calligraphers today, results in a paper that is as glossy and smooth as though it had been calendered between rollers.

Vegetable dyes are generally used to color the paper. The dye material is boiled in water, which is then poured into a trough. The paper is soaked in the dye until it reaches the desired color, then set aside to dry. A cream or tan color produced from tea is the most popular. Among the other substances used to dye papers, and the colors they produce, are pomegranate skins and the green outer skins of walnuts (brown); seeds of *cehrî*, or dyer's buckthorn (yellow); red logwood (red); purple logwood (purple); the dark brown soot formed in the chimney of a confectioner's stove during the production of caramel (yellowish white); and onion skins (reddish). If desired, the margins of the paper can be dyed a different color from the writing area. A paper prepared this way is called *akkâse* (fig. 13).

After dying, according to the ancient rules, a coating of *âhâr* size is applied over the paper surface to prevent the soot-based ink from penetrating the fibers of the paper. Because the ink remains on the surface, imperfections in the writing, such as the ragged edges that are sometimes produced on letters during the pen stroke, may be removed by wiping the area with a bit of cotton, licking the surface, or scraping it with a special knife called the *tashih kalemtıraşı* (correction knife; fig. 4). Papers prepared with *âhâr* also improve with age. The most common size is egg whites mixed with alum and applied with a sponge. Starch or flour boiled with water into a thin paste can also be used. If the raw paper is not burnished within a week after being sized, the size will crack during the burnishing process, and the paper will be ruined.

The paper is burnished with the *çakmak mühre* (fig. 4), a wooden tool with handles on either end and a protruding piece of polished flint in the center. The paper is laid on a large, smooth panel of wood. To ensure that the *mühre* glides evenly over the surface of the paper, the paper is rubbed first with a piece of woolen fabric that has itself been rubbed over a bar of soap. Then, holding the *mühre* by its two handles, stone down, the calligrapher exerts pressure on the stone and moves it forward and backward over the paper, which is free to move on the wooden panel. Soon the paper begins to acquire a bright sheen. The paper is then stored for at least a year, until it is ready for use. Only when the paper has been sized, burnished, and aged will the pen glide

easily over it. And only then is it possible to correct errors by wiping or
scraping. (Official documents of the Ottoman Empire, however, were
written on burnished but unsized paper—which absorbed ink—so as to
prevent forgery or alteration.)

To write on sized paper, it is necessary to wipe the paper lightly first
with a piece of woolen fabric dusted with chalk. The chalk removes the
slippery finish created by the soap that was used when the paper was
burnished. It also removes any trace of oil transferred to the paper by
handling, as ink will not take on an oily surface.

The palette in calligraphy is generally black lines, produced with
lampblack ink, on a light background (see fig. 1). The soot that is the
principal ingredient of lampblack ink (*is mürekkebi*) is obtained by
burning such substances as linseed oil, beeswax, naphtha, or kerosene.
Gum arabic, the other ingredient, serves to bind the carbon particles to
the paper. From the many formulas for producing this ink that have
been preserved, it is clear that the process has changed over time. The
final, most-developed formula calls for soot, dissolved gum arabic, and
distilled water, which are mixed and ground together for a long time.
This ink never fades.

In the case of artistic calligraphy, the ink was left to dry naturally.

But for official correspondence, a fine, colored sand called *rıh* or *rîk* was sprinkled over the writing (fig. 7). Literate people carried lampblack ink with them wherever they went, in portable inkwells.

In Ottoman calligraphy, the most commonly used of the many different colored inks were yellow, or *zırnık*, made of orpiment (a compound of sulfur and arsenic); red, or *lâl;* white, or *üstübeç*, made of white lead; and gold, or *zer*.

To make yellow ink—according to Ottoman tradition—the natural pigment called orpiment was combined with sodium, then vigorously ground with gum arabic and mixed with water. (*Altınbaş zırnığı*, or realgar, was sometimes used instead of orpiment, producing a more orange yellow.) Ruby red ink required mixing a substance called *lotur*, which has not been identified, with soapwort, alum, and water and then boiling them. Pulverized cochineal was added to this liquid, which was boiled again, yielding an extremely attractive red color. White ink was made using the same method as for yellow ink, substituting white lead for the orpiment. This white ink was primarily used for writing the *sûre*, or chapter, headings in illuminated Qur'ans. Gold ink was made by pulverizing high-karat gold leaf (fig. 8) into a fine powder in a thick solution of gum arabic or honey in a porcelain dish. Once this laborious task was accomplished, the substance was rinsed in water to remove the gum or honey, and the gold strained into another dish, leaving the finest gold dust. Gelatin dissolved in water was added (fig. 8). The gold ink was applied to the nib of the pen with a special brush as needed. This was the basis of the *zer-endûd*, or gold-painted, method.

In an age when all writing was done with reed pens and lampblack ink, the inkwell, or *hokka*, was a part of every ceramic writing set, wooden writing casket, and portable pen case. Inkwells could be ceramic or glass, but more frequently they were made of metal, such as brass, copper, or silver (figs. 6–7). The ink was not poured directly into these inkwells. Rather, a small wad of raw-silk fiber called *lika* (fig. 7) was inserted into the inkwell and the ink poured over it. The *lika* absorbed the ink like a sponge, ensuring that the pen would take up just the right amount of ink. The *lika* also ensured that the ink would not spill should the inkwell be overturned.

How letters and words are positioned, how they are arranged in relation to a straight line, and how far apart the lines are spaced are all dictated by calligraphic rules. To aid in his writing, the calligrapher created guidelines on the paper using a simple tool called a *mıstar*—a piece of cardboard with strands of thread stretched taut across it at regular intervals (fig. 9).

To make the *mıstar*, the calligrapher first calculated the proper spacing of lines on the manuscript page, according to the size of the measuring dot produced by the reed pen he was to use. He then drew the lines on a piece of cardboard the same size as the page, and, using a needle and a single strand of fine silk thread, made holes at the end

Figure 9. A sahife mıstarı, *or page ruler (top), and a* kıt'a mıstarı, *or* kıt'a *ruler (bottom). Derman Collection, Istanbul*

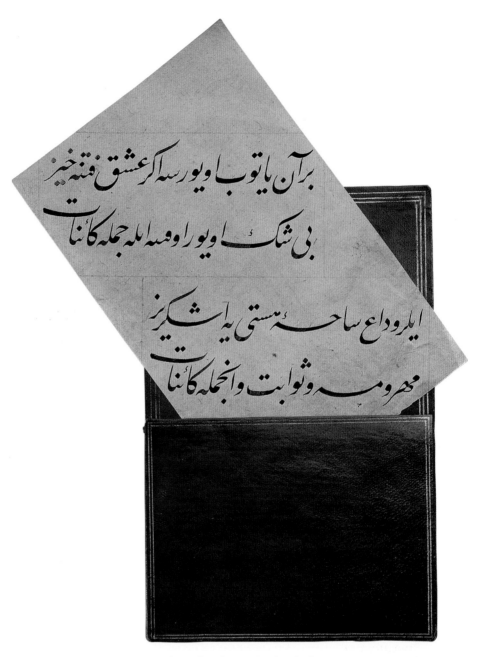

Figure 10. A ta'lîk yazı altlığı, *or leather cushion that simplifies writing a* mâil ta'lîk kıt'a. *The* kıt'a *is by Necmeddin Okyay (1300/1883–1396/1976). Derman Collection, Istanbul*

of each line and drew the silk through the hole at one end and across the cardboard to the hole at the other. The thread was also used to create guidelines indicating right and left margins. To use the *mıstar*, the calligrapher placed the prepared paper on the thread side of the cardboard and traced the threads with his finger, pressing hard enough to leave subtle impressions of the lines.

In Ottoman times, calligraphers did not sit on chairs and write at tables. They sat on sofas or cushions with their right knee raised and with the paper resting against the knee, a position that kept the paper perpendicular to the calligrapher's line of sight. To support the paper against the knee, the calligrapher used an *altlık*, a flexible pad of rough paper approximately eight inches by ten inches in size. Unlike a hard surface, a flexible pad allowed for movements of the hand. A special, differently shaped *altlık* was employed for writing *ta'lîk* script (fig. 10).

Ottoman scissors are handsome implements with long blades, designed for cutting sheets of paper evenly from larger sheets. Some pairs of scissors were produced with their owner's name in openwork on the handles (fig. 4). It is a great pleasure to use such a tool. Indeed, calligraphers relied on the high quality of all their tools and materials to produce the finest work.

THE EARLY TURKISH CONTRIBUTION TO CALLIGRAPHY

The Turks converted to Islam and adopted the Arabic alphabet by the tenth century, a century before the Turkish migrations into Anatolia. No artworks that would demonstrate an interest in calligraphy at this early date have survived. The earliest examples of the Turks' use of Arabic writing date from the Anatolian Seljuk period (1092–1308). During this time, the *kûfî* script was largely abandoned in favor of the "six scripts." *Kûfî* was reserved for book headings and monuments, where foliated or interlaced versions of it are found. In its architectural application, a geometrical version called *satrançlı* (chessboard) or *murabba'lı* (squared) *kûfî* was used; some sources call these scripts *ma'kılî* or *bennâî* (architectural). During the Beylik period (thirteenth to fourteenth century), when independent Turkish principalities succeeded the Seljuks, and from the beginning of the Ottoman Empire until the conquest of Constantinople (1299–1453), calligraphy in Anatolia appears to have been a continuation of the ʿAbbasid school. The calligrapher Şeyh Hamdullah (833/1429–926/1520; see cat. nos. 1–2) marks the beginning of the Ottoman predominance in calligraphy. Thereafter, the art followed a steady course of development into the twentieth century.

Before discussing the great masters who contributed to the evolution of the art, let us look at the scripts used in Ottoman calligraphy.

The six scripts can be divided into three groups, each consisting of two natural partners: *sülüs* and *nesih; muhakkak* and *reyhânî;* and *tevkî'* and *rıkâ'*. The first partner in each group (*sülüs, muhakkak,* and *tevkî'*) is written with a pen whose nib is approximately 2 millimeters (³⁄₃₂ inch) in width. The second partner (*nesih, reyhânî,* and *rıkâ'*) is written with a pen whose nib is approximately 1 millimeter (³⁄₆₄ inch) in width. *Muhakkak* and *tevkî'* are larger-scale versions of *reyhânî* and *rıkâ'*, respectively. *Sülüs* and *nesih*, however, do not fit this scheme, diverging substantially in form as well as in style. The very fine version of *nesih* is called *gubârî* (like dust), because the letters appear as small as motes of dust.

Of the six scripts, *sülüs* and *nesih* were especially compatible with Turkish taste. *Sülüs*, which is called the "mother of calligraphy" in historical sources, is the most amenable of the six scripts to artistic treatment. Its rounded and taut letters can attain great richness. Moreover,

this script gives calligraphers the greatest scope for creating *istifler*, or compositions (fig. 11). The advantages of *sülüs* are especially striking in the case of *celî sülüs* (*celî* means "large" here), which can be written with a broad-nibbed pen or enlarged for architectural inscriptions by means of squaring. A *sülüs* or *celî sülüs* line in which words or groups of letters are joined is known as *müselsel* (like a chain). An *istif* that uses a word or group of words written twice as a symmetrical mirror image, interlocked down the center, is known as *aynalı* or as a *müsennâ*. The terms are also applied when the two sides of a visually symmetrical composition have different texts, one side written normally and one in reverse. As for *nesih*, even though its letters are curved, they must be arranged in lines, making the script unsuitable for *istifler*. Instead, it is used for long texts. *Mushaflar* are commonly written in *nesih*, and early printing fonts were based on it.

Muhakkak and *reyhânî* are also suited to arrangement in lines, due to the predominance of straight lines in their letters. Until the sixteenth century, large-format Qur'ans were written in *muhakkak*, and smaller ones in *reyhânî*. These scripts were, however, for the most part eventually forgotten. Yet in order to improve their dexterity, calligraphers continued to copy the old masters' works in these scripts, which were found in *kıt'alar* (see pages 27–29) and albums. In addition, *muhakkak* has continued to be used for writing the *besmele*, the Qur'anic formula "In the name of God, the Compassionate, the Merciful." The *besmele*, which occurs at the beginning of each chapter of the Qur'an except chapter 9 (*Tevba*), is without doubt the phrase most often written in Ottoman calligraphy. (The *besmele* in *muhakkak* can be seen in the top line of the *hilye* in figure 19.)

The *tevkî'* and *rıkâ'* scripts were mainly used for official purposes and rarely for copying manuscripts. *Rıkâ'* was developed into a more

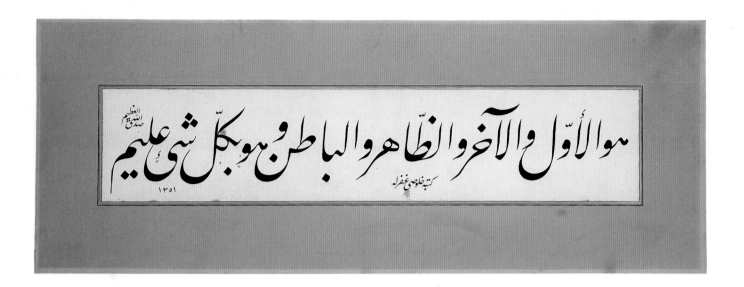

*Figure 12. Mehmed Hulûsi Yazgan
(1286/1869–1358/1940), Levha, 1351/1931.
Ink on paper, celî ta'lîk, 38.7 × 90 cm
(15 × 35⅛ in.). Sakıp Sabancı Collection,
Istanbul (82)*

attractive form called *hatt-ı icâze*, used especially by calligraphers to write their signatures and diplomas for their students.

The vowel signs and other marks that aid in the reading of Arabic can be used in all six of the scripts, although with Turkish-language texts, *nesih, tevkî', and rıkâ'* are sometimes written without these signs.

A version of *tevkî'* that originated in fourteenth-century Persia, where it was used primarily for writing official documents, was called *ta'lîk.* Later, it evolved into a different script named *nesh-i ta'lîk;* in time, this name was changed to the more easily pronounced *nesta'lîk.* Although it bore no relationship to the original Persian *ta'lîk* script, *nesta'lîk* became known as *ta'lîk* after it arrived in Istanbul, in the second half of the fifteenth century. This graceful, delicately formed script is written without vowel signs, which are optional in Persian and Turkish. It has a light and poetic air, in comparison to the majesty of *sülüs.* A small version of Ottoman *ta'lîk*, called *hurde* or *hafî*, was used for literary works and collections of poetry. *Hurde ta'lîk* was also the official script used by *kâdılar* (judges) and by muftis, judges entitled to write a *fetvâ*, or *fatwā* (an opinion on *şeriat*, or Islamic canon law), in the *fetvâhâne*, or *fetvâ* department of the office of the highest Islamic authority of the state. *Hurde ta'lîk*, as well as *nesih* and *rıkâ'*, was used to write *vakfiyeler* (endowment deeds; cat. no. 22), which were an important feature of Ottoman social life. *Celî ta'lîk* was, after *celî sülüs*, the most common *celî* script used on monuments and *levhalar* (large paper and cardboard panels that can be framed and hung on the wall). The difference between the two scripts can be gauged by comparing the *celî ta'lîk levha* in figure 12 with the *celî sülüs levha* in figure 11; both *levhalar* use the same text: "He [God] is the First and the Last, the Manifest, the Hidden" (Qur'an 57:3). Regular-size *ta'lîk*, written with a nib 2 millimeters (³⁄₃₂ inch) wide, was largely used for writing *kıt'alar.*

The original *ta'lîk* script used for official correspondence in Persia was also brought to Ottoman Turkey, by the Akkoyunlular Turkomans

(1467–1501), at some point after 1473. Within a short while, changes were introduced, and because the script was restricted to use in the Imperial Council of State (Dîvân-ı Hümâyun), it became known as *dîvânî*. In the sixteenth century, a new variety of the script was derived from the unvocalized *dîvânî* script. The new version was called *celî dîvânî*. (In calligraphy, the term *celî* generally means "large," but here it means "clear" or "evident.") This majestic version of *dîvânî* was written with vowels, reading signs, and decorative features and was used to write only the most significant documents and proclamations. Both forms of the script are written in lines that curve up toward the left, and both require considerable skill to read and write. Moreover, it is almost impossible to add extra words or letters to a line of text. Those characteristics made *dîvânî* and *celî dîvânî* useful for official documents, as they prevented forgeries and ensured confidentiality.

THE OTTOMANS AND THE ART OF CALLIGRAPHY

The Kayı tribe of the Oğuz Turks came from Central Asia to Anatolia and, under the leadership of Osman Bey, the son of Ertuğrul Gâzi, founded the Ottoman Beylik, or principality, in 1299. After 1360 the principality expanded into southern Europe, quickly becoming a state. The invasion of the Central Asian warlord Timur (Tamerlane) in 1402 put the state's existence in jeopardy. In 1453, however, the Ottomans conquered Constantinople, and under Sultan Mehmed the Conqueror (r. 1451–81), the Ottoman Empire became a world power. In the eighteenth and nineteenth centuries, the empire's fortunes declined, and, in 1923, after a bitter war of independence, the Ottomans ceded to the victorious new Turkish Republic the land that had been the site of their history.

To understand why Ottoman calligraphy is so little known in the West, compared with the calligraphy of the Arabs, Persians, and Central Asians, one must understand something of the relationship between Europe and the Ottoman Empire. From the end of the fourteenth century, the European states attempted by political and military means to prevent the expansion of the Ottoman state. For almost four hundred years (from 1299 to 1683), however, the Ottoman domain continued to grow. To the Europeans, the Ottomans were nothing more than armed invaders on horseback—invaders who followed a religion different from their own. The Christian church encouraged this hostility, fueling the anti-Ottoman alarms that followed the Ottoman siege of Vienna in 1683. With their own land and way of life threatened, the Europeans did not look beyond that threat to see the Ottomans' powerful state legal system or their refined culture, art, and architecture. Ottoman art was assumed to be primitive and the Ottomans, barbarians. Not until the nineteenth century was the value of Turkish art recognized in Europe. Joseph von Hammer (1774–1856) was the first Westerner to explain the special place of calligraphy in Ottoman culture, in his ten-volume *Geschichte des Osmanischen Reiches* (1827–35). Clément Huart

(1854–1926) continued this line of scholarship, in *Les Calligraphes et les miniaturistes de l'Orient musulman* (1908). Today, many works of Ottoman calligraphy are scattered in various American museums. It is hoped that this exhibition of calligraphy from the Sakıp Sabancı Collection will provide the American viewer with a concentrated overview of the subject.

Following the conquest of Constantinople, a succession of Ottoman master calligraphers shaped the practice of their art by building on the work of their predecessors and altering the shapes of letters, changing the relationship of words to the line, and reconfiguring the internal geometry of letters and words.

The first great calligrapher in this period, Şeyh Hamdullah (833/1429–926/1520; see cat. nos. 1–2) began by emulating the best works executed in the style of Yāqūt al-Mustaʿsimī (Yāqūt). Encouraged by his patron and student Sultan Bâyezid II (r. 1481–1512), however, he went on to subject the works of Yāqūt to critical scrutiny. He developed a new style of calligraphy about 890/1485, incorporating his own artistic values. Known as Şeyh's Manner, the new method brought the Yāqūt period of Ottoman calligraphy to a close. In the age of Sultan Süleyman the Magnificent (or the Lawgiver; r. 1520–66), the calligrapher Ahmed Karahisârî (875/1470?–963/1556; see cat. no. 6) revived the Yāqūt school with unsurpassed brilliance, but it fell into oblivion after his death and could not prevail against the method of Şeyh Hamdullah.

Şeyh's Manner continued in use for more than 150 years, during which *sülüs* and *nesih* spread rapidly. Finally, Hâfız Osman (1052/1642–1110/1698; see cat. nos. 14–16), another genius of the art, streamlined the style of Şeyh Hamdullah, in the process developing his own style of writing. The Şeyh style was soon abandoned for that of Hâfız Osman, which remained in the ascendant for a century.

The next important Ottoman calligraphers were İsmail Zühdi (d. 1221/1806; see cat. no. 26) and his brother, Mustafa Râkım (1171/1758–1241/1826; see cat. no. 27), who developed their own styles, inspired by the finest work of Hâfız Osman. Although masterful work had been written in *sülüs*, calligraphers had been unable to achieve an aesthetically satisfying version of *celî sülüs*. Even the *celî sülüs* of Hâfız Osman was not worthy of an artist of his caliber. It was in the hands of Mustafa Râkım that *celî sülüs*, as well as *sülüs* and *nesih*, reached a level of excellence, with regard to both the letters themselves and the design of complex compositions. Mustafa Râkım's approach was to apply to *celî sülüs* the principles Hâfız Osman developed for *sülüs*. Râkım also perfected the imperial *tuğra* (calligraphic emblem), which is why both *celî sülüs* and the *tuğra* can be classified as "pre-Râkım" or "post-Râkım."

Another master of *celî* and a successor to Râkım was Sâmi Efendi (1253/1838–1330/1912; see cat. nos. 49–52), who, in a variation on Râkım's method, applied the *sülüs* letters of İsmail Zühdi to *celî*. Sâmi Efendi also designed the most attractive forms for the vowel signs and other reading aids, and for the *tezyînat* (decorations) and numbers, which were used to fill in the empty areas of an *istif*. Today, Sâmi Efendi's method still predominates.

Mahmud Celâleddin (1163/1750?–1245/1829; see cat. nos. 32–33), who was Râkım's contemporary, adapted the style of Hâfız Osman to his own taste; in his *sülüs* and *nesih* he achieved firm and confident writing. His *celî*, however, was rigid and static. For this reason, Celâleddin's style was abandoned, and Râkım's prevailed.

Although the great calligrapher and musician Kâdıasker Mustafa İzzet Efendi (1216/1801–1293/1876; see cat. nos. 36–37) and his students all adopted a style that included characteristics of the writing of Hâfız Osman, Celâleddin, and Râkım, it was their contemporary Şevki Efendi (1245/1829–1304/1887; see cat. nos. 40–41) who developed *sülüs* and *nesih* to a height of perfection never attained previously or surpassed since.

The *dîvânî* and *celî dîvânî* scripts reached their peak at the end of the nineteenth century as well (see cat. no. 70). The Ottomans in Istanbul had used these scripts since the second half of the fifteenth century. After the Persian *nesta'lîk* master Mīr ʿImād al-Hasanī (961/1554?–1024/1615) devised the best system for writing *nesta'lîk*, the Turkish calligraphers adopted his method in great numbers. A Turkish style of *nesta'lîk* was born when Mehmed Es'ad Efendi (d. 1213/1798; see cat. no. 28) integrated the most beautiful letters of Mīr ʿImād into his own style. (Mehmed Es'ad Efendi, it should be noted, was a remarkable calligrapher who was known by the epithet Yesârî, or the Left-Handed, because the right side of his body was paralyzed, obliging him to write with his left hand.) His son, Yesârîzâde Mustafa İzzet Efendi (d. 1265/1849), elaborated detailed rules for this method and in Istanbul developed a style of *celî ta'lîk* that had no match even in Persia. Sâmi Efendi, who was as much a master of *ta'lîk* and *celî ta'lîk* as he was of *celî sülüs*, passed the Turkish style of *ta'lîk* down to our day in its most perfect form.

Two scripts, it should be noted, were not recognized by the Ottomans as being worthy of artistic consideration. The first was *rık'a*. Despite the similarity of their names, *rık'a* bears no resemblance to *rıkâ'*, the sixth of the six scripts. *Rık'a* was the script for daily use by every literate Ottoman subject. It was always written with a reed pen whose nib was less than 1 millimeter (³⁄₆₄ inch) wide. In earlier times, the script was written differently by different calligraphers, with no rules or conventions. Mümtaz Efendi (1225/1810–1287/1872) devised a method of writing *rık'a* called *bâbıâlî rık'ası*, for use in government offices. Mehmed İzzet Efendi (1257/1841–1302/1903) developed a *rık'a* script that had strict rules of execution and could be written very quickly, with some letters simplified in comparison to *bâbıâlî rık'ası*.

The second script that did not merit artistic treatment was *siyâkat*, which was reserved for treasury documents and title deeds. This script was so difficult to read and write, in fact, that it was almost a cipher script.

Clearly, Ottoman calligraphers did not use unchanged the writing that they had originally borrowed from other Islamic countries. Rather, the stylistic evolution of Ottoman calligraphy involved a continual process of sifting, refining, and elaborating new methods according to the calligraphers' own tastes, without distorting the essential forms of the letters. Moreover, unlike Ottoman architecture, music, and fine and decorative arts, calligraphy did not degenerate under Western influence. Calligraphy was spared this decline for three reasons: the absence in Europe of a comparable art that could exert an influence on calligraphy; the continuation of the master-and-apprentice system among classically trained calligraphers, in which established principles were transmitted from generation to generation; and calligraphy's capacity for self-renewal.

In the Islamic world, there is a widespread adage that "the Qur'an was revealed in the Hijaz; it was best recited in Egypt and best written in Istanbul." Indeed, taking into account the length of time that the Ottomans maintained this art in its highest form, one cannot label it chauvinism to celebrate the "Turkish art of calligraphy." There is no denying that in Ottoman Istanbul the miraculous Qur'an was made art on paper. The pearls of the Prophet of Islam's words and deeds, the *hadîsler*, became pearls of calligraphy. Examples of such works will be found in this catalogue. Here, too, the reader will find other works of art by calligraphers too numerous to mention individually here—artists whose works include everything from collections of poetry to *fermanlar* (imperial edicts), from inscriptions carved in marble on public fountains to gravestones.

CALLIGRAPHY DECORATION

Although calligraphy arose as an independent art, a great deal of attention was soon paid to decorating it with *tezhip* (gold illumination) or *ebrû* (Turkish paper marbling), or both. These colorful decorations added to the attractiveness of the calligraphy, with its limited color range.

The word *tezhip* (or *tezhîb*) refers primarily to the application of pure gold with a special brush, but it also encompasses the use of a varied palette of colors accompanying the gold. Both yellow (23- to 24-karat) gold and green (18-karat) gold are used, with different burnishing techniques employed to achieve different effects, such as brilliant or matte gold. Another style of ornamentation, *halkârî* (dissolved-gold work), uses no color except for the color of the background paper. In this technique, the motifs are painted in a wash of gold ink, giving a subtle shaded effect, and outlined in full-strength gold ink. First, however, the design must be drawn. The type of calligraphy, the proportions of the work, and its overall size all play a role in determining an appropriate design.

The art of illumination was developed to a high degree in Iran in the early fifteenth century, during the Timurid period (1370–1507). By the end of the fifteenth century, the Ottomans began to take the art to further heights, using stylized images from the animal and vegetable kingdoms to develop a classic style of ornamentation marked by flat surfaces and, often, brilliant color. At the end of the seventeenth

Figure 13. Hâfiz Osman (1052/1642–1110/1698), Folios 11v (Qur'an 112–14) and 12r (Fâtiha) *from a collection of chapters from the Qur'an, 1086/1675. Ink, colors, and gold on* akkâse *paper, nesih, 22.2 × 14.8 cm (8⅝ × 5¾ in.). Sakıp Sabancı Collection, Istanbul (284)*

century, Ottoman illumination entered a period of stagnation, and in the eighteenth century, under the influence of Western art, it began to lose its identity altogether. By the nineteenth century, the borders of calligraphic works were decorated with derivative designs that gave the illumination a strange quality. Beginning in the mid-twentieth century, however, artists seeking to revive the classic styles have brought about a renaissance in the art.

Illumination is a costly process, because of the gold and the labor involved. An economical alternative to an illuminated border is a border made of *ebrû* paper (cat. nos. 1, 13–14, 19, 21, 23, 33, 39, 54, 57, and 59). *Ebrû*—the word comes from the Persian *abrī*, meaning "cloud"—is made with a bath of water thickened with gum tragacanth (*kitre*) and contained in a special trough. Pigments from natural earths and other sources are ground and mixed with water and ox gall, which causes them to float and expand when sprinkled on the surface of the tragacanth bath. Designs are made by drawing a stylus through the pigments. When a piece of paper is laid on the bath, the pigments adhere to it. When the paper is raised, the design is lifted off the water. The paper is then dried. Later, it is cut and pasted onto the desired areas of the work.

THE USES OF CALLIGRAPHY
BOOKS

Before the invention of the printing press, the most important use of calligraphy was to make a copy (*mushaf*, or codex) of the Qur'an (fig. 13; see also cat. nos. 3, 5–7, 9, 11, 15, 20, 40, 43, 45, and 47–48). Prayer handbooks (see cat. nos. 4 and 42) and scientific and literary works were of secondary importance. The earliest Qur'ans were written in *kûfî;* later, such scripts as *muhakkak, reyhânî,* and *nesih* were used. By the sixteenth century, *mushaflar* were being written in combinations of scripts—*muhakkak* with *nesih* or *reyhânî,* for example, or even three scripts per page: *muhakkak, sülüs,* and *nesih.* According to Ottoman taste, *nesih* was the most suitable script for the sacred task of copying the Qur'an. And in the hands of the Ottomans, over the course of four centuries from Şeyh Hamdullah on, *nesih* developed an easy readability.

Although there are no comprehensive historical sources that give the exact dimensions of the different types of Qur'ans, various references yield the following standard sizes:

1. *cami mushafı:* the mosque Qur'an; the largest Qur'an, written for and donated to a specific mosque
2. *büyük (kebîr) kıt'a mushaf:* the large Qur'an; one-half the size of the mosque Qur'an
3. *vezirî kıt'a mushaf:* the *vezir* (wazir) Qur'an; one-half the size of the *büyük* Qur'an
4. *küçük (rubu') kıt'a mushaf:* the small Qur'an; one-half the size of the *vezirî* Qur'an and one-quarter the size of the *büyük* Qur'an
5. *sümün kıt'a mushaf:* the one-eighth-size Qur'an; one-half the size of the *küçük* Qur'an and one-eighth the size of the *büyük* Qur'an
6. *sancak mushafı:* the emblem Qur'an; the smallest Qur'an, of no fixed size, but usually hexagonal or octagonal in format; affixed to the tip of the pole of a military standard

Qur'ans are encountered that do not conform to this classification, of course. But regardless of their proportions, Ottoman Qur'ans were always vertical in orientation. Use of the *mıstar* ruler allowed the calligrapher to lay out and repeat perfect guidelines for the text, page after page, cleanly and simply.

Before the printing press was introduced into the Ottoman world, large numbers of calligraphers earned their living by copying the Qur'an, which has more than six hundred pages. Everyone wanted his own Qur'an—by an outstanding calligrapher or by an ordinary one, according to the commissioner's financial means. A person who could afford no Qur'an at all could read one at a mosque or Sufi lodge where a charitable donor had paid for a *cami mushafı.* Many calligraphers could write quickly: Çemşir Hâfız Salih (d. 1236/1820) completed a record 454 *mushaflar* in his lifetime, and Ramazan bin İsmail (d. 1091/1680; see cat. no. 9) made 400. These masters and others could be thought of as living printing presses, given the swiftness of their work. In general, however, meticulously prepared Qur'ans with high artistic value took a long time to complete. The length of time depended on the speed and mood of the calligrapher, which could vary not only from calligrapher to calligrapher but even from moment to moment in the same calligrapher's life, as illustrated by the story of

Yahya Hilmi Efendi (1249/1833–1325/1907; see the entry for cat. no. 47).

Traditionally, calligraphers who copied Qur'ans would begin at the tenth section, or *cüz* (there are thirty sections in all, generally twenty pages each), write to the end, and then return to the *Fâtiha* (opening chapter) and finish the first nine sections. By this means, the calligrapher was able to work out any difficulties with the script in section 10 through section 30, ensuring a perfect *nesih* for the opening sections.

After finishing the lettering of each page, the calligrapher would go back and, using a smaller pen, write in the vowel signs and reading signs. Finally, using red (*lâl*) ink, the calligrapher would add the *secavend* (stop, pause, and other instructions for recitation, whether informally by the individual or formally in the mosque). During these final operations, the calligrapher would check for mistakes, removing any page on which there was an error and substituting a correct page. The extracted page, known as a *muhrec sahife*, was given to an illuminator to use as a sample to display his gilding talent to potential customers.

Once the text was finished, the Qur'an was illuminated. Especially rich designs were used on the first two pages, which consist of the first chapter (*Fâtiha*) and the beginning of the second chapter (*Bakara*). These two most imposing pages of a handwritten Qur'an are called the *serlevha* (cat. nos. 3, 5, 40, 43, and 48). Exceptional Qur'ans aside, the remaining pages are not illuminated but decorated with a ruled frame around the text. The frame, called the *cedvel*, is gold, outlined with delicate black or colored lines called *tahrirler*, which are also used to enhance other gilded designs.

The illuminator filled the spaces between each *âyet*, or verse, with a rosette-type decoration called a *durak*, or stop. The most inventive illuminators came up with a large number of designs for these decorations so they would not be repeated too often—quite a feat, considering that there are more than six thousand stops in a single Qur'an. In addition, the illuminator put various section marks in the border. A *cüz gülü* (one-thirtieth-section rosette) appeared every twenty pages, and a *hizib gülü* (one-quarter-section rosette) every five pages. A *secde gülü* (prostration rosette) was placed in the border next to each place in the text where the reader must prostrate himself. After each ten *âyetler* came a special marker called the *aşere gülü* (ten rosette), and at the beginning of each chapter, or *sûre*, is a *sûre başı tezhîbi* (chapter-head illumination; see especially cat. nos. 20 and 47). Two of these headings appear in the *serlevha*, and there are 112 more in the text. At the end of the *mushaf*, a page called the *hâtime tezhîbi* was also illuminated, giving the artist an opportunity to demonstrate his skill. The calligrapher's signature is found on this page.

Following the illumination, the calligrapher used white-lead ink (*üstübeç*) to write in, on the gilded areas and rosettes, the titles of the chapters, as well as the *cüz*, *hizib*, *secde*, and *aşere* titles.

The finest *mushaflar* were joint productions, especially in the sixteenth century. Designs and motifs were conceived and planned by a

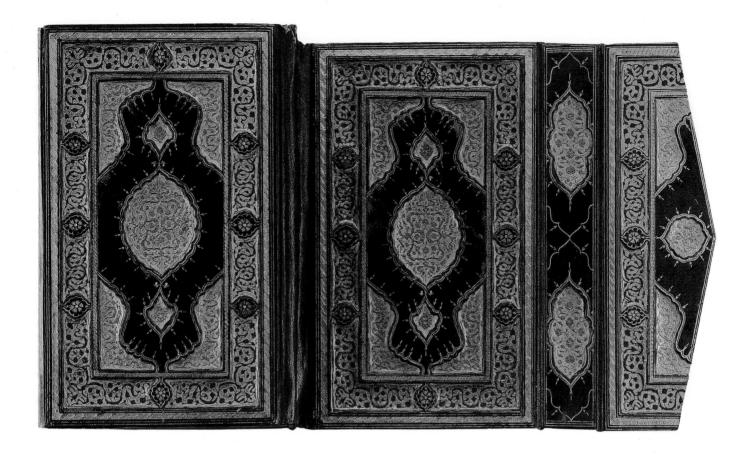

group of artists called *tarrahlar*, or planners. The gold *cedveller* were prepared by artists called *cedvelkeşler*, or frame drawers. A separate group was responsible for putting the black outlines, or *tahrirler*, around the gold illumination. Still other artists would produce the *duraklar*. One group would supply the gold ink, a second would apply the gold ink in the designs, and a third would apply the colors. This was the method used to illuminate precious manuscripts at the palace *nakışhâne*, or department of illuminators and miniaturists. The most delicate work was done by young artists whose eyes were not yet weakened, under the supervision of master illuminators. In later centuries, however, a master illuminator would undertake all these tasks with a few pupils in what was, at best, a slow process.

The final step was binding the volume. Many illuminators were also bookbinders who produced the classic bindings called *şemse kap*. In this style of binding, carved dies are used to stamp the *şemse* (sunburst design) and other motifs into the leather binding, according to formal design rules. The embossed leather was generally decorated with gilding (fig. 14). A unique feature of an Islamic binding is the envelope flap, or *mıkleb*, on the left side of the back cover. This flap can be tucked between the pages to serve as a bookmark. In addition to being bound as a single-volume *mushaf*, the Qur'an can be bound in thirty-volume sets, one volume per *cüz*. Sometimes the thirtieth *cüz—Amme cüzü*,

Figure 14. Ottoman şemse *binding, 17th century. Embossed leather decorated with gold, 21.1 × 14.4 cm (8¼ × 5⅛ in.). From the left: front cover, spine, back cover,* sertâb *(a flexible connecting piece between the back cover and the* mıkleb*);* mıkleb. *Sakıp Sabancı Collection, Istanbul (191)*

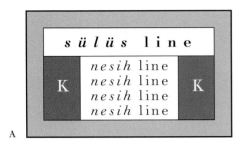

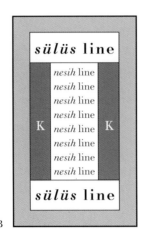

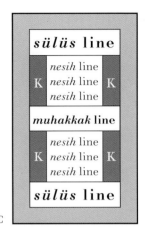

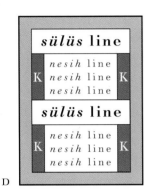

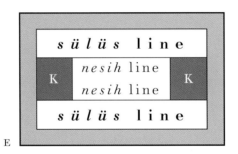

Figure 15. Traditional kıt'a *layouts*

Qur'an 78–114—was bound separately (cat. no. 38). The chapter called *En'âm* (cat. nos. 2 and 16), plus the chapters most frequently recited (during worship and on prescribed occasions), is sometimes produced as a volume called *En'âm-ı Şerîf* (cat. no. 24).

In addition to the Qur'an, other popular religious books are the *Delâilü'l-Hayrât* (cat. no. 31), a prayer book that often contains miniatures of Mecca and Medina, and the *Evrâd-ı Şerîfe*, which includes special prayers for use in Sufi orders. These books do not have an illuminated double-page spread like the Qur'anic *serlevha*. Rather, only the right-hand *unvan sahifesi* (title or opening page) is heavily illuminated (see cat. nos. 2, 16, and 38).

For books written in the Turkish language, *nesih* script without vowels, and the naturally unvocalized small *ta'lîk*, was preferred (fig. 23). It would not be an exaggeration to say that *hurde ta'lîk* raises the level of a work, such as a collection of the poetry of a single poet, called a *dîvân*.

Fetvâlar (opinions on Islamic canon law) and *vakfiyeler* (endowment deeds; cat. no. 22) were also bound into books.

The word *kıt'a*, which means "piece" or "section," has come to be used as a technical term to describe a specific type of calligraphic work that is rectangular in shape, is oriented either vertically or horizontally, and has writing on one side of the paper only (cat. nos. 1, 10, 12–14, 18–19, 21, 23, 25–26, 28–29, 33, 36–37, 41, 53, 55, and 57). (Square *kıt'alar* are made occasionally when there is no other choice—when, for instance, the amount of text alters the border proportions, or when the *kıt'a* needs to be fitted into an album [see cat. no. 10].) Commonly, the paper on which the calligrapher writes is pasted in the center of a larger cardboard backing, leaving four equal margins for later decoration with illumination, *ebrû* paper, or even plain polished paper. The narrow band surrounding the writing is called the *iç pervaz*, or inner border; outside of it is the *dış pervaz*, or outer border. In place of the *iç pervaz* there can be one or two *ara pervazlar*, or interval borders. The entire border area is also called the *kenar suyu*.

Kıt'alar are classified according to the kinds of scripts used in them. There are *sülüs*-and-*nesih kıt'alar*; *muhakkak*-and-*reyhânî kıt'alar*; and so forth. Among the Ottoman calligraphers, the most widespread kind of *kıt'a* is the *sülüs*-and-*nesih kıt'a*, which typically has a line of text in *sülüs* and three to five lines of *nesih* underneath. Sometimes the *nesih* lines are written on a slant, from upper right to lower left.

Figure 15 shows common *kıt'a* layouts. In diagram A, the area where the text appears resembles a human torso. For that reason, the rectangular spaces that are left open for decoration (marked K) are called *koltuklar*, or armpits. On a vertical layout, such as in diagram B, the preference is to write the first and last lines in *sülüs*, with eight to ten lines of *nesih* in between. Sometimes an additional line of *sülüs* (or, in early *kıt'alar*, *muhakkak*) is written in the middle, as in diagram C. Some nineteenth-century *kıt'alar* were made by putting two *sülüs*-and-*nesih kıt'alar* together, one on top of the other (see diagram D). In these double *kıt'alar*, the lower *nesih* section was sometimes written on a slant to break the visual uniformity.

A special form of *kıt'a* was used for a student exercise (*meşk*). In this format (diagram E), there is one line of *sülüs*, followed by two lines of *nesih*, followed by one more line of *sülüs*. As in all formats, the *nesih* lines are shorter than the *sülüs* lines to leave room for the *koltuklar*. There are also *kıt'alar* written only in *nesih* or only in *sülüs*.

Although the dimensions of *sülüs*-and-*nesih kıt'alar* vary, most are in the range of 4 to 6 inches in height; the widths range from 1.5 to 2 times the height. (Proportions differ for vertical *kıt'alar*.) The *sülüs*-and-*nesih kıt'alar* in this exhibition will give an idea of both common and not-so-common dimensions (cat. nos. 1, 10, 12–13, 19, 21, 23, 25–26, 33, 36–37, 41, and 57).

The *ta'lîk kıt'a* was usually used for poetry. In general, the text of a *ta'lîk kıt'a* is two *beyitler*, or poetic verses, written one under the other. The verses can be separated by a gilded rule, or *cedvel*. When the writing

Figure 16. Kâdıasker Mustafa İzzet Efendi (1216/1801–1293/1876), Murakkaa, 1265/1849. Ink, colors, and gold on paper mounted on cardboard, sülüs and nesih, 18.7 × 26.3 cm (7¼ × 10¼ in.). Sakıp Sabancı Collection, Istanbul (164)

slants upward, from the lower right to the upper left, as in diagram F, the work is called a *mâil kıt'a*, or inclining *kıt'a* (see also figs. 10 and 21). The smaller the angle of inclination of the text, the wider the *kıt'a* will be. The preferred angle is forty degrees. The triangular areas marked K in diagram F are called *muska koltuklar* (triangular *koltuklar*) or *köşelikler* (corner pieces). These areas can be illuminated. (Occasionally, there are *ta'lîk kıt'alar* with no illumination at all—not even border lines.) In those *ta'lîk kıt'alar* that were laid out with the *mıstar*, triangular areas were always right triangles. Later on, however, this rule was not always followed, except in the four corners of the piece. It was the practice of the Persian (Herat) school to make the top margin of the *ta'lîk kıt'a* twice as wide as the side and bottom margins. This practice was adopted in some Ottoman *kıt'alar* (see fig. 15, diagram F; and cat. no. 28).

When the lines of text in a *ta'lîk kıt'a* are horizontal, it is called a *düz ta'lîk kıt'a*, or level *ta'lîk kıt'a*. Most of these were written by the calligraphy teacher (*hoca, muallim,* or *üstâd*) for the student to study and copy; they are called *meşk kıt'aları,* or exercise *kıt'alar* (cat. nos. 28, 29, 53, and 55).

Another form of *kıt'a* is the *karalama* (blackening), a practice piece filled with line after line of calligraphy, complete with measuring dots (fig. 7). A calligrapher would work on a *karalama* in his spare time, to maintain his technique. Today, many collectors prize these handsome pieces and consider them akin to abstract art.

Until the fourteenth century, *kıt'alar* were pasted not to boards but edge to edge so they could be rolled up like a scroll (*tomar*) and kept in an accompanying leather case. (Some calligraphic works are actually made as scrolls.) The edge-to-edge arrangement was later abandoned in favor of calligraphy albums called *murakkaalar.* Most *kıt'alar* were originally part of such an album and, after coming loose from the album, would be framed and hung on a wall.

MURAKKAALAR

To make a calligraphy album, all the *kıt'alar* to be included are pasted on specially prepared pieces of cardboard, then trimmed to the same dimensions. Pairs of *kıt'alar* are placed back to back and bound at all four edges with thin strips of leather or cloth, which not only hold the pieces together but also protect the edges from wear and tear. The attached pairs are then bound between covers. This kind of album is called a *düz murakkaa* (simple album), *kitap murakkaa* (book-type album), or simply *murakkaa.* The oldest examples of the book-type album date from the end of the fifteenth century. This format had two advantages: besides protecting the edges of the pages, it allowed different works by different calligraphers and even from different eras to be compiled into a single unit. Although miniatures or illuminations were sometimes made into albums, the majority of *murakkaalar* consisted of calligraphy.

In the *körüklü murakkaa* (bellows album), the pairs of *kıt'alar* are bound at one edge only. Then the pairs are joined together so that they can be opened out accordion-fashion and viewed all at once. All four edges are protected by leather strips. In this type of album, only the first page is attached to the binding (fig. 16; see also cat. nos. 10, 18, and 36).

Another kind of *murakkaa* is made up of teaching exercises. Albums could be made from lessons on single or double letters, which are called *müfredât* (singles; cat. nos. 28 and 41), or from lessons consisting of sentences, usually from poetic odes, prayers, Qur'anic verses, or *hadîsler* (sayings of the Prophet Muhammad), which are called *mürekkebât* (compounds; cat. nos. 29, 53, and 55). If the *kıt'alar* were created especially for a *meşk murakkaa* (exercise album), the calligrapher signed only the final *kıt'a* of the series.

Figure 17. Sâmi Efendi (1253/1838–1330/1912), Kalıp for a levha, 1318/1900, detail. Orpiment ink on dark brown paper, celî sülüs. Türkpetrol Foundation, Istanbul

When a series of *kıt'alar* is written in a specific order for a *murakkaa*, the text of each script runs from *kıt'a* to *kıt'a*. In other words, one reads the *sülüs* lines continuously through the entire *murakkaa*, and then the *nesih* lines. For that reason, *murakkaa kıt'alar* that have been unbound often include sentences with no beginning or end. In such a *müteselsil murakkaa*, or sequential album, only the final *kıt'a* is signed (cat. no. 13).

In an album composed of independent *kıt'alar*, each *kıt'a* is signed by its calligrapher. Such an album, which may include works by a number of calligraphers, is called a *toplama murakkaa*, or collection album. If one *kıt'a* in a *toplama murakkaa* is smaller than the others, the inner border may be widened, or an extra strip of paper, illumination, or *ebrû* called a *takoz* (chock) may be pasted on one or more edges of the inner border. There are also *murakkaalar* in which the *kıt'alar* have not been assembled in so scrupulous a fashion (cat. no. 1).

LEVHALAR

In the nineteenth and twentieth centuries, especially among the Ottomans, a demand developed for the *levha*, or panel, an art form that (with some exceptions) uses the *celî* sizes of scripts (cat. nos. 27, 32, 34, 39, 44, 46, 49, 51–52, 54, and 58–59). The resulting work is framed and hung on the wall, to be appreciated as a whole composition as well as read for its text. (A special category of *levha*, the *hilye*, is discussed below.)

Successful *celî*—writing large enough to be read from a distance—requires skill in both hand and eye. (In order to print examples of *celî* writing in a book, they must be reduced from their original size. And when a *celî sülüs* work or a *celî ta'lîk* work is reduced for publication, it is nearly indistinguishable from regular-size *sülüs* or *ta'lîk*.) In comparison with normal-size writing, *celî* writing—especially the *istif*, a composition of superimposed and interlaced letters and words—is very difficult and represents the ultimate achievement in calligraphy.

Calligraphers could choose various formats for their compositions in *celî sülüs:* the writing area could be square, nearly square (cat. no. 27), rectangular (fig. 11 and cat. no. 34), circular (cat. no. 58), or elliptical (cat. nos. 46 and 54). In rarer cases, the composition took the shape of a bird, flower, or fruit.

The difficulty of producing *celî* compositions led to a practical way of obtaining multiple copies from a single original. First, the calligrapher practices a passage over and over to get the composition just right. Then, using the final work, the calligrapher makes a *kalıp*, or stencil. If the inscription is too large to be executed directly by hand, it is first written on a smaller scale, then enlarged by squaring. That is, the calligrapher writes the inscription in a convenient size, then divides the work into squares, as on graph paper. Next, he divides a piece of paper the same size as the desired finished inscription into an equivalent number of squares, proportionally larger. Then he copies the calligraphy from the original work, square by square, to the larger paper and from it makes the stencil. (This is the same method used to embellish mosques, teaching institutions, and fountains with inscriptions carved in marble.)

In the early days, before the *celî* scripts were perfected, stencils were written on white paper with lampblack ink, and any necessary corrections were made by scraping with the correction knife. By the end of the eighteenth century, however, calligraphers had begun to write their stencils with orpiment ink on black or dark brown paper (fig. 17; for a *levha* prepared from this stencil, see cat. no. 51). This method was preferable for two reasons. First, orpiment ink does not cause a thick buildup of ink on the paper; and second, corrections can be made by covering the mistake with lampblack ink and then writing over it with orpiment ink. It is possible to perform this operation several times over without damaging the paper.

The stencil is made by placing a few sheets of white paper the same size as the original under the composition and securing them lightly with paste. The calligrapher then uses a fine needle, held in a watchmaker's pin vise, to pierce holes all along the borders of the letters and other elements of the composition. When all the parts of the composition have been outlined with tiny holes, the white papers underneath the original are separated from each other. These *alt kalıplar* (bottom stencils) are inspected carefully to be sure the holes faithfully represent the calligraphy. The original copy, on black or brown paper, is called the *üst kalıp*, or top stencil.

To transfer the calligraphy to another piece of paper or to marble or some other surface, the calligrapher places an *alt kalıp* on the new surface. If the background is light in color, the calligrapher uses a small cotton bag filled with finely powdered willow charcoal to transfer the design. As the bag is moved over the *alt kalıp* and patted, the charcoal filters through the bag and through the holes of the stencil, leaving small black dots on the light background. If the calligrapher wishes to transfer the composition to a dark background, for subsequent reproduction with gold ink, he uses a bag filled with chalk powder, which leaves small white dots. This operation is called *yazı silkmek* or *yazı silkelemek* (to pounce the writing). (The top stencil is never used for this purpose, because it will get soiled with charcoal or chalk. Instead, the top stencil is used as a guide, so that the calligraphy can be transferred and reproduced perfectly. Unless the exact relation of the perforations to the original writing is understood, the reproduced writing can be too thick or too thin.)

After pouncing, the calligrapher uses a small-tipped pen and lampblack ink to trace the dots and establish the outline of the writing, which will be filled in with ink. Or, if he trusts his hand, he will use a pen of the same width as that used to produce the original work and simply rewrite the text by following the dots (cat. no. 54). (The charcoal or chalk can be brushed away later.) Copies made from a stencil are most highly esteemed if they are made by the calligrapher himself. Sometimes, however, inferior *celî* copies were made by people whose skills were not up to the task. For this reason, calligraphers kept their stencils away from unskilled copyists.

Copies made in gold ink, rather than lampblack ink, were often executed by illuminators rather than calligraphers. The process for producing a *levha* of this kind is called *zer-endûd* (painted in gold; fig. 11). In this method, a panel of high-quality cardboard is coated with a non-water-soluble mineral pigment bound with gelatin and applied while hot. Among the colors used are black, ultramarine, "duck's-head green," "fez red," and brown. After the panel is prepared, the design is transferred via the stencil and chalk powder. Then the contours (*tahrirler*) are carefully drawn with a thin gold ink and a fine brush. The area within these lines is filled with a full-strength gold ink. After the work is dry, it is burnished to a matte finish using the *zermühre*, or gold burnisher (fig. 8), a highly polished, specially shaped stone, usually agate, set in a handle. This tool is used only for burnishing gold. The resulting work can be truly magnificent. Indeed, when the gilding was done by master illuminators, these *zer-endûd levhalar* were as valuable as the originals. Some of the *levhalar* in the Sakıp Sabancı Collection were made in this way (cat. nos. 27, 34, 49, 51–52, and 58).

As the size of gold *celî* works increases, so does the expense of the gold ink. To keep costs at a reasonable level, very large *zer-endûd levhalar* are produced by applying gold leaf directly to the panel, rather than making it into ink. The background material for such pieces may be a special cloth, called *muşamba* (originally, *muşamma'*, a cloth coated with colored beeswax), or it may be a painted wooden or zinc panel. The writing is transferred to the background material by pouncing the stencil with chalk powder. The letters and other elements are painted with an adhesive varnish size. In Ottoman times, this size was called *lika* or *lâk* and was made from linseed oil; today, a substance called *mixtion* is used. After the size has reached the desired tack, the gold leaf is laid on it. The gold leaf adheres to the size, producing an attractive matte appearance. Gold leaf applied in this way is resistant to every weather condition. All the large gold inscriptions in mosques, as well as those cut in marble in low relief, are prepared in this way.

The *celî* forms of *sülüs* and *ta'lîk* are the most dazzling. After the advances made by Mustafa Râkım, *celî sülüs*—above all in the *zerendûd* style—gained a magnificence no other writing can match. Whether executed with a pen or enlarged by squaring, the forms of *celî* writing are not exactly the same as those of normal-size writing. The smaller scripts have been likened to a child, the larger ones to a mature adult. Just as the proportions of a child's limbs differ from those of an adult, normal-size writing, too, differs from *celî*. The great writers of *celî* were aware of the principles of perspective. While composing their inscriptions, they took into account the height at which the writing was to be placed and adjusted the dimensions of the letters accordingly, to ensure the correct visual effect.

MOSQUE CALLIGRAPHY

As gathering places for Muslims to worship, mosques are decorated with clear *celî* inscriptions that all may see. The most commonly used texts come from the Qur'an and *hadîs* literature, which are in Arabic. The preferred script for these texts is fully vocalized *celî sülüs*. A band of writing called the *kuşak yazısı* winds around the upper part of the mosque walls and around the drum of the dome (or, when there is more than one, around the drums of all the domes). The crowns of the domes and semidomes are decorated with special circular or semicircular compositions called *kubbe yazısı*, or dome writing. All these inscriptions are in *celî sülüs*.

The mosque inscriptions are done by a professional painter called a *nakkâş*, or decorator, who specializes in calligraphy and decoration. The work is executed in gold leaf against a dark background or carved in marble in low relief, which is more durable. An attractive way of finishing a marble relief is to paint the recessed background a dark color and gild the writing with gold leaf. Until the seventeenth century, the bands of writing were generally done in glazed tile; subsequently, the preferred method has been to paint or gild them. Inscriptions in domes and over windows are also done either in paint or in gold leaf. The customary circular *levhalar* in mosques are written on *muşamba* cloth or on wooden or metal panels that have been painted a dark color. The writing is in *celî sülüs*, executed in gold leaf. The customary texts are the *ism-i celâl*, the name of God; the *ism-i Nebî*, the name of the Prophet; the *çiharyâr*, the names of the Four Friends, that is, Abū Bakr, ʿUmar, ʿUthmān, and ʿAlī, the first four caliphs; and the *Hasanayn*, the names of Hasan and Husayn, grandsons of the Prophet.

INSCRIPTIONS

The term *kitâbe*, or inscription, refers to writing on the exterior facade (occasionally the interior) of a monument or public building, such as a mosque, Sufi lodge, educational institution, religious school, caravansary, small neighborhood water fountain (*çeşme*), bathhouse, grand public fountain (*sebil*), library, and so forth. Inscriptions are also found on such freestanding stone markers as archery target stones and gravestones. Most inscriptions are carved in marble in low relief. Like the *kuşak* inside a mosque, these inscriptions can be made with the raised writing gilded with gold leaf and the recessed background painted a dark color. *Celî sülüs* and, especially for Turkish-language inscriptions, *celî ta'lîk* were the most commonly used scripts, and the most beautiful examples are to be found in Istanbul. In the United States, a lovely example of an unpainted marble inscription is to be found on the seventeenth level of the Washington Monument in Washington, D.C. It was presented to the United States in 1853 as a symbol of Ottoman friendship. The inscription was copied by Kâdıasker Mustafa İzzet Efendi (see cat. nos. 36–37).

Apart from these uses, calligraphic inscriptions have appeared throughout history on such materials as wood, leather, metal, and ceramics and on such objects as seals, rings, mosque lamps, helmets, swords, and various tools (fig. 6). But with the great majority of such works, the beauty of the writing is lost, because the calligraphy is too modified and far removed from its pen-written original.

HİLYELER

Islam rejects the depiction of anyone who could be idolized. For this reason, aside from a few insignificant miniatures, there have been no pictures of the Prophet Muhammad. Nevertheless, in reliable original sources contemporaries of the Prophet of Islam vividly describe him in words, allowing each believer to picture the Prophet in his own heart and mind—an approach that is clearly more in keeping with an iconoclastic faith than depicting the Prophet in drawings or paintings would be. These descriptions are called *hilyeler*, as are calligraphic works made from the descriptions (fig. 19; see also cat. nos. 17, 35, and 56). In addition to meaning "description," the word *hilye* (Arabic *hilya*) means "ornament" and "adornment."

The most commonly used *hilye* is that of the Prophet's son-in-law ʿAlī, which can be translated as follows:

Transmitted from ʿAlī, may God be pleased with him, who, when asked to describe the Prophet, peace be upon him, would say: He was not too tall or too short. He was medium-size. His hair was not short and curly, nor was it lank, but in between. His face was not narrow, nor was it fully round, but there was a roundness to it. His skin was white. His eyes were black. He had long eyelashes. He was big-boned and had wide shoulders. He had no body hair except in the middle of his chest. He had thick hands and feet.

Figure 18. The general layout of a hilye

Figure 19. Hâmid Aytaç (1309/1891–
1402/1982), Hilye, 1369/1950. Ink, colors,
and gold on paper, muhakkak, sülüs, and
nesih, 65.7 × 47.2 cm (25⅝ × 18⅜ in.). The
illumination is by Muhsin Demironat
(1325/1907–1403/1983). Sakıp Sabancı
Collection, Istanbul (395)

When he walked, he walked inclined, as if descending a slope.
When he looked at someone, he looked at them full-face. [Part A]

Between his shoulders was the seal of prophecy, the sign
that he was the last of the prophets. He was the most generous-
hearted of men, the most truthful of them in speech, the most
mild-tempered of them, and the noblest of them in lineage.
Whoever saw him unexpectedly was in awe of him. And
whoever associated with him familiarly, loved him. Anyone who
would describe him would say, I never saw, before him or after
him, the like of him. Peace be upon him. [Part B]

(A number of other *hilye* texts are also available, taken from *hadîs* literature.)

In its complete form, this text is called the *hilye-i şerif* (the illustrious *hilye*), *hilye-i saadet* (the felicitous *hilye*), and *hilye-i Nebevî* (the *hilye* concerning the Prophet), terms that imbue the concept with a deeper meaning. Since the early days of Islam, this text has been written in tiny *nesih* in a small format for carrying in the breast pocket as a sign of love and esteem for the Prophet. In the last quarter of the seventeenth century, Hâfız Osman developed the stunning graphic form of the *hilye* that is familiar to us today.

Figure 18 shows the various sections of the *hilye:*

1. *baş makam* (the head station): The *besmele* is always written here.
2. *göbek* (the belly): Part A of the *hilye* text is written in this central cartouche, which is usually circular, oval, or square in shape.
3. *hilâl* (the crescent): The Prophet Muhammad, who illuminated this world with his light, is often likened to the sun and moon. The *göbek* symbolizes the sun and the *hilâl* the crescent moon that surrounds it. The *hilâl* is not a requisite part of the *hilye*, however; the *göbek* can appear without it. When it is used, the crescent can be decorated with gold or gold-illuminated designs.
4, 5, 6, 7. From the standpoint of embellishment, the richest part of the *hilye* is the square that contains the *göbek* and the *hilâl*. In the four corners, it also contains the names of the *çiharyâr*, Abū Bakr, ʿUmar, ʿUthmān, and ʿAlī. In place of the four caliphs' names, four names of the Prophet can be written instead: Ahmad, Mahmūd, Hāmid, and Hamīd. On some *hilyeler*, this area is used for the names of the *aşere-i mübeşşere*, that is, the ten companions of the Prophet who were promised eternal life in heaven. (On occasion, some of their names are found in the *koltuklar*, areas 10 and 11 in the diagram.)
8. *âyet* (Qur'anic verse): In this section, a Qur'anic verse about the Prophet is written. The most common is: "And We [God] did not send you [Muhammad] except to be a mercy to the universe" (Qur'an 21:107). Two other verses are also used: "Truly, you [Muhammad] are of a tremendous nature" (Qur'an 68:4); or "And God is significant witness that Muhammad is the messenger of God" (Qur'an 48:28–29).
9. *etek* (the skirt, or lower part): This area contains Part B of the *hilye* text, along with a prayer for the Prophet and the calligrapher's signature.
10, 11. *koltuklar* (armpits): On either side of the *etek* are empty spaces called *koltuklar*, which may be illuminated.

Note that this is a general scheme; many different models of the *hilye* also exist (see cat. no. 17 for an example).

TUĞLAR

ZÜLFELER

SULTAN'S TITLE
OR HONORIFIC

DIŞ BEYZA

İÇ BEYZA

HANÇER

CALLIGRAPHER'S
SIGNATURE

KÜRSÜ

The most popular *hilyeler* are written in *sülüs* and *nesih;* in *muhakkak,* *sülüs,* and *nesih;* and in *ta'lîk.* In the last century, large *hilye levhalar,* using *celî* scripts, were made to be hung on walls. Early *hilye levhalar* were pasted on wooden panels, as large paper for making big sheets of cardboard was not available. Most of these pieces are now full of holes, having fallen victim to woodworms. As more-sizable paper became available, subsequent *hilye levhalar* have escaped this fate.

Illuminators took great pains to decorate *hilye levhalar* with the art of *tezhîb* (illumination). The pieces were gilded abundantly with yellow and green gold. To make them worthy of depicting the dignity of the Prophet, some *hilyeler* were even written in gold ink in the *zerendûd* method. Occasionally, too, one comes across a *hilye* with miniatures of Mecca and Medina just above the *besmele.*

FERMANLAR, BERATLAR, AND MENŞÛRLAR

Specialists at the Ottoman Imperial Council of State prepared various official documents, including *fermanlar* (imperial edicts; cat. no. 67), *beratlar* (which included imperial titles of privilege and grants of freehold property [*mülk beratı*]; cat. nos. 61, 63–66, and 68–69), and *menşûrlar* (imperial appointments; cat. nos. 70–71). The *tuğra* (calligraphic emblem) of the reigning sultan was inscribed at the head of the document, and before it came a short prayer. Originally, these documents were made as *tomarlar* (scrolls) or pleated for safekeeping. In recent times, people have begun to frame such pieces and hang them as

Figure 20. The elements of the tuğra. *This* tuğra *was created by Mustafa Râkım (1171/1758–1241/1826) for Sultan Mahmud II (r. 1808–39).*

works of art. Here, these documents will be discussed from the standpoint of their calligraphy and illumination, rather than their content and meaning.

Just as nations today represent themselves with symbols or emblems, so in Ottoman times a calligraphic emblem represented the state. That emblem was the *tuğra*, a calligraphic treatment of the reigning sovereign's name that would be official so long as that sovereign remained on the throne. The earliest example is the simple *tuğra* of Sultan Orhan Gâzi (r. 1326–59).

The *tuğra* consists of the sovereign's name, his patronymic, and the invocation *el-muzaffer dâimâ* (the ever-victorious), written in a special shape. *Tuğralar* are also encountered consisting of the names of Sufi saints, a verse from the Qur'an, or a *hadîs* (saying of the Prophet Muhammad). Figure 20 shows the main elements of the *tuğra*: the *kürsü* or *sere*, which is the monogram proper; the *tuğlar* or *elifler* (shafts); the *zülfeler* (tassels); the *iç beyza* and *dış beyza* (inner and outer ovals); and the *hançer* or *kollar* (dagger or arms—the double tail-like projections growing out of, and to the right of, the ovals).

The *tuğra* developed slowly, achieving its basic form in the reign of Sultan Mehmed the Conqueror (1451–81). It reached its classic, lavish form during the reign of Sultan Süleyman I, the Magnificent (or the Lawgiver; 1520–66), in keeping with the splendor of that period. The *tuğra* was written in gold ink, delicately outlined in black ink. From the period of Mehmed the Conqueror on, the spaces between the letters were illuminated, a practice that continued until the mid-nineteenth century. All the skills of the illuminator were displayed in these works so that, from time to time, the *tuğra* itself was nearly hidden behind the decoration, like a bride behind her veil (cat. nos. 64–65). From the first quarter of the seventeenth century, a certain coarseness was sometimes evident in the illumination, and from then on, the *tuğra* began to degenerate.

With the revolution of shape and dimension in calligraphy brought about by Mustafa Râkım at the beginning of the nineteenth century, the *tuğra* was transformed into a masterpiece of proportion. It was no longer thought necessary to illuminate it, but, under Western influence, the *tuğra* was often surrounded with radiating sun rays in gold. While Râkım's style of *tuğra* is frequently found on monumental inscriptions, it is rarely seen on documents issued by the Imperial Council of State. The most beautiful examples of the *tuğra*, simple and without illumination, were produced from the reign of Sultan Abdülaziz until the end of the Ottoman epoch (1861–1922; cat. nos. 50, 70, and 71).

In early Ottoman times, official documents were written only in *tevkî'* or *rıkâ'*, because these scripts are easy to read. Beginning in the sixteenth century, however, the more difficult *dîvânî* and *celî dîvânî* were used and thus entered their most perfect and regularized period. Although it is the right of the calligrapher to sign his work, the documents that came from the Imperial Council of State never bore

Figure 21. Necmeddin Okyay (1300/1883–1396/1976), İcâzetnâme, 1322/1905. Ink, colors, and gold on paper, ta'lîk, 29.2 × 19.8 cm (11⅜ × 7¾ in.). The icâzetnâme *was granted by Sâmi Efendi (1253/1838–1330/1912). The illumination is by Bahaddin Tokatlıoğlu (1283/1866–1358/1939). Derman Collection, Istanbul*

signatures for the *tuğra* or the text. It is said that the official calligraphers who worked at the Council of State had to take an oath never to use either *dîvânî* or *celî dîvânî* outside the council.

Black, red, green, and blue inks, as well as gold, were used to write the *tuğralar* and the *dîvânî* and *celî dîvânî* scripts on *fermanlar*, *beratlar*, *menşûrlar*, and other official documents. The choice of which of the two scripts to use, which colors, and whether or not to use a gold-sprinkled background (*zer-efşan*) was not arbitrary. Each had a specific meaning in Ottoman protocol.

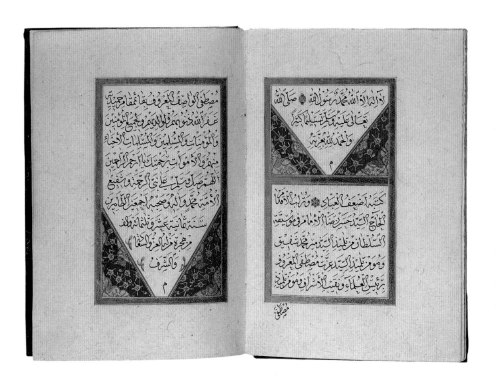

A CALLIGRAPHER'S TRAINING

Children would begin to study calligraphy at their local elementary school to determine if they had any talent for it. To work at beautiful writing at a young age trains the eye in visual proportion and aesthetic value. Early lessons were a means of advancing those with talent and inclination for the art.

The great masters of calligraphy received a regular monthly or daily salary from their positions at the Imperial Council of State, the Imperial Palace Service (Enderûn-ı Hümâyun), or the like, or from teaching posts at a school or endowed institution such as the *meşkhâne*, which was a calligraphy studio attached to a religious college. Master calligraphers also gave private lessons at their homes on appointed days. Even the poorest of these calligraphers expected no remuneration from their students, however, not even gifts. This tradition has been scrupulously observed up to the present.

From the earliest days, calligraphers were required to have the proper certification to practice the art. The novice calligrapher had to have his teacher's written permission, the *icâzetnâme*. Without it, he could not put his signature on his work.

To learn calligraphy, the student (*talebe*) goes to the *hoca*, or teacher, who writes a model line, while the student is watching, for the student to study and copy. This text is called a *meşk* (model or lesson). To receive this model for study is called *meşk almak*, to take the model; to teach it is called *meşk etmek*, to do the model. (*Meşkler* are discussed in the entries for cat. nos. 28–29 and 41.)

The student studies the *meşk* of the teacher and makes copies that are as close to the original as possible. This practice is called *taklîd*. To correct the lesson, the *hoca* writes the correct forms, measured in dots, directly beneath any letters or words that do not meet his approval. This is called *çıkartma* (extraction). Using the corrected lesson as a guide, the student prepares a new *meşk*. If the teacher or master (*üstâd*) sees a shortcoming, he again writes his *çıkartma* under that part of the lesson (fig. 2).

In *meşk* exercises, the *sülüs* and *nesih* scripts are shown sometimes separately (cat. no. 18) but most often together (cat. no. 41). The same teacher teaches both scripts. *Ta'lîk* is always studied separately, and usually with a different teacher (cat. nos. 28, 29, 53, and 55). Because their use was confined to the Imperial Council of State, the *tuğra* and the *dîvânî* and *celî dîvânî* scripts were taught only there. *Rık'a*, which had utilitarian rather than artistic value, was first taught at elementary school and later was quickly mastered at the various official departments and offices.

Novices whose aptitude was weak were eliminated while still practicing the *müfredât* (singles) exercises (cat. nos. 28 and 41); that is, *meşkler* composed of single and double letters. Those who passed this stage could look forward with hope to a future as a calligrapher. The next step would be the exercises called *mürekkebât* (compounds; cat. nos. 29, 53, and 55), which involved words and sentences of more than two letters. Students studying *sülüs* and *nesih* would copy in Arabic one of the long poetic odes called *kasîdeler* (cat. nos. 30 and 36). Those studying *ta'lîk* would write a *kasîde* in Persian or Turkish (cat. nos. 29, 53, and 55). Finally, the novice would practice writing well-known Qur'anic verses, *hadîsler*, prayers, letters of the alphabetic numbering system (*abced hesabı*, a series of mnemonic words arranged in alphabetical order from one to a thousand, and heavily used for dating purposes), and epigrams concerning the art of calligraphy. Writing these texts would help the student develop an understanding of composition. Students who made steady progress and continued with weekly lessons could work through these stages in three to five years. Those who finished would receive diplomas. The diploma, which gave them the right to sign their own works, is called an *icâzetnâme* (permission document); receiving the document is called *icâzet almak* (receiving permission). When signing a work, the calligrapher writes, in Arabic, *katabahu* (he wrote it; Turkish spelling: *ketebehû*) in front of his name, so the diploma can also be referred to as the *ketebe kıt'ası* (the "he wrote" *kıt'a*; fig. 21).

Students earn their teacher's *icâzet* (permission) by copying a suitable work by one of the great masters, selected by their teacher. Like the practice of copying the teacher's *meşk*, this process is also known as *taklîd*, or imitation, which has a special meaning in regard to calligraphy. The calligrapher carefully observes the selected composition, imprinting it on his memory. He then writes it on paper with near-photographic fidelity (cat. no. 33). The writing must be so close to the original that if the student's work were superimposed over the master's, no difference would be visible. This difficult feat requires the calligrapher to analyze thoroughly the style and technique of the calligrapher he is copying. Even calligraphers at the height of their art take pleasure in *taklîd*, as a sign of reverence for the work of a great master. No tracing is employed in this process, and forgery is not an issue. Rather, the calligrapher indicates in the signature that the work is a *taklîd* and cites the name of the person whose work is imitated. The *kıt'a* format is usually selected for imitation, and the finished copy constitutes the student calligrapher's *icâzetnâme*. Sometimes, however, a section of the Qur'an, or even the whole *mushaf*, is written as an *icâzetnâme* for a student of *nesih*. The *hilye-i saadet* can also serve as an *icâzetnâme* for a student of *sülüs* and *nesih*.

After the student has written the imitation for an *icâzetnâme* in *sülüs* and *nesih* and it is approved by the teacher, the teacher writes under it, in *rıkâ'* (or, as it was later called, *hatt-ı icâze*, or *icâzet* script), the permission text, *izinnâme*, granting the student's diploma. For a student of *ta'lîk*, the *izinnâme* is written in *hurde ta'lîk*. The wording of this text, which is in Arabic, is traditional (fig. 21). The permission formula that is generally used, with some changes or additions, can be translated as follows: "I give permission [*icâzet* or *izin*] to the writer of this beautiful *kıt'a* [student's name] to sign his name under his work. May God prolong his life and increase his knowledge. I am his teacher." Here the teacher writes his name and the date.

At last the student has earned the right to the title *hattat*, or calligrapher. At an *icâzet cemiyeti* (*icâzet* assembly), which usually takes place in a mosque, the new calligrapher's illuminated work is presented to a "jury" composed of masters of calligraphy. This pleasant and auspicious ceremony has been maintained into our own time. Even renowned calligraphers who, for whatever reason, could not receive their *icâzet* at the usual time would not break with this tradition and so received their *icâzet* later in their careers.

Throughout the Ottoman era, the most advanced calligrapher in terms of ability, sagacity, and seniority, as determined by the calligraphers themselves, was called the *reisü'l-hattâtîn*, or chief of the calligraphers. On his death, another would be named. The eldest of the living calligraphers was called the *şeyhü'l-hattâtîn*, or the sheikh of the calligraphers, out of respect, but this title was honorary, not official.

Finally, a word about signatures. Over the centuries, the tradition took root to sign a calligraphic work in Arabic, regardless of whether the text was in Turkish, Arabic, or Persian. There were various signature formulas beginning with an Arabic verb: *katabahu, namaqahu, harrarahu*, or *sawwadahu* (Turkish spellings: *ketebehû, nemekahû, harrerehû*, and *sevvedehû*), all of which mean "he wrote it." The word preferred among calligraphers to mean "signature" was *ketebe*. If the work were a *meşk* or a *karalama*, it would generally be signed *meşekahû* (he wrote it as a *meşk*) or with the calligrapher's name only.

The calligrapher would add Arabic qualifiers to his name, such as *fakîr* (the poor), *hakîr* (the lowly), and *müznib* (the sinful)—all terms of humility to deflect any charge of conceit. To show gratitude to his teacher, the calligrapher would cite his teacher's name and sometimes even add a genealogical tree of the calligraphers of his particular school. At the end of the signature, the calligrapher would ask God to forgive them all, even those who would look at the work.

Works were usually signed in the same script as the text. The *hurde ta'lîk* script was considered the most appropriate for signing *ta'lîk kıt'alar* and *celî ta'lîk levhalar*. Signatures for works in *sülüs* or *nesih* can be signed in *rıkâ'*, which has come to be called *icâzet yazısı*. *Rıkâ'* calligraphy can be used to write *icâzetnâmeler* for other branches of knowledge, such as for classical religious education, Sufism, and so forth (fig. 22).

Figure 23. Calligrapher unknown, Folios 1v and 2r from the Persian-language Most Eloquent Odes *for Sultan Bâyezid II (r. 1481–1512), 15th–16th century. Ink, colors, and gold on paper,* hurde ta'lîk, *20.5 × 13.2 cm (8 × 5⅛ in.). Sakıp Sabancı Collection, Istanbul (318)*

TURKISH CALLIGRAPHY TODAY

Turkish calligraphy reached its height of perfection in the nineteenth and early twentieth centuries. But in 1928, it received a heavy blow when the Turkish Republic supplanted the Arabic alphabet with a modified version of the Latin alphabet. Even though formal instruction in the art was reinstituted at the Academy of Fine Arts (now Mimar Sinan University), Istanbul, in 1936, the academy was unable to ensure the training of new calligraphers. As the remaining Ottoman calligraphers died, one by one, this historical chapter seemed closed.

In fact, however, the master-and-student system has continued to produce new calligraphers, with the help of the Center for Islamic History, Art, and Culture (IRCICA), in Istanbul. In addition to its program of publications and conferences, this organization announced in 1986 an international calligraphy competition, to be held every three years. Calligraphers from all Islamic nations, and the United States, participated in the most recent competition. It is pleasing to see that the young Turkish calligraphers are reaching a professional level in the art and are once again increasing in number.

Legibility is the prime goal of the art of calligraphy. While this is indeed the essence of the art, the splendid beauty that resides in the calligraphic strokes should be appreciated as well. "To read beautiful calligraphy," Kâdıasker Mustafa İzzet Efendi noted, "is like smelling the aroma of a tulip." Even for those who cannot read the texts, this volume gives a glimpse of the spiritual elegance and grace that was to be found in the Ottoman tulip garden.

Catalogue

ŞEYH HAMDULLAH

833/1429–926/1520

Şeyh Hamdullah was born in the north-central Anatolian town of Amasya. According to one source, his birth occurred in 833/1429; another source has it as 840/1436. To judge by the features of an undated Qur'an (now in the collection of the Süleymaniye Library, Istanbul) that we know he wrote at the age of eighty-nine, the first source is probably the more accurate. His father, Mustafa Dede, was a sheikh of the Sühreverdî order and a member of the Turkish community of Bukhara, in Central Asia, who had migrated to Amasya. Şeyh Hamdullah Efendi signed his works İbni'ş-Şeyh (Son of the Sheikh) or Hamdullah—never Şeyh (Sheikh) Hamdullah. (Şeyh Hamdullah was also an accomplished archer, and acquired his title as sheikh of the Atıcılar Tekkesi [marksmen's lodge] then located in Ok Meydanı, the archers' grounds reserved for this purpose after the conquest of Constantinople.)

In addition to studying the traditional curriculum in Amasya, he learned the six scripts there under the tutelage of Hayreddin Mar'aşî, a follower of the style of Yāqūt al-Mustaʿsimī (Yāqūt; d. 698/1298). Şeyh Hamdullah also studied the calligraphic works of Abdullah al-Sayrafī (active 14th century). When he was governor of Amasya, Bâyezid (1450–1512), son of Sultan Mehmed the Conqueror (r. 1451–81), befriended Şeyh Hamdullah and studied calligraphy with him. When the sultan died and Bâyezid succeeded to the throne in Istanbul in 886/1481, he invited his calligraphy master to the capital. Şeyh Hamdullah accepted the invitation and became master calligrapher at the Ottoman palace.

This was the beginning of a new phase in his artistic career. Sultan Bâyezid II esteemed his teacher so highly that he would hold the sheikh's inkwell and put a pillow behind his back as he wrote. The sultan wished that Yāqūt's style be developed and, for this purpose, gave Şeyh Hamdullah the most beautiful of Yāqūt's works kept at the court so that he might study them carefully. This event probably took place in 890/1485. After careful scrutiny of these works, Şeyh Hamdullah was able to elaborate a style of his own; thereafter, he became known as the calligrapher's lodestar (kıbletü'l-küttâb).

Şeyh Hamdullah was a master of all six scripts. He spent the better portion of his life copying the Qur'an, producing forty-seven copies in all. He also produced a large number of En'âm-ı Şerîfler (special collections of Qur'anic chapters), separate cüzler of the Qur'an, collections of prayers, tomar scrolls, kıt'alar, murakkaalar, collections of meşkler (exercises), and so forth.

He was also responsible for the inscriptions in the Bâyezid, Fîruzağa, and Davud Paşa mosques in Istanbul, and in the Bâyezid Mosque in Edirne. Although these inscriptions illustrate his achievement in celî sülüs, they are rather primitive in comparison with the celî that was to appear after him.

1. **Murakkaa**
Istanbul, 15th–early 16th century
Sülüs and nesih
Ink, colors, and gold on paper mounted on cardboard
Each kıt'a 21.4 × 30 cm (8⅜ × 11⅛ in.)
(243)

Illustrated here are the thirteenth and fourteenth kıt'alar, in sülüs and nesih, from a murakkaa composed of fourteen kıt'alar by Şeyh Hamdullah. Early kıt'alar were often restored to preserve their value. Most such restorations date to the reign of Sultan Ahmed III (1703–30) and the years following his reign. The dış pervaz (outer border) on murakkaalar restored in this period is often made with ebrû paper created by the great marbling master Hatib Mehmed Efendi (d. 1187/1773). Such is the case here. Mehmed Efendi's papers are characterized by extraordinary color and animation.

Mehmed Efendi was the hatib of the Ayasofya Mosque, and the ebrû style he developed (hatib ebrûsu; see cat. no. 14) also bears that name. (A hatib is the religious official who gives the Friday sermon in a congregational mosque.) Hatib Mehmed Efendi studied the sülüs and nesih scripts with the calligrapher İsmail Zühdi (d. 1144/1731), but his primary art was marbling. His subtle palette and alluring designs make Hatib Mehmed Efendi a great figure in the art of ebrû. He died in the month of Muharrem 1187/April 1773, when his house in the Hocapaşa (Sirkeci) district of Istanbul caught fire. His marbled papers were all destroyed.

When this album was being restored, the defects in the paper were covered using the eighteenth-century

beyne's-sütur (often referred to as cloud-cartouche) style of illumination. The gold frames (cedveller) were redrawn, and the iç pervaz between them was illuminated in the style of the period. The outer borders were decorated with a marbled paper called şal (shawl), which in turn was decorated with zer-efşan, or flecks of gold ink or gold leaf. The outer borders of kıt'alar are normally equal in width. The borders here, however, are not equal, probably because the pieces were adapted to fit a very fine şemse kap binding originally made for another purpose. It was the practice to decorate facing kıt'alar in an album in an identical manner, as was done in this murakkaa.

It is impossible to say exactly how many students learned calligraphy from Şeyh Hamdullah, but the most prominent of his students were his son, Mustafa Dede (900/1495–945/1538), whom he named after his own father, and his son-in-law, Şükrullah Halîfe. Their children and grandchildren also learned the art and taught it to succeeding generations, thereby making Şeyh Hamdullah's family the most prolific in the number of master calligraphers it produced. Şeyh Hamdullah died toward the end of 926/1520 and was buried in the Karacaahmed Cemetery, in the Üsküdar quarter of Istanbul. Later calligraphers considered burial near his grave a great honor. They called the area around his grave Şeyh Sofası, or Hall of the Sheikh. Some novice calligraphers buried their pens for a week in the soil near his grave, hoping for a blessing from his spiritual power.

2. En'âm

Istanbul, 15th–early 16th century
Nesih
Ink, colors, and gold on paper
Binding 19.2 × 12.9 cm (7½ × 5¼ in.)
(283)

This work contains only the chapter of the Qur'an titled *En'âm*, or The Cattle (Qur'an 6:1–165). This chapter of the Qur'an is read in hope of receiving spiritual blessings and, in this case, was written, illuminated, and bound as a small separate book. A more common volume is the *En'âm-ı Şerîf* (cat. no. 24). In that format, the chapter *En'âm* comes first, followed by other frequently recited chapters of the Qur'an, such as *Yâsîn* (36); *Rahman*, or The Compassionate (55); and *Mülk*, or The Sovereignty (67).

This volume was written by Şeyh Hamdullah in *nesih* script, ten lines per page. Although the work is undated—Şeyh Hamdullah rarely dated his work—it was done after he developed his new style. Folios 1v and 2r are shown here.

At court, Sultan Bâyezid II (r. 1481–1512) would seat Şeyh Hamdullah in the place of honor during discussions of religion, a sign of favor that rankled the learned theologians who were also present. At one such session, it is said, the sheikh displayed a Qur'an he had written, and the theologians expressed great admiration of it. After the meeting, as the scholars stacked their papers and books, the sultan asked where the Qur'an should be placed. "No book may ever be placed on top of the Qur'an," said the theologians. "It must therefore be placed on top of our works." Smiling, Bâyezid responded, "No one has revived the writing of the Qur'an as much as Şeyh Hamdullah. How, then, can I seat him in a place inferior to yours?" The theologians had no reply.

بِسْمِ اللَّهِ الرَّحْمَٰنِ الرَّحِيمِ

الْحَمْدُ لِلَّهِ الَّذِي خَلَقَ السَّمَاوَاتِ وَالْأَرْضَ
وَجَعَلَ الظُّلُمَاتِ وَالنُّورَ ثُمَّ الَّذِينَ كَفَرُوا
بِرَبِّهِمْ يَعْدِلُونَ ۝ هُوَ الَّذِي خَلَقَكُمْ مِنْ طِينٍ
ثُمَّ قَضَى أَجَلًا وَأَجَلٌ مُسَمًّى عِنْدَهُ ثُمَّ أَنْتُمْ
تَمْتَرُونَ ۝ وَهُوَ اللَّهُ فِي السَّمَاوَاتِ وَفِي الْأَرْضِ
يَعْلَمُ سِرَّكُمْ وَجَهْرَكُمْ وَيَعْلَمُ مَا
تَكْسِبُونَ ۝ وَمَا تَأْتِيهِمْ مِنْ آيَةٍ مِنْ آيَاتِ

رَبِّهِمْ إِلَّا كَانُوا عَنْهَا مُعْرِضِينَ ۝ فَقَدْ
كَذَّبُوا بِالْحَقِّ لَمَّا جَاءَهُمْ فَسَوْفَ يَأْتِيهِمْ
أَنْبَاءُ مَا كَانُوا بِهِ يَسْتَهْزِئُونَ ۝ أَلَمْ يَرَوْا
كَمْ أَهْلَكْنَا مِنْ قَبْلِهِمْ مِنْ قَرْنٍ مَكَّنَّاهُمْ
فِي الْأَرْضِ مَا لَمْ نُمَكِّنْ لَكُمْ وَأَرْسَلْنَا السَّمَاءَ
عَلَيْهِمْ مِدْرَارًا وَجَعَلْنَا الْأَنْهَارَ تَجْرِي مِنْ
تَحْتِهِمْ فَأَهْلَكْنَاهُمْ بِذُنُوبِهِمْ وَأَنْشَأْنَا
مِنْ بَعْدِهِمْ قَرْنًا آخَرِينَ ۝ وَلَوْ نَزَّلْنَا عَلَيْكَ
كِتَابًا فِي قِرْطَاسٍ فَلَمَسُوهُ بِأَيْدِيهِمْ
لَقَالَ الَّذِينَ كَفَرُوا إِنْ هَٰذَا إِلَّا سِحْرٌ مُبِينٌ

ŞEHZÂDE KORKUT
822/1467–919/1513

Ebu'l-Hayr Mehmed Korkut was born in Amasya, the son of then Prince Bâyezid (1450–1512) and the second of eight brothers. He was the most beloved grandchild of Sultan Mehmed the Conqueror (r. 1451–81), who saw to it that Prince Korkut received the most rigorous education in his palace. After Bâyezid became sultan in 1481, Prince Korkut intermittently held the governorship of Manisa, Antalya, and, again, Manisa between 1484 and 1512.

In the last days of his father's reign, Prince Korkut wished to succeed him to the throne. In 1512, when his brother Prince Selim became Sultan Selim I, the Grim, Korkut would not oppose him and returned to Manisa as governor. Concerned about the possible fragmentation of the empire, Selim I (r. 1512–20) had his brother captured and strangled. He died on Muharrem 5, 919/March 13, 1513, and was buried next to the tomb of Sultan Orhan Gâzi (r. 1326–59), in Bursa.

Prince Korkut wrote six highly regarded works on religious subjects and, under the pen name Harîmî, a collection of poems. This talented prince also composed musical works and zealously promoted the development of Ottoman scholarship.

3. Qur'an
Istanbul?, late 15th century
Nesih
Ink, colors, and gold on paper
Binding 21.3 × 16.3 cm (8¼ × 6⅜ in.)
(279)

Many members of the Ottoman dynasty were trained in the arts. A number of sultans, in fact, had a serious interest in poetry, music, and calligraphy. Şehzâde (Prince) Korkut Çelebi wrote the Qur'an whose *serlevha* (illuminated opening spread; folios 1v and 2r) is shown here. The scion of a family that distinguished itself in science and culture, Prince Korkut studied calligraphy with Şeyh Hamdullah (see cat. nos. 1–2) while the sheikh still lived in Amasya. This Qur'an is the only known extant example of the prince's work. It is written in an amateurish *nesih* script, thirteen lines per page, on 350 folios. Had Prince Korkut lived longer, he would undoubtedly have become one of Şeyh Hamdullah's noted followers.

This undated Qur'an is a fine example of the art of Ottoman illumination in the late fifteenth century.

HÜSEYİN ŞAH

D. AFTER 965/1557

A native of Istanbul, Hüseyin Şah was always close to Şeyh Hamdullah (see cat. nos. 1–2) and received calligraphy training from him alongside the sheikh's own son, Mustafa Dede. The prayer handbook shown here provides evidence that Hüseyin Şah was Şeyh Hamdullah's slave. (Any discussion of slavery is problematic, but it is worth noting that most faithful Muslims tried to bring a measure of humanity to the practice.)

The child could already have been named Şah (Shah), implying kingship, when he was purchased, or Şeyh Hamdullah could have given Hüseyin the name Şah afterward. In any event, he took the child under his wing and raised him as an elder brother to his own son. He not only taught the boy his art but considered him to be his successor. (Other slaves also learned calligraphy from their masters. Two Caucasian slaves stand out: the sixteenth-century Hasan Çelebi, the slave of Ahmed Karahisârî [see cat. no. 6], and Mehmed Hâşim [d. 1261/1845], the slave of Mustafa Râkım [see cat. no. 27]. After being emancipated, both were adopted by their former owners and were taught calligraphy and became masters of the art.)

It is reported that when he liked a particular work by Hüseyin Şah, Şeyh Hamdullah would sign it with his own name, a mark of high esteem. After the sheikh's death, Hüseyin Şah was known as Hüsameddin Halîfe and wrote primarily in the *nesih* script. He lived a long life and died sometime after 965/1557. His burial place is unknown.

4. **Prayer Handbook**
Istanbul, before 926/1520
Nesih
Ink, colors, and gold on paper
Binding 21.2 × 14.5 cm (8¼ × 5⅝ in.)
(361)

These are the last two pages, folios 5v and 6r, from a handbook of prayers written by Hüseyin Şah on six folios. This volume, with its format of eight lines per page, clearly shows how close Hüseyin Şah's *nesih* script was to that of his master, Şeyh Hamdullah.

Although the book is undated, it was apparently written before the death of Şeyh Hamdullah in 926/1520. It was common in practice (though not a matter of law) that the bond of slavery was broken on the death of the master. Hüseyin Şah indicates in the colophon, on folio 6r, that he was still a "slave of the sheikh," however, and there is no reference in the colophon to the death of Şeyh Hamdullah. Regarding his own name, Hüseyin Şah mentions in the colophon of a later work (965/1557) now in the Topkapı Sarayı Museum Library, Istanbul, that his father was Abdullah (slave of God). (Because slaves' lineages were not tracked, they were assigned a patronymic, frequently Abdullah.) Hüseyin Şah sometimes signed himself "son of Abdullah."

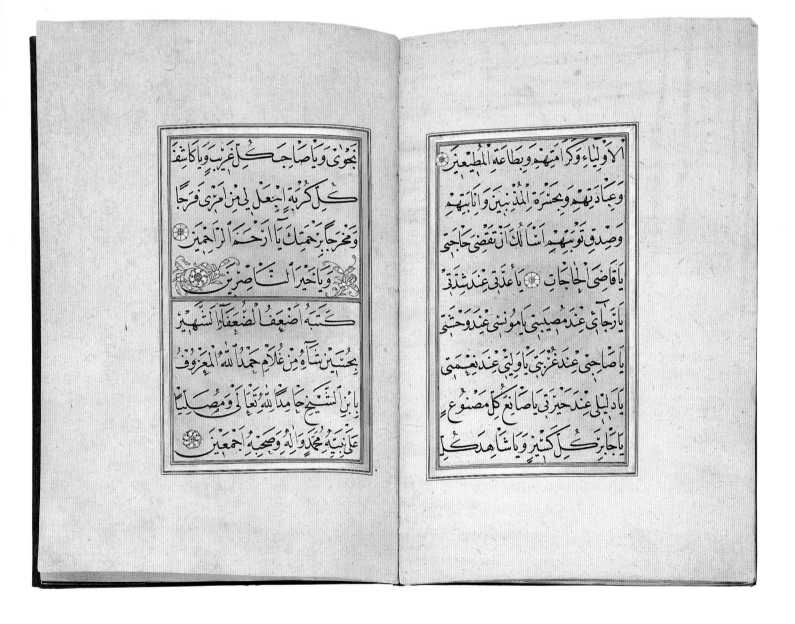

CALLIGRAPHER UNKNOWN

5. Qur'an
Istanbul, 16th century
Nesih
Ink, colors, and gold on paper
Binding 27.3 × 18.5 cm (10⅞ × 7¼ in.)
(56)

This fine Qur'anic codex, or *mushaf*, was written in the style of Şeyh Hamdullah (see cat. nos. 1–2), probably by one of his students. It was copied in an excellent *nesih* script, thirteen lines per page, on 348 folios. The *hâtime tezhîbi* (colophon illumination) and *ketebe* (signature), which occur at the end of the volume, have been cut out, perhaps by a thief years ago. With the *hâtime* missing, it is impossible to know whether the director of the illumination signed the work. (Because the illumination of most *mushaflar* was a joint effort by different artists, their individual signatures were not given; only the director signed.) Judging by the style of illumination of the *serlevha* (the two illuminated opening pages, folios 1v and 2r, shown here), this Qur'an can be dated to the late days of the reign of Sultan Süleyman I, the Magnificent (or the Lawgiver; r. 1520–66).

In a *serlevha*, the entire text of the *Fâtiha*—the opening chapter of the Qur'an—is written on the right-hand page (folio 1v). The first verses of the second chapter, *Bakara* (The Cow), are written on the left-hand page (folio 2r), following the layout of the *Fâtiha:* the number of lines and the dimensions of the writing space are identical. The top, bottom, and outside margins are illuminated, but not the gutter where the pages join. The color scheme of the two illuminated pages is the same; the design of the left is a mirror image of that of the right, making the two pages a unified whole. Although subsequent pages reserve larger areas for the text, their layout echoes that of the *Fâtiha*.

In this example, the design elements are very well balanced. The verse stops in the text portion of the *serlevha* are in the style called *havalı* or *çift tahrir;* empty areas are filled with leaf and branch motifs. The *tuğ* motifs in the margins—lancetlike floral and geometric designs alternating between the pages' dominant lapis lazuli blue and gold—are in the same style. They emerge from golden *bulut* (cloud) motifs that contain the text area. All the colors and designs serve to harmonize the sixteenth-century-style illumination with the cream-colored paper.

The *rumîli koltuk* (rectangular area) on each side of the text space is painted on a gilded background. The designs in these areas can also be seen on Iznik tiles decorating the Salon of Sultan Murad III (r. 1574–95) at the Topkapı Sarayı, Istanbul.

On the other pages of this *mushaf*, the *sûre başları* (chapter heads) and the *aşere, hızib,* and *secde* rosettes are executed in lapis and gold.

AHMED KARAHİSÂRÎ
875/1470?–963/1556

Ahmed Şemseddin Karahisârî was born in Afyon Karahisar, a west-central Anatolian city, but his exact date of birth is unknown. We do know, however, that he died in 963/1556, aged nearly ninety, so we can safely assume he was born a little before 875/1470. One report states that his first master was Yahyâ es-Sûfî (d. 882/1477), one of the calligraphers of the age of Sultan Mehmed the Conqueror (r. 1451–81), but the reliability of this report is suspect, for Ottoman sources regularly confuse this Yahyâ es-Sûfî with a later namesake. It is likely, however, that Karahisârî benefited from the calligraphic works of the earlier Yahyâ es-Sûfî. The master to whom Karahisârî always acknowledged apprenticeship, as he did in the Qur'an illustrated here, is Esedullâh-ı Kirmânî (d. 893/1488), but we do not know where he studied with him.

Karahisârî is known as the reviver in the Ottoman state of the style of Yāqūt al-Mustaʿsimī (Yāqūt; d. 698/1298), thereby earning him the title of *Yâkût-i Rûm*, or the Yāqūt of Asia Minor. There is a *mushaf* dating from the later years of his life which, in his own words, he "copied in imitation of Yāqūt" in finely written *nesih*. This style could not compete with Şeyh Hamdullah's style (see cat. nos. 1–2), however, and so was abandoned by the following generation. We may say that Karahisârî's style accomplished a double task: putting an end to Yāqūt's style and bringing three of the six scripts—*sülüs, nesih,* and *rıkâ'*—closer to the Ottoman taste. Only in *celî sülüs* was Karahisârî's style more effective than that of the sheikh.

Karahisârî's surviving works include Qur'ans, prayer handbooks, *kıt'alar,* and *murakkaalar.* Although there are surviving *celî* works cut in marble and worked on tiles, these bear no signature, and it is impossible to tell whether they are by him or by his student Hasan Çelebi (d. after 1002/1594), whose method was identical. In addition to Hasan Çelebi, Karahisârî's students Derviş Mehmed (d. 1000/1592), Ferhad Paşa (d. 982/1575), and Muhiddin Halîfe (d. 983/1575) are worthy of mention.

Karahisârî died in 963/1556. It is said that he copied the inscription for his gravestone himself, but the exact location of his grave, in the Sütlüce quarter of Istanbul, is unknown.

6. Qur'an
Istanbul, 948/1541
Nesih
Ink, colors, and gold on paper
Binding 19.6 × 12.8 cm (7⅝ × 4⅞ in.)
(278)

Ahmed Karahisârî was about seventy when he copied this Qur'an, dated 948/1541. It is written in a small *nesih* script, seventeen lines per page, which allowed him to complete the *mushaf* in only 236 folios.

This Qur'an is notable for its extremely fine example of the *zahriye,* or frontispiece. Islamic bound manuscripts always begin the text on the right-hand page (folio 1v). The back of the first page of text (folio 1r) is called the *zahriye,* from the Arabic word for "back," *zahr.* This page can be left plain so that notations concerning the book or its owner can be added, or it can be illuminated. The financial resources of an Islamic state or dynasty would determine whether works prepared under its patronage would be finely illuminated with one, two, or, more rarely, four *zahriyeler.* In a Qur'an, the *zahriye* could consist of a simple illumination, or it could include one or more Qur'anic verses worked into the design. The central element could be circular, elliptical, or shuttle-shaped. In works other than Qur'ans, the *temellük kitâbesi* (ownership inscription) could be on this page. In short—until the sixteenth century, when the practice fell out of use in the interest of economy—the *zahriye* gave illuminators an opportunity to create an artistic tour de force, independent from the calligraphy.

The double *zahriye* shown here includes a passage from *Isra,* or The

Night Journey (Qur'an 17:88): "Say: If all mankind and Jinns got together to produce the like of this Qur'an, they could never produce it, even if they supported each other to try." The verse is written at the center of circular cartouches, on a gold background, in white-lead ink.

This magnificence is continued in the extraordinarily fine illumination of the *serlevha*, *hâtime*, and chapter headings of this *mushaf*.

Mustafa bİn İbrahİm

ACTIVE 16TH CENTURY

7. Qur'an
959/1552
Nesih and *rıkâ'*
Ink, colors, and gold on paper
Binding 31 × 20.5 cm (12⅛ × 7⅞ in.)
(345)

Nothing is known of Mustafa bin
İbrahim, who completed this Qur'an in
Muharrem 959/January 1552, except
that he was from Salonika (present-day
Thessaloníki), as is indicated by his
signing himself Selânikî. The *mushaf*
has thirteen lines per page, on 336
folios. Written in an attractive *nesih*
script, it gives the impression of having
been copied quickly and easily.
Compared to the double *zahriye* in
Karahisârî's *mushaf* (cat. no. 6), the
single *zahriye* in this volume is quite
uninspired: verses 77–89 of chapter 56
of the Qur'an are written within a
circle, in a thickish *rıkâ'* script. The
pages shown here—folios 137v and
138r—consist of verses 125–28 from
chapter 16 through verses 1–10 of
chapter 17.

The *serlevha* in this *mushaf* is
rather heavily decorated with gold-
and-lapis-lazuli-blue illumination that
is of middling quality. The chapter
headings are not illuminated; instead,
the titles are written in *rıkâ'* script, in
gold ink outlined in black. The *aşere*
symbols are without illumination, and
the *duraklar* (verse stops) are quite
plain. The volume has been rebound.

It is not known where this *mushaf*
was written.

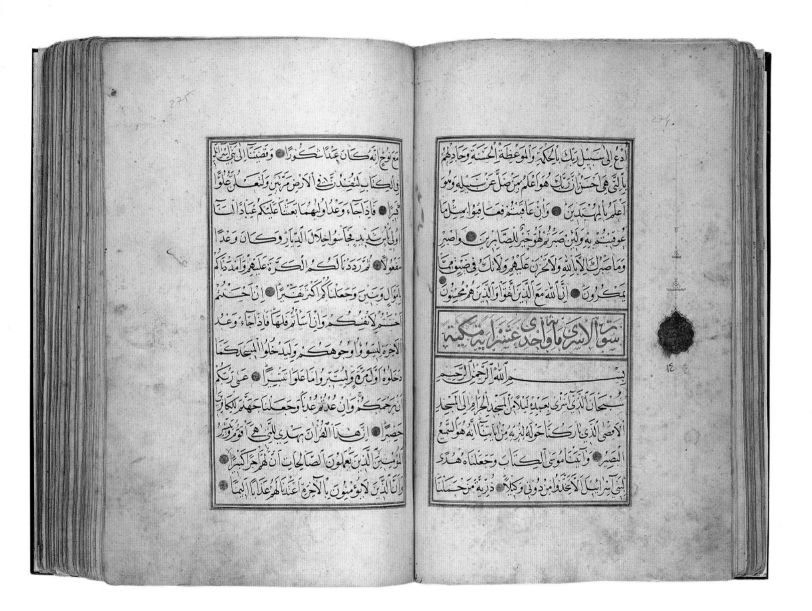

KÂDI MAHMUD EFENDİ

D. 985/1575

Mahmud Efendi studied calligraphy with Selânikli Mustafa bin Nasuh, who had been a student of Şeyh Hamdullah's (see cat. nos. 1–2) while the sheikh still lived in Amasya. Mahmud Efendi's first employment was as a scribe at the religious court. Later, he was appointed *kâdı* (judge of Islamic law), first of Baghdad and then of Diyârıbekir. He died while in that post. Mahmud Efendi trained his son, Ahmed Paşa, in the calligraphic method of Şeyh Hamdullah. Ahmed Paşa served as a *vezir*, or minister of government, and as a *beylerbeyi*, or governor general. He died in 1020/1611.

8. *Kehf*

966/1559
Muhakkak, sülüs, and *rıkâ'*
Ink, colors, and gold on paper
Binding 28 × 19.7 cm (10⅞ × 7⅞ in.)
(210)

This work by Kâdı Mahmud Efendi consists of only chapter 18 of the Qur'an, written on twenty folios. Both the ink and the variety of scripts are noteworthy. The pages shown here are folios 19v and 20r, which include the end of the chapter and the calligrapher's signature. The seven-line format is organized as follows: the first line is written in *muhakkak* script with blue ink; the following two lines are in *sülüs* script in black ink; next is one line of *muhakkak* in gold ink, two lines of *sülüs* in black ink, and, finally, one line of *muhakkak* in blue. In the triangular corner areas of the last page, the calligrapher extolled the virtues of the chapter—*Kehf*, or The Cave—in *rıkâ'* script, using black ink. His signature appears in red (*lâl*) ink in the lower part of the left triangle, along with the date 966/1559. All the scripts are smaller than customary, and the text areas are not framed with golden *cedveller*. In addition, instead of golden *duraklar* (verse-stop rosettes) between the verses, as was usual, there is simply a space.

Şeyh Hamdullah had abandoned the practice of writing Qur'ans using multiple scripts from the group known as the six scripts. Here, Mahmud Efendi used two of the six—*sülüs* and *muhakkak*—in alternating lines and in different colors, almost as a reminder of an earlier epoch.

It is not known where Mahmud Efendi wrote this work.

صنعا أُولَئِكَ الَّذِينَ كَفَرُوا بِآيَاتِ

رَبِّهِمْ وَلِقَائِهِ فَحَبِطَتْ أَعْمَالُهُمْ فَلَا نُقِيمُ لَهُمْ

يَوْمَ الْقِيَامَةِ وَزْنًا ذَلِكَ جَزَاؤُهُمْ جَهَنَّمُ

بِمَا كَفَرُوا وَاتَّخَذُوا آيَاتِي وَرُسُلِي هُزُوًا

إِنَّ الَّذِينَ آمَنُوا وَعَمِلُوا الصَّالِحَاتِ كَانَتْ لَهُمْ

جَنَّاتُ الْفِرْدَوْسِ نُزُلًا خَالِدِينَ فِيهَا لَا يَبْغُونَ

عَنْهَا حِوَلًا قُلْ لَوْ كَانَ الْبَحْرُ مِدَادًا لِكَلِمَاتِ

رَبِّي

رَبِّي لَنَفِدَ الْبَحْرُ قَبْلَ أَنْ تَنْفَدَ كَلِمَاتُ

رَبِّي وَلَوْ جِئْنَا بِمِثْلِهِ مَدَدًا قُلْ إِنَّمَا أَنَا

بَشَرٌ مِثْلُكُمْ يُوحَى إِلَيَّ أَنَّمَا إِلَهُكُمْ إِلَهٌ

وَاحِدٌ فَمَنْ كَانَ يَرْجُو لِقَاءَ

رَبِّهِ فَلْيَعْمَلْ عَمَلًا صَالِحًا وَلَا يُشْرِكْ

بِعِبَادَةِ رَبِّهِ

أَحَدًا

RAMAZAN BİN İSMAİL

D. 1091/1680

Ramazan Efendi was the imam of a mosque in the neighborhood of the Mevlevî Sufi Lodge (Mevlevîhâne) in the Yenikapı district of Istanbul, a position he held for life. Aside from this work, he would allot a portion of each day to copying the Qur'an in *nesih* script. It is reported that visitors to his house, even important personages such as the *vezir*, would wait outside while he worked at this blessed occupation and that his house was always filled with people who came to do benevolent works.

A *mushaf* is composed of thirty *cüzler*, and Ramazan Efendi wrote half a *cüz*, or ten pages, every day. In this manner, he completed an entire volume in two months, and a total of four hundred copies of the Qur'an in his lifetime—certainly a record for his era. Although the date of his birth is not known, he must have lived a long life, for to write four hundred Qur'ans at his rate would have taken sixty-six years. Whenever he fell ill, he would request that his visitors—the calligraphers Derviş Ali (see cat. no. 10), Suyolcuzâde Mustafa (see cat. no. 12), and Hâfız Osman (see cat. nos. 14–16)—finish the works he had started but had not been able to complete before his illness.

Ramazan Efendi's *şecere*, or pedigree, in the art of calligraphy, like that of Derviş Ali, reaches back to Şeyh Hamdullah (see cat. nos. 1–2). Ramazan Efendi's teacher Abdullah bin Cezzar (d. 1074/1663) was the student of Imam Mehmed Tokâtî (d. 1052/1642); Imam Mehmed Tokâtî studied calligraphy with Hasan Üsküdârî (d. 1023/1614).

Hâfız Halil Efendi (d. 1115/1703), Çinicizâde Abdurrahman Efendi (d. 1137/1725), and Seyyid Hasan Hâşimî Efendi (d. 1098/1687) were the best known of Ramazan Efendi's students.

He died on Ramazan 27, 1091/October 21, 1680, and was buried outside the Yenikapı Mevlevî Sufi Lodge, which no longer exists. His son Derviş İbrahim (d. 1131/1719) assumed his father's position at the mosque. Derviş İbrahim had learned calligraphy from his father and also worked at copying Qur'ans. When he died, he was buried in the same tomb as his father, inseparable in death as in life.

9. Qur'an
Istanbul, 1053/1643
Nesih and *rıkâ'*
Ink, colors, and gold on paper
Binding 20.8 × 14.5 cm (8⅛ × 5 ⅝ in.)
(254)

This *mushaf* by Ramazan bin İsmail is written in *nesih* script on 337 folios and is bound in its original *şemse kap* (sunburst-design) binding. There are thirteen lines per page. The text area is framed with a gilded *cedvel*, and the verses are separated by decorated *duraklar* (verse stops). The *sûre başları* are written in red ink in *rıkâ'* script, between lightly gilded endpieces. The pages shown here—folios 192v and 193r—are near the beginning of the nineteenth *cüz* (section), which is noted in the upper right-hand corner of the margin of folio 192v. The text on these pages is from chapter 25 of the Qur'an (*Furkan*, or The Criterion), beginning with the end of verse 20 and running through the beginning of verse 42. The *serlevha* in this *mushaf*, by an unknown artist, is a typical example of seventeenth-century illumination.

Ramazan Efendi had a quick and flowing way of writing. Throughout his life, he restricted himself to the *nesih* script, which the Ottomans called the "servant of the Honorable Book" (that is, the Qur'an).

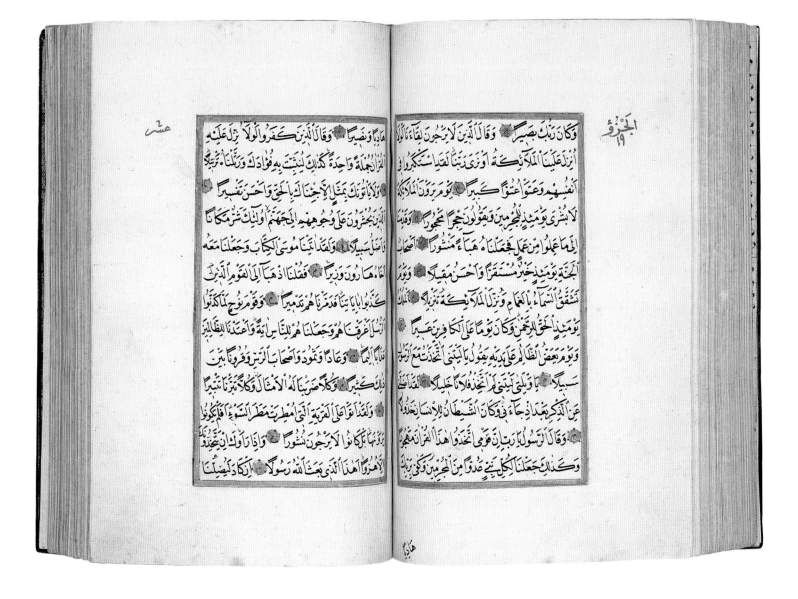

DERVİŞ ALİ
D. 1084/1673

Derviş Ali was born in Istanbul. His pedigree in calligraphy begins with Şeyh Hamdullah (see cat. nos. 1–2) and includes Şükrullah Halîfe, Pîr Mehmed bin Şükrullah (d. 988/1580), Hasan Üsküdârî (d. 1023/1614), and Derviş Ali's teacher, Hâlid Erzurumî (d. after 1040/1631). Derviş Ali taught a number of apprentices, and copied more than sixty *mushaflar*. (A *mushaf* by him dated 1075/1664, his sixty-third, is in the Sakıp Sabancı Collection.) He also wrote a large number of *En'âm-ı Şerîfler* (collections of Qur'anic chapters), *kıt'alar*, and albums. Derviş Ali died, advanced in years, in Ramazan 1084/December 1673. The inscription on his tombstone (the location of which is now unknown) indicated that he was an excellent archer. He is called Derviş Ali the Great, or the First, to distinguish him from two later namesakes.

Derviş Ali taught the highly honored calligraphers Suyolcuzâde Mustafa Eyyûbî (see cat. no. 12), Ağakapılı İsmail bin Ali (see cat. no. 13), and Hâfız Osman (see cat. nos. 14–16). Another of his students was Sadrâzam (Grand *Vezir*) Köprülüzâde Fâzıl Ahmed Paşa (1635–1676), who, when he visited Derviş Ali, would kiss his hand in the manner reserved in Ottoman protocol for the *şeyhülislâm*, the highest religious authority in the empire. Since the state had an interest in calligraphy, and the men of state were connoisseurs of the art, calligraphers were highly regarded.

10. **Murakkaa**
Istanbul, 1075/1664
Sülüs, nesih, and *rıkâ'*
Ink, colors, and gold on paper mounted on cardboard
Each *kıt'a* 20.5 × 21.5 cm (7⅞ × 8⅜ in.)
(391)

These two *kıt'alar* by Derviş Ali are from a six-*kıt'a körüklü murakkaa* (bellows or accordian album). Each *kıt'a* is square, save the final, signature *kıt'a*, which is rectangular. (The top and bottom borders of this *kıt'a*, shown here, have been widened to match the square format.) The format of the first five *kıt'alar* is one line in *sülüs*, two or three lines in *nesih*, one line in *sülüs*, and two or three in *nesih*. The final *kıt'a* in the album is signed, under the line of *sülüs* and to the left, in *rıkâ'* (*icâzet*) script. The *koltuk* areas have been left unilluminated and the *duraklar* (stops) and inner and outer borders are not exceptional.

تقع ولا بكثير تستبع

قال رسول الله صلى الله عليه وسلم
سيكون بعدي أمراء يظلمون ويكذبون
فمن صدقهم بكذبهم وأعانهم على ظلمهم

اللهم صل وسلم على أشرف الخلق

فليس مني ولست منهم ولم يرد على الحوض
وصلى الله على خير خلقه محمد وآله الطيبين

محمد وآله الطيبين الطاهرين

الطاهرين كتبه أضعف عباد الله الرؤوف
ده وثبره على جامع الله بعد الله عرضه مصطفى
عن سيد محمد وآله المنتجب النبين الطيبين الطاهرين

65

NEFESZÂDE SEYYİD İSMAİL EFENDİ

D. 1090/1679

Nefeszâde Seyyid İsmail Efendi was related to Nefeszâde Seyyid İbrahim Efendi (d. 1060/1650), who was the author of a very important source for historians of calligraphy, *Gülzâr-ı savab* (The Rose Garden of the Correct Way of Working). Like Derviş Ali (see cat. no. 10), he studied calligraphy with Hâlid Erzurumî (d. after 1040/1631). His pedigree reaches back to Şeyh Hamdullah (see cat. nos. 1–2). During his lifetime, Seyyid İsmail Efendi was considered the unique representative of the sheikh's method, and it is known that he taught the method to Hâfız Osman (see cat. nos. 14–16), who became a master of it.

We know that Seyyid İsmail Efendi was large in stature. According to Müstakîmzâde's *Tuhfe-i hattâtîn* (The Rare and Valuable Lives of the Calligraphers), "If he were not such a fat-bellied man and could easily have held his writing pad on his knee, it would have been impossible to distinguish his writing from that of Şeyh Hamdullah."

Seyyid İsmail Efendi died in 1090/1679. The location of his grave is unknown.

11. Qur'an

Istanbul, 1075/1644
Nesih
Ink, colors, and gold on paper
Binding 21.4 × 15 cm (8⅜ × 5⅞ in.)
(261)

Nefeszâde Seyyid İsmail Efendi followed the method of Şeyh Hamdullah when he wrote this fine Qur'an in 1075/1644, 160 years after the sheikh's heyday. It is written in *nesih* script, thirteen lines per page. The binding and illumination are original. The chapter titles are written, within the chapter-head illuminations, in white-lead ink on a gilded background. The pages shown are folios 375v and 376r, with the final two verses of chapter 87 (*Âlâ*, or The Most High), all of chapter 88 (*Gâşiye*, or The Calamity), and most of chapter 89 (*Fecr*, or The Dawn).

In the Islamic tradition, the first word of a bound-manuscript page is written in the lower left-hand corner of the preceding page, as is shown here, to ease the transition to the following page (see also cat. nos. 8–9, 15–16, 20, 22, 30–31, 42, and 45). The purpose of this repeated word was twofold: it helped prevent confusion and lost time during recitation of the Qur'an; and, because it was not the custom to number the pages of manuscripts, it made collation of the pages for binding foolproof. In Turkish, this repeated word is known as the *müş'ir* (pointer), *rakîb* (watchman), or *çoban* (shepherd).

Suyolcuzâde Mustafa Eyyûbî

1028/1619?–1097/1686

Suyolcuzâde Mustafa was born in the Eyüb district of Istanbul and thus acquired the name Eyyûbî. The name Suyolcuzâde means "son (*zâde*) of the *suyolcu*," or of the man in charge of maintaining the city's water conduits. Suyolcuzâde began his studies with a calligrapher known as Dede and, upon Dede's death, became a student of Derviş Ali's (see cat. no. 10). After receiving his *icâzet*, Suyolcuzâde devoted his life to calligraphy and teaching. His best-known students were Hocazâde Mehmed (d. 1106/1695), Câbîzâde Abdullah (d. 1149/1736), and Hâfız Osman (see cat. nos. 14–16), with whom Suyolcuzâde had an especially close relationship.

Hâfız Osman would walk all the way from his home in the Haseki quarter of Istanbul to Eyüb—a distance of some four miles—to take his lessons from Mustafa Efendi, then walk all the way back. He even walked barefoot to his lesson one snowy winter day, which endeared him to Suyolcuzâde. It is said that once, when Hâfız Osman had become a great master in his own right, he attended a gathering at which his former master was present. When the grand *vezir* asked with whom he had studied, Hâfız Osman turned toward Suyolcuzâde and said, "I am a graduate of His Excellency." Mustafa Efendi was so deeply moved by these words that, as they were leaving, he kissed Hâfız Osman on the forehead and, with tears in his eyes, bade him good wishes.

Suyolcuzâde wrote more than fifty *mushaflar* and many *En'âm-ı Şerîfler*, *evrâdlar* (collections of personal prayers), and *murakkaalar*. He died in 1097/1686 and was buried in the Hamamarkası Cemetery, in the Eyüb district where he had passed his whole life. His grandson, Suyolcuzâde Mehmed Necib (d. 1137/1725), was the author of a collection of biographies of calligraphers, *Devhatü'l-küttâb* (The Genealogical Tree of Calligraphers). He also copied the epitaph for his grandfather's gravestone, which was eventually broken and is now in the Museum of Turkish and Islamic Art, Istanbul. The exact location of Suyolcuzâde's grave is unknown.

12. *Kıt'a*

Istanbul, 17th century
Sülüs and *nesih*
Ink, colors, and gold on paper mounted on cardboard
14.1 × 22.4 cm (5½ × 8¾ in.)
(151)

This undated *kıt'a*, with one line of *sülüs* and two of *nesih*, appears to have been written extremely quickly. These well-balanced and mature lines seem almost to have gushed spontaneously from the writer's pen. When Sâmi Efendi (see cat. nos. 49–52) saw this work, he said, "It is my conviction that Hâfız Osman did not become Hâfız Osman until he met Suyolcuzâde."

The signature of the calligrapher is written in angled lines in the left *koltuk*. The illumination was done at a later date.

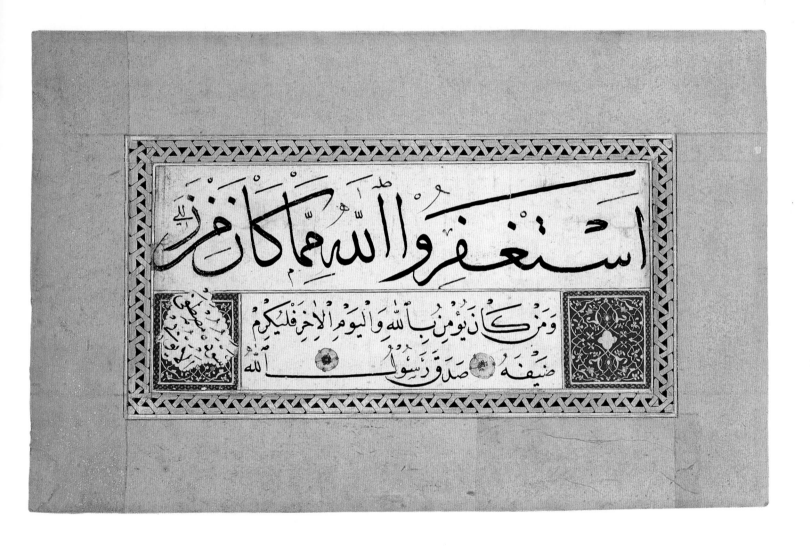

AĞAKAPILI İSMAİL EFENDİ

D. 1118/1706

Born in Istanbul, İsmail Efendi was known as Ağakapılı because he taught at the Janissary officers' school in Ağakapı (now the site of the mufti's office in the Süleymaniye quarter). Although he did not do so on the *kıt'a* shown here, Ağakapılı usually signed himself İsmail bin Ali (son of Ali). An outstanding student of Derviş Ali's (see cat. no. 10), he trained many calligraphers himself. He was one of the last calligraphers to be able to trace his artistic pedigree directly back to Şeyh Hamdullah (see cat. nos. 1–2). The sheikh's method was soon to become obsolete, however, and although Ağakapılı was Hâfız Osman's contemporary, he did not follow Osman's new treatment of the six scripts (see cat. nos. 14–16). Nevertheless, Ağakapılı greatly admired Hâfız Osman and said of him, "We knew calligraphy, but Hâfız Osman wrote it." After Ağakapılı's death, his writing chest was found to contain a number of fine *kıt'alar* by Hâfız Osman.

Ağakapılı wrote more than forty Qur'ans and many *En'âmlar*, *aklâm-ı sitte kıt'alar*, and albums, which were greatly admired. When he reached the age of eighty, his hand began to tremble. Nevertheless, in his old age, he executed inscriptions in the *celî sülüs* script of the period for the Şeyhülislam Feyzullah Efendi *medrese* (Islamic theological school) and its library (now the State Library), in Istanbul. These inscriptions are still extant.

The epitaph for the grave of Hâfız Osman, which was in the *hazîre* (enclosed burial precinct) of the Sünbül Efendi Sufi Lodge, Istanbul, was Ağakapılı's work. He died eight years after completing this epitaph, and was buried in the Kasımpaşa district's Darıderesi Cemetery, which no longer exists. The epitaph he copied for Hâfız Osman was copied on his own gravestone as well, with Ağakapılı's name substituted for Hâfız Osman's.

İkinci (the Second) Derviş Ali (d. 1128/1716), who is not represented in this catalogue, studied with Ağakapılı İsmail and Hâfız Osman. He appears in the genealogy of calligraphers (see the appendix to this volume) as a point of transmission between these masters and later generations.

13. *Kıt'a*
Cenkâr, 17th century
Sülüs and *nesih*
Ink, colors, and gold on paper mounted on cardboard
14.3 × 23.1 cm (5⅝ × 9 in.)
(144)

This is the final *kıt'a* of a sequential album (*müteselsil murakkaa*) of 131 *kıt'alar*. Ağakapılı İsmail Efendi signed the piece simply "İsmail." Written immediately after the signature is a device that indicates that the work has been proofread. The signature also states that the writing was done in Cenkâr, a village on the Anatolian shore of the Bosphorus opposite from where Ağakapılı lived. (Today, Cenkâr is called Çengelköy and is a district of Istanbul.) This *kıt'a* is testimony that, even while the calligrapher was traveling, the pen never left his hands.

The text of the *kıt'a* is a *hadîs*, or saying of the Prophet: "I was sent only to perfect nobility of character in people."

71

HÂFIZ OSMAN

1052/1642–1110/1698

Hâfız Osman was born in Istanbul in 1052/1642. His father, Ali Efendi, was the muezzin of the Haseki Sultan Mosque. The young Osman zealously memorized the Qur'an, achieving the title *hâfız*. (This title, which means "one who memorizes the Qur'an," was used as a first name by those who earned it.) His family was very poor, and he was educated under the patronage of Fâzıl Mustafa Paşa (1638–1691), of the illustrious Köprülü family. His first calligraphy teacher was Derviş Ali (see cat. no. 10), who, believing he was too old to provide the quality of teaching the talented young man deserved, eventually sent him to his own student Suyolcuzâde Mustafa Eyyûbî (see cat. no. 12), whom he considered most distinguished. Hâfız Osman received his *icâzet* from Suyolcuzâde in 1070/1660, at the age of eighteen.

As can be seen from his early works done under the tutelage of Derviş Ali, Hâfız Osman initially followed the method of Şeyh Hamdullah (see cat. nos. 1–2). To perfect this style, he felt the need to begin his apprenticeship again as the student of Nefeszâde Seyyid İsmail Efendi (see cat. no. 11). So successful at the sheikh's method was Hâfız Osman that, years later, his works became a major source for understanding the style of Şeyh Hamdullah in the six scripts. After finishing his studies with Nefeszâde, Hâfız Osman began a direct study of the sheikh's original works, increasing his skill by using the *taklîd* method of imitation (for a description of this method, see the entry for catalogue number 33).

In 1090/1679, however, Hâfız Osman abandoned the sheikh's method and developed his own style. Just as Şeyh Hamdullah, in his day, originated a style by building on the works of Yāqūt al-Mustaʿsimī (Yāqūt; d. 698/1298), so Hâfız Osman sifted and purified Ottoman calligraphy, reaching a new stage in the development of the art characterized by a greater refinement in the letter shapes and, in general, a less cramped, livelier line. Although at first this new method encountered criticism as well as envy, it was accepted in a short time, and the sheikh's style was abandoned. A further development occurred about 1100/1689, when Hâfız Osman began to reduce the size of his *nesih* script. Connoisseurs believe his best work in *nesih* was that done between 1090 and 1100.

In 1106/1695, Hâfız Osman was appointed calligraphy teacher to Sultan Mustafa II (r. 1695–1703) and his son, the future sultan Ahmed III. While in the sultan's presence, Hâfız Osman was seated on a special sofa as a mark of respect. Moreover, while Hâfız Osman was preparing the sultan's *meşk* (lesson), the sultan would honor him by holding his inkwell. These favors did not spoil Hâfız Osman, in whom asceticism and humility were lifelong traits. One day, during a lesson, the sultan is reported to have exclaimed admiringly, "There will never be another Hâfız Osman Efendi!" Hâfız Osman replied, "My sovereign, as long as sultans like you hold the inkwell for their teacher, there will be many Hâfız Osmans."

14. ***Murakkaa***
Istanbul, 1080/1669
Sülüs and *muhakkak*
Ink, colors, and gold on paper mounted on cardboard
Each *kıt'a* 28.3 × 19.7 cm (11⅛ × 7⅞ in.)
(343)

This eleven-folio collection was written by Hâfız Osman in 1080/1669, when he was still a young man. In this album, only the *besmele*, the first line of the right-hand folio shown here, is written in *muhakkak*. The rest is in *sülüs* script, five lines per page.

The original borders of this work were replaced a century later using *ebrû* (marbled paper) made by Hatib Mehmed Efendi (d. 1187/1773; see cat. no. 1). This type of *ebrû* is called *hatib ebrûsu* in honor of its inventor. It is made by floating a background color on the tragacanth bath described on page 22, releasing drops of another color onto the background, and then applying still other colors on top of these drops, making concentric circles of pigment. A stylus is then drawn through the colors to create the design.

The borders were restored following a method that is still in use today: the original borders of the *kıt'a* are cut off. Two pieces of *ebrû* are put back to back, marbled sides out. A window is cut through both papers, just a bit smaller than the text area of the *kıt'a*, in order to leave a slight overlap. The *kıt'a* is then pasted between the two sheets of *ebrû* and the assemblage is dried under pressure. The same procedure is used for all the folios in the album. The new border is called the *vassâle*. (The original process for applying a *vassâle*—in the restoration of a *mushaf*—is described in the entry for catalogue number 20.)

بِسْمِ اللهِ الرَّحْمٰنِ الرَّحِيمِ

قَالَ الْإِمَامُ أَبُو الْعَبَّاسِ

الْمُسْتَغْفِرِيُّ رَحِمَهُ اللهُ

قَصَدْتُ دِيَارَ مِصْرَ أُرِيدُ

طَلَبَ الْعِلْمِ مِنَ الْإِمَامِ

أَبِي حَامِدٍ أَحْمَدَ بْنِ حَيُّوةَ

الْمِصْرِيِّ رَحِمَهُ اللهُ وَالْتَمَسْتُ

حَدِيثَ خَالِدِ بْنِ الْوَلِيدِ

رَضِيَ اللهُ عَنْهُ فَأَمَرَنِي بِصَوْمِ

سَنَةٍ كَامِلَةٍ ثُمَّ عَاوَدْتُهُ فِي

Because Hâfız Osman held no government office, he was free to travel. He often visited Bursa and Edirne, in Turkey, and he went to Egypt in 1083/1672 and to the Hijaz in 1087–88/1676–77 to make the pilgrimage to Mecca. Whenever he traveled, he continued to practice calligraphy, noting in his signature where he was when he wrote a particular piece. The signatures on his works attest to the many stops along the way at which he wrote *karalamalar* or *cüzler*.

Over his forty-year artistic career, Hâfız Osman worked continuously. He made twenty-five copies of the Qur'an, among them the charming *mushaf* in this volume (cat. no. 15). Hâfız Osman also wrote innumerable *En'âmlar*, *cüzler*, *kıt'alar*, and *murakkaalar* using the six scripts. While there are no references to Hâfız Osman's composing poetry, he generally took great care to write the colophons for his works in rhyming Arabic prose.

Although Hâfız Osman's *celî sülüs* was not up to the level of his other scripts, it is worth noting that Mustafa Râkım (see cat. no. 27), who was to make the great revolution in *celî sülüs* a century later, took his inspiration from Hâfız Osman's regular-size *sülüs*. Hâfız Osman is also remembered for developing the *hilye-i saadet* from an Arabic text to the *levha* format we know today. It was also he who established for the prayer book *Delâilü'l-Hayrât* the layout that is now universally followed.

As a teacher, Hâfız Osman was scrupulous in adhering to the custom of charging nothing for lessons. He would teach the poor at his home on Sundays and the children of the well-to-do on Wednesdays. It is said that, after finishing a lesson, he would often go out on his horse and come across a student who had been delayed and missed the session. Instead of upbraiding the student, Hâfız Osman would get off his horse and give the student a lesson at the side of the road. He is known to have had at least fifty students, the best-known of whom include Yedikuleli Seyyid Abdullah (see cat. nos. 17–18), Yusuf Rûmî (d. 1121/1709), Rodosîzâde Abdullah (d. 1116/1704), Yusuf Mecdî (d. 1133/1731), and Mehmed Girîdî (d. 1165/1765).

A few years before he died, Hâfız Osman suffered a slight stroke but recovered enough that the quality of his late works did not deteriorate. He died three hundred years ago, in his home, on Cemâzilûlâ 29, 1110/December 3, 1698. He was interred in the cemetery of the Sünbül Efendi Sufi Lodge, Istanbul. Ağakapılı İsmail Efendi (see cat. no. 13) copied the epitaph for his gravestone, which still stands.

The path that Hâfız Osman opened in the *sülüs, nesih,* and *rıkâ'* scripts has since branched in other directions but is still valid today.

15. Qur'an

Istanbul, 1093/1682

Nesih

Ink, colors, and gold on paper

Binding 18.2 × 12.7 cm (7⅛ × 4⅞ in.)

(348)

This Qur'an clearly displays Hâfız Osman's special style of writing. Shown here are folios 462v and 463r, comprising the end of chapter 94 (*Inşirâh*, or The Expanding), all of 95 (*Tîn*, or The Fig), and all of 96 (*Alak*, or The Clot). The *mushaf* was finished in the last days of Ramazan 1093/September 1682. The perfectly realized *nesih* script is written eleven lines per page on 470 folios. An artist named Hasan bin Mustafa decorated the *mushaf*. The *serlevha* and *sûre başları*, and the *cüz, durak,* and *aşere* rosettes, are very elegant and appropriate to the calligraphy. It is possible that the fine *şemse kap* binding is also the work of Hasan bin Mustafa. (Very little is known about Hasan bin Mustafa, except that he was raised by Beyâzî Mustafa and was the student of Sürâhi Mustafa. Two other illuminators are known to have decorated Hâfız Osman's works: Hâfız Mehmed Çelebi and Ahdeb Hasan Çelebi, also known as Kanbur Hasan Çelebi [both Ahdeb and Kanbur mean "Hunchback"].)

Hâfız Osman is said to have received about 350 *kuruş* (piasters) for each of the three *mushaflar* he wrote between 1080/1669 and 1088/1677. That would equal approximately twenty ounces of gold, or almost six thousand dollars in today's currency.

In 1967, after five years of preparation, a facsimile edition of this Qur'an was printed by the Doğan Kardeş Institution, Istanbul.

بِسْمِ اللَّهِ الرَّحْمَنِ الرَّحِيمِ

اقْرَأْ بِاسْمِ رَبِّكَ الَّذِي خَلَقَ ۞ خَلَقَ الْإِنْسَانَ مِنْ عَلَقٍ ۞ اقْرَأْ وَرَبُّكَ الْأَكْرَمُ ۞ الَّذِي عَلَّمَ بِالْقَلَمِ ۞ عَلَّمَ الْإِنْسَانَ مَا لَمْ يَعْلَمْ ۞ كَلَّا إِنَّ الْإِنْسَانَ لَيَطْغَى ۞ أَنْ رَآهُ اسْتَغْنَى ۞ إِنَّ إِلَى رَبِّكَ الرُّجْعَى ۞ أَرَأَيْتَ الَّذِي يَنْهَى عَبْدًا إِذَا صَلَّى ۞ أَرَأَيْتَ إِنْ كَانَ عَلَى الْهُدَى ۞ أَوْ أَمَرَ بِالتَّقْوَى ۞ أَرَأَيْتَ إِنْ كَذَّبَ وَتَوَلَّى ۞ أَلَمْ يَعْلَمْ بِأَنَّ اللَّهَ يَرَى ۞ كَلَّا لَئِنْ لَمْ يَنْتَهِ لَنَسْفَعًا بِالنَّاصِيَةِ ۞ نَاصِيَةٍ كَاذِبَةٍ خَاطِئَةٍ ۞ فَلْيَدْعُ نَادِيَهُ ۞ سَنَدْعُ الزَّبَانِيَةَ ۞ كَلَّا لَا تُطِعْهُ وَاسْجُدْ وَاقْتَرِبْ ۞

فَإِذَا فَرَغْتَ فَانْصَبْ ۞ وَإِلَى رَبِّكَ فَارْغَبْ ۞

سُورَةُ التِّينِ مَكِّيَّةٌ وَهِيَ ثَمَانُ آيَاتٍ

بِسْمِ اللَّهِ الرَّحْمَنِ الرَّحِيمِ

وَالتِّينِ وَالزَّيْتُونِ ۞ وَطُورِ سِينِينَ ۞ وَهَذَا الْبَلَدِ الْأَمِينِ ۞ لَقَدْ خَلَقْنَا الْإِنْسَانَ فِي أَحْسَنِ تَقْوِيمٍ ۞ ثُمَّ رَدَدْنَاهُ أَسْفَلَ سَافِلِينَ ۞ إِلَّا الَّذِينَ آمَنُوا وَعَمِلُوا الصَّالِحَاتِ فَلَهُمْ أَجْرٌ غَيْرُ مَمْنُونٍ ۞ فَمَا يُكَذِّبُكَ بَعْدُ بِالدِّينِ ۞ أَلَيْسَ اللَّهُ بِأَحْكَمِ الْحَاكِمِينَ ۞

سُورَةُ الْعَلَقِ مَكِّيَّةٌ تِسْعَ عَشْرَةَ آيَةً

16. *En'âm*

Istanbul, 1095/1684

Nesih

Ink, colors, and gold on paper

Binding 18.2 × 12.3 cm (7⅛ × 4¾ in.)

(285)

Hâfız Osman was at the height of his
artistic powers when he wrote this copy
of the chapter *En'âm*, or The Cattle
(Qur'an 6:1–165) in *nesih* script in
1095/1684. This often-recited chapter
was written ten lines per page on
twenty-three folios; shown here are
folios 1v and 2r. As is the custom in an
En'âm volume, only the right-hand
opening page has been illuminated. It
is called the *unvan sahifesi* and is an
unpretentious and charming example
of the illuminator's art. The binding
is stamped with *şemse* motifs. In its
simplicity and elegance, this book gives
us a hint of the nobility of the age of
Hâfız Osman.

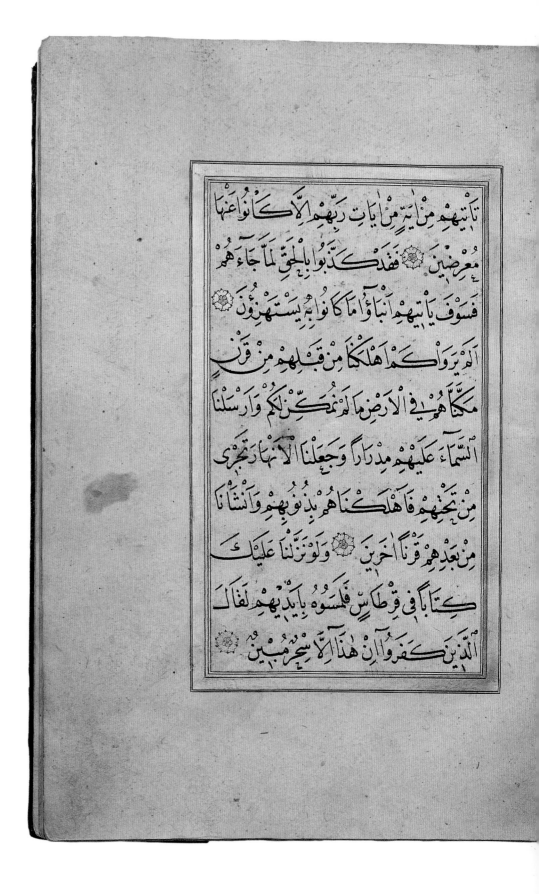

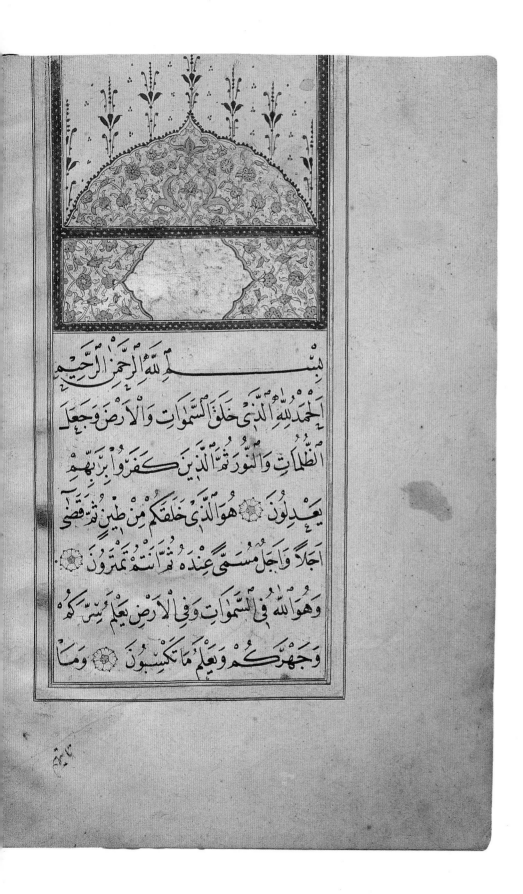

بِسْمِ اللهِ الرَّحْمٰنِ الرَّحِيمِ

اَلْحَمْدُ لِلّٰهِ الَّذِى خَلَقَ السَّمٰوَاتِ وَالْأَرْضَ وَجَعَلَ
الظُّلُمَاتِ وَالنُّورَ ثُمَّ الَّذِينَ كَفَرُوا بِرَبِّهِمْ
يَعْدِلُونَ ۝ هُوَ الَّذِى خَلَقَكُمْ مِنْ طِينٍ ثُمَّ قَضَى
أَجَلًا وَأَجَلٌ مُسَمًّى عِنْدَهُ ثُمَّ أَنْتُمْ تَمْتَرُونَ ۝
وَهُوَ اللهُ فِى السَّمٰوَاتِ وَفِى الْأَرْضِ يَعْلَمُ سِرَّكُمْ
وَجَهْرَكُمْ وَيَعْلَمُ مَا تَكْسِبُونَ ۝ وَمَا

YEDİKULELİ SEYYİD ABDULLAH EFENDİ

1081/1670–1144/1731

Abdullah Efendi was born in the Yedikule district of Istanbul in 1081/1670 and is therefore known by the appellation Yedikuleli. Because he was descended from the Prophet Muhammad on both parents' side, he signed himself *seyyid* (sayyid). He is also called emir. His father, Seyyid Hasan Hâşimî (d. 1098/1687); his son, Seyyid Abdülhalim Hasib (1117/1705–1172/1759); and his grandson, Seyyid Mehmed Said (1152/1739–1172/1758), shared his occupation, making four generations of calligraphers in the family.

Abdullah Efendi's father was the imam of the Imrahor (Mîrâhûr) Mosque in Yedikule. The young Abdullah memorized the Qur'an, completed his education, and began his study of calligraphy with his father. At the age of seventeen, he began to practice the six scripts with Hâfız Osman (see cat. nos. 14–16) and received his *icâzet* in just forty months, winning the appreciation of his teacher. When his father died, Abdullah Efendi became the imam of the Imrahor Mosque, a post he held until the end of his life. He copied twenty-four *mushaflar*, about a thousand *En'âmlar* and *evrâdlar* (collections of personal prayers), countless *kıt'alar*, albums, *hilyeler*, and books, in addition to teaching calligraphy to many students. Among the best-known were Eğrikapılı Mehmed Râsim Efendi (see cat. no. 19) and Şekerzâde Mehmed Efendi (see cat. no. 21).

In 1120/1708, Sultan Ahmed III (r. 1703–30) appointed Abdullah Efendi to be the *meşk* teacher at the Topkapı Sarayı, where he was always received with affection. One day, the story goes, the sultan heard of the high quality of the ink made by Abdullah Efendi. The sultan immediately sent an imperial halberdier to the calligrapher to obtain a sample. The halberdier took the inkwell Abdullah Efendi was using and brought it to the sultan, who drained the ink and filled the inkwell with gold. The inkwell was returned to the calligrapher along with other presents.

Yedikuleli Seyyid Abdullah Efendi was the most outstanding student of Hâfız Osman, especially in the *nesih* script, in which he was a master—so much so, in fact, that once, in introducing his student, Hâfız Osman is reported to have said, "He writes more beautifully than I."

Abdullah Efendi died on Rabi 8, 1144/September 10, 1731. He was buried in the cemetery facing the Şah Sultan Lodge, in the Eyüb district of Istanbul.

17. *Hilye*
Istanbul, 1110/1698
Celî muhakkak, *sülüs*, and *nesih*
Ink, colors, and gold on paper mounted on board
58 × 41.5 cm (22⅞ × 16⅜ in.)
(91)

This *hilye-i saadet* was written by Abdullah Efendi in a form that departs from Hâfız Osman's model. The *besmele* is written in *celî muhakkak*. Two Qur'anic verses are written in *sülüs*: "And We [God] did not send you [Muhammad] except to be a mercy to the universe" (Qur'an 21:107), beneath the *besmele*; "And We [God] did not send you [Muhammad] except to be a bringer of good news, and a warner" (Qur'an 25:56), beneath the *hilâl* (crescent). Below the second verse are the customary names of the Seven Sleepers and their dog; their story is found in *Kehf*, or The Cave (Qur'an 18:9–27). Directly above the *hilâl*, God's name and the Prophet's name are written in *sülüs*. Surrounding the crescent, also in *sülüs*, are the names of the so-called Ten Who Were Promised Paradise, including the four successors of the Prophet, or the Four Friends. To the right of the *hilye* proper is a column containing the ninety-nine names of God, and to the left is a column listing names that describe the Prophet. The illumination of the piece is typical of the period.

As was the practice at the time, this *hilye* was originally pasted onto a wooden panel and hung on a wall, illuminated by an oil lamp. Because it was not protected by glass, the paper darkened, and woodworms riddled the panel with holes.

بسم الله الرحمن الرحيم

قال الله سبحانه وتعالى وما ارسلناك الا رحمة للعالمين

الله جل جلاله   محمد عليه الصلاة والسلام

ابو بكر رضي الله عنه   عمر رضي الله عنه

عثمان رضي الله عنه   علي رضي الله عنه

حسن رضي الله عنه   حسين رضي الله عنه

قال الله سبحانه وتعالى وما ارسلناك الا مبشرا ونذيرا

قططنه   كسطنطبوس

18. *Murakkaa*
Istanbul, late 17th–18th century
Nesih
Ink, colors, and gold on paper mounted
on cardboard
Each *kıt'a* 20 × 24.1 cm (7¾ × 9⅜ in.)
(213)

In Ottoman calligraphy, a *meşk*
(teaching exercise) generally combined
sülüs and *nesih* scripts (see cat. no. 41),
while *ta'lîk* was usually studied
separately (see cat. nos. 28, 29, 53, and
55). In this album, Abdullah Efendi
has written four *müfredât kıt'aları* and
one *mürekkebât kıt'ası* in *nesih* script
only. (For an explanation of the terms
müfredât and *mürekkebât*, see catalogue
numbers 28 and 41.) In this undated
körüklü murakkaa (accordion album),
Yedikuleli has produced a *nesih* perfectly
in accord with that of his teacher Hâfız
Osman (see cat. nos. 14–16).

EĞRİKAPILI MEHMED RÂSİM EFENDİ

1099/1688–1169/1756

Because Mehmed Râsim Efendi was born in the Eğrikapı district of Istanbul, he was known as Eğrikapılı. His father, Yusuf Efendi (d. 1142/1729), who was also a calligrapher, was the imam of the Molla Aşkî section of the same district. Early in his career, Mehmed Efendi signed himself Imamzâde (Son of the Imam) Mehmed, but this appellation was not specific enough and led to confusion. After the age of forty, he used the signature Mehmed Râsim (*râsim* means "artist"), a fact that is useful in dating the *kıt'a* shown here. He began to learn the six scripts with his father, then continued his studies with Yedikuleli Seyyid Abdullah Efendi (see cat. nos. 17–18), the favorite pupil of Hâfız Osman (see cat. nos. 14–16). Mehmed Râsim received his *icâzet* in 1117/1705.

Educated in religion and literature, Mehmed Râsim Efendi was a specialist in *inşâ* (the art of composing elegant correspondence) and left many works of poetry. He was appointed calligraphy teacher at the Galata Sarayı in 1126/1714 and then named to the same post at the Topkapı Sarayı in 1150/1737. He died on Şa'ban 14, 1169/May 13, 1756, and was interred in the cemetery just outside the Eğrikapı district. His student Mestçizâde Ahmed Efendi (d. 1174/1761) copied the epitaph for the gravestone, which still stands today.

In the course of his two official appointments, Mehmed Râsim Efendi is said to have trained approximately a thousand calligraphers. He was Yedikuleli Abdullah Efendi's finest student. Once, a *mushaf* was commissioned from Abdullah Efendi when he was short of time. He had Mehmed Râsim Efendi write it but signed his own name to it, then gave his student the entire payment for the work.

Mehmed Râsim Efendi wrote sixty *mushaflar* and many *En'âm-ı Şerîfler, kıt'alar, murakkaalar,* and *hilyeler*. He also wrote a number of inscriptions in *celî sülüs*, the best-known of which appear on the Sâliha Sultan Fountain, in Istanbul's Azapkapı quarter. (These inscriptions, it should be noted, were written in a pre-Râkım *celî* style.) He also wrote *ta'lîk*, which he learned from the master at that time, Hekimbaşi Kâtipzâde Mehmed Refi' Efendi (d. 1183/1769). He earned his *icâzet* in this script at the age of fifty-two. In a rare turnabout, he taught *sülüs* and *nesih* to his *ta'lîk* teacher and gave him an *icâzet* for these scripts.

19. *Kıt'a*
Istanbul, after 1139/1727
Sülüs and *nesih*
Ink, colors, and gold on paper mounted on cardboard
16.6 × 24.5 cm (6½ × 9½ in.)
(154)

This *sülüs*-and-*nesih kıt'a* was signed simply Mehmed Râsim. From the style of the floral illumination and of the *ebrû* paper used on the borders, the piece can be dated to shortly after 1139/1727.

The text reads: "Be sagacious, generous, and a keeper of secrets."

YAHYA FAHREDDİN

D. 1169/1756

Hâfız Yahya Fahreddin was nicknamed Sarı, or Yellow, apparently because of his hair color or complexion. The son of a man named Osman, he was from the Tophâne quarter of Istanbul. The story goes that one day, while he was tending the grave of the calligrapher Demircikulu Yusuf Efendi (d. 1020/1611), in front of the Karabaş Sufi Lodge in Tophâne, he found a reed pen buried in the ground near the grave. This sparked a desire in him to learn calligraphy, and he began studying with İkinci Derviş Ali (d. 1128/1716). When his teacher died, he continued his studies with the teacher's son-in-law and student, Hüseyin Hablî (d. 1157/1744). Masters such as Yedikuleli (see cat. nos. 17–18) and Eğrikapılı (see cat. no. 19) were among the calligraphers who formed the jury during his *icâzet* ceremony in 1135/1723. One of the other calligraphers in attendance, Abdullah Vefâî (d. 1144/1729), claimed that Yahya Fahreddin's teacher had written the *icâzet kıt'ası*, whereupon Yahya Efendi began to write a new *kıt'a* in front of the masters. Yedikuleli Abdullah Efendi dismissed Vefâî from the jury with the mocking words, "See here, sir. Can't you distinguish the calligraphy of a master from that of a student?"

In addition to writing fifteen Qur'ans, Yahya Fahreddin Efendi wrote some very fine *murakkaalar* in *sülüs* and *nesih*. He took particular pains with the *hareke* (vowel signs) and other reading aids, writing them beautifully. In addition, using pre-Râkım *celî sülüs*, he wrote inscriptions for the Âtıf Efendi Library, in Istanbul's Vefa district, and for the Imperial Arsenal of Ordnance and Artillery. Laying out architectural inscriptions takes a good deal of space, and while Yahya Fahreddin Efendi was working on inscriptions for the interior of the Nuruosmaniye Mosque, he said he needed a house with a very large hall—big enough to shoot a cannon in. Yirmisekiz Çelebizâde Mehmed Said Paşa (1701?–1761) was moved by this remark, and, as soon as he became grand *vezir* in 1755, purchased a mansion for Yahya Fahreddin. The calligrapher was able to write only two inscriptions in his new home, however, before he died, in Recep 1169/April 1756. He was buried in the cemetery opposite the Şeyh Murad Lodge, in the Eyüb quarter. The location of his grave is no longer known.

20. **Qur'an**
Istanbul, 1157/1744
Nesih
Ink, colors, and gold on paper
Binding 18.3 × 12 cm (7⅛ × 4⅝ in.)
(258)

Shown here are folios 396v and 397r from a Qur'an written in 1157/1744. This *mushaf* was copied thirteen lines per page on 402 folios. On folio 402r, Yahya Fahreddin signed his name and stated that Hüseyin Hablî bin Ramazan was his teacher. The illuminator, one Mustafa, wrote his name in a golden *durak* rosette in the lower left-hand corner of the same page. (An eighteenth-century illuminator from Bursa, Mustafa Efendi went by the patronymic Tuzpazarı İmamı.) In this volume, the *duraklar* are plain, in contrast to the *serlevha* illumination, which was executed in the flowery and colorful style, new at that time, called Turkish Rococo. The chapter heads are similarly illuminated, with the chapter titles written in white-lead ink. The margins of each page are decorated with *zer-efşan* (flecks of gold ink or gold leaf).

The manuscript has been restored and the margins replaced by the *vassâle* method. Over time, the margins of manuscript pages become worn from handling, especially at the lower outside corners. The craftsman who restored these margins was called a *vassal;* his craft, *vassâlecilik.* Briefly, the process is as follows: the text area of each page is carefully cut from its margins, and the four edges of the text area are thinned (by beating with a special hammer) and beveled. The paper that will form the new border is cut to conform to the size of the book and folded in the middle to form the

gutter, which will be bound to the spine of the book. The text pieces are then placed, in the proper order, on the new pages, which are marked and in which windows the size of the text areas are cut. On each page, the inner edges of the window are beaten with the hammer to thin and expand the paper a bit, so that it will overlap the text area slightly. The text piece is lightly edged with glue, put in place, and pasted down. When the pages are dry, the seams are pounded lightly with the hammer to smooth them, so that the bound volume will not be too thick. A golden *cedvel* (frame) is then drawn over the seams to hide them. Only careful examination will reveal that the manuscript has been restored. When the process is complete, the double-folio sheets are collated into *cüzler* (one-thirtieth parts of the Qur'an), pierced, sewn, and bound. (For another use of the *vassâle* process, see the entry for catalogue number 14.)

This Qur'an was probably restored in the nineteenth century.

ŞEKERZÂDE MEHMED EFENDİ

D. 1166/1753

Mehmed Efendi was the son of Abdurrahman Efendi, a confectioner (*şekerci*) in the western Anatolian city of Manisa, where the calligrapher was born. Instead of calling himself Şekercizâde, or Son of the Confectioner, Mehmed Efendi shortened the name to Şekerzâde (Son of Sugar). Indeed, it is tempting to say he deserved the name, so sweet and cheerful is his work.

Şekerzâde studied calligraphy with İbrahim Kırımî (d. 1150/1737) before moving to Istanbul, where he studied with Yedikuleli Abdullah Efendi (see cat. nos. 17–18). He wrote Qur'ans, *kıt'alar*, and *murakkaalar* and was an expert at *taklîd*, the imitation of the work of other calligraphers. With the encouragement of Sultan Ahmed III (r. 1703–30), he spent several years in Medina, copying the *mushaf* donated to the mosque adjoining the tomb of the Prophet. When he returned to Istanbul, Sultan Mahmud I (r. 1730–54) had ascended to the throne, and Şekerzâde presented the copy to him. It is now kept in the Süleymaniye Library (Yeni Cami K.3), Istanbul. A facsimile was issued in 1291/1874, the first officially printed *mushaf* in Ottoman history.

Şekerzâde also taught calligraphy to those employed in the private gardens of the Topkapı Sarayı, and gave calligraphy lessons in his own house in the Ayasofya quarter of Istanbul. He died in Cemâziyelevvel 1166/March 1753 and, like many other calligraphers, was buried near the grave of Şeyh Hamdullah, in the Karacaahmed Cemetery in the Üsküdar quarter.

21. *Murakkaa*
Istanbul, 1158/1745
Sülüs and *nesih*
Ink, colors, and gold on paper mounted on cardboard
Binding 28.3 × 20.8 cm (11 × 8⅛ in.)
(208)

Şekerzâde Mehmed Efendi wrote this twelve-*kıt'a düz murakkaa*, or album arranged to open like a book, in *sülüs* and *nesih*. Because this is a sequential album, the signature and date (1158/1745) occur only on the final *kıt'a*. In each *kıt'a*, the top and bottom lines are in *sülüs*, with three shorter lines of *nesih* in between, leaving space for an illuminated *koltuk* on either side. This work and others testify that Şekerzâde, like his contemporaries, followed the method of Hâfız Osman (see cat. nos. 14–16).

The decoration of this album was done at the time it was written. The outer borders are of *kumlu ebrû* (sand-patterned marbled paper), articulated with simple gold motifs.

CALLIGRAPHER UNKNOWN

22. *Vakfiye*
Istanbul, 1169/1756
Nesih
Ink, colors, and gold on paper
Binding 30.7 × 19 cm (11⅛ × 7⅜ in.)
(341)

Charitable foundations called *vakıflar* existed in many Islamic nations, each of which molded the concept according to its customs and understanding of Islam. The Ottomans developed *vakıflar* into lasting institutions. A *vakıf* consisted of the property of a person or group of persons that had been dedicated to a purpose pleasing to God and that could not be transferred to another use. The *vakıf* transformed personal property into collective property that brought great benefit to the common people. Many social services were delivered to Ottoman subjects in this way, and many religious, architectural, cultural, and artistic works were supported by *vakıflar*. The *vakıf* was self-supporting, generating income in perpetuity.

The *vakfiye* is the official document that stipulates the purpose of a particular *vakıf*, its financial worth, its income and expenses, its administrators (*mütevellîler*), and its donor (*vâkıf*). Such documents assured the administrative and financial autonomy of the *vakıf*. These documents generally include praise for the donor, as well as Qur'anic verses, *hadîsler*, or sayings that describe the consequences of altering the terms of the *vakıf*. This section is usually written in Arabic. Following it, in Turkish, are the conditions concerning the establishment of the *vakıf*. Finally, the donor and a *kâdı* (judge of religious law) sign the document in the presence of witnesses, thereby putting it in force.

The donor could have the document written in calligraphy, then illuminated and bound. The *unvan sahifesi* (opening page; folio 1v) of such a *vakfiye* is shown here. This book is a complete *vakfiye*, written in a large *nesih* script, on sixteen folios. It stipulates that Hacı Ahmed Ağa, one of the palace eunuchs at the time of Sultan Osman III (r. 1754–57), has set up a *vakıf* to secure the perpetual support of a school and *sebil* (public water fountain) that he established in Cairo, which was then a part of the Ottoman Empire. One condition reads: "Every year, may ten thousand *paralar* [a unit of coinage] be allotted to transport, during the summer, delicious water from the blessed Nile River to the aforementioned public water fountain." The names of nine witnesses are written at the end of the document, which is dated Şevvâl 18, 1169/July 16, 1756. The calligrapher and illuminator are unknown, as it was not customary to sign these works.

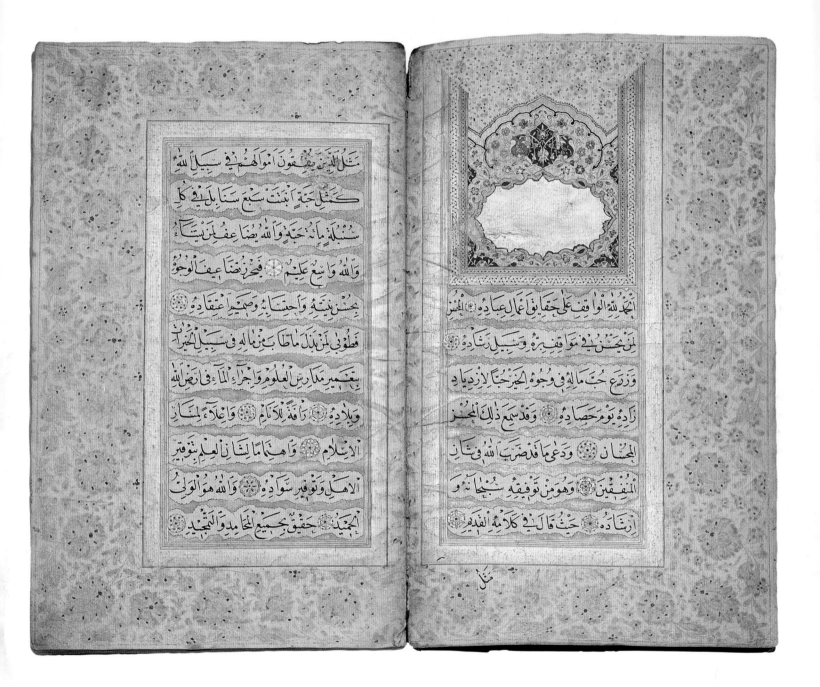

Mustafa Kütâhî

D. AFTER 1201/1787

Born in the west-central Anatolian city of Kütahya, Mustafa Kütâhî was the nephew of a sheikh and liked to be called Şeyhzâde (Son of the Sheikh). After receiving his education, he became a teacher in Istanbul, where he studied calligraphy with İbrahim Rodosî (d. 1201/1787). Although the date of his death cannot be established for certain, Mustafa Kütâhî was clearly still alive in 1201/1787, for a *levha* he wrote bears that date. He also wrote a number of *sülüs*-and-*nesih kıt'alar* and *celî sülüs levhalar*. He was buried in the Karacaahmed Cemetery, in the Üsküdar quarter of Istanbul.

Mustafa Kütâhî's daughter, Şerife Emine Safvet Hanım, was also a calligrapher. An undated *levha* in *sülüs* by her is in the collection of the Museum of Turkish and Islamic Art (3274), Istanbul.

The artistic pedigree of the great nineteenth-century calligrapher Şevki Efendi (see cat. nos. 40–41) reaches back to Mustafa Kütâhî, via Mahmud Râci and Mehmed Hulûsi (d. 1291/1874).

23. *Murakkaa*
Istanbul, 1181/1767
Sülüs and *nesih*
Ink, colors, and gold on paper mounted on cardboard
Each *kıt'a* 15.4 × 23.2 cm (6 × 9⅛ in.)
(386)

The last two *kıt'alar* of a nine-*kıt'a murakkaa* by Mustafa Kütâhî are shown here. One of the most memorable calligraphers of the eighteenth century, Mustafa Efendi of Kütahya was known for his extremely stylish writing. Most of the *kıt'alar* in this album are signed, the last dated 1181/1767. The style of these *kıt'alar* is reminiscent of that of Şeyh Hamdullah (see cat. nos. 1–2). Moreover, the signatures on most of them include the phrase *ibni'ş-şeyh*, or son of the sheikh, which likewise calls to mind Şeyh Hamdullah, who used the same patronymic.

The *sülüs* line of the lower *kıt'a* consists of a famous Arabic tongue twister, which repeats the letter *cim* (ج) nine times, producing a complex pattern of letters in relation to the baseline of the writing. Because it requires great mastery to write this sentence in *sülüs*, first-rate calligraphers enjoy writing it as a way of testing themselves. If any of the *cimler* are out of place, the entire work fails—no matter how perfectly the letters are formed. In this piece, Kütahyalı Mustafa Efendi has arranged the letters most effectively, showing great mastery.

The borders of these *kıt'alar* are decorated with light-toned *kumlu* (sand-patterned) and *kılçıklı* (fishbone-patterned) marbled paper.

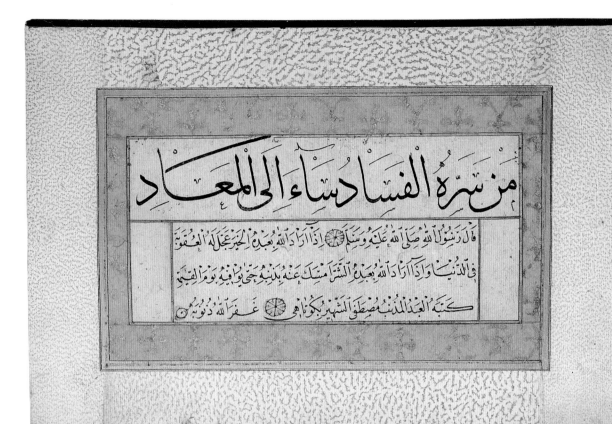

من سرة الفساد ساء الى المعاد

قال رسول الله صلى الله عليه وسلم ۞ اذا اراد الله بعبد الخير عجل له العقوبة
فى الدنيا واذا اراد الله بعبد الشر امسك عنه بذنبه حتى يوفيه يوم القيمة
كتبه العبد المذنب مصطفى الشهير بكوتاهى ۞ غفر الله ذنوبه ۞

قال رسول الله صلى الله عليه وسلم ۞ ما من مولود الا ويولد على فطرة
الاسلام ۞ ثم ابواه يهوّدانه وينصّرانه ويمجّسانه ۞ صدق رسول الله
اللهم صل وسلم على نبيّ الرحمة وشفيع الامة الضعيفة محمد واله وصحبه
اجمعين ۞ كتبه المذنب مصطفى العزيف ابن الشيخ الكوتاهى

ABDULLAH EDİRNEVÎ

D. 1201/1787

Abdullah bin İsmail was born in Edirne, a city in Thrace, near the borders of Greece and Bulgaria. He studied calligraphy in Edirne with Şuglî Ahmed Dede (d. 1140/1728), then became the student of Şekerzâde Mehmed Efendi (see cat. no. 21) in Istanbul. He received his *icâzet* from Şekerzâde and died in 1201/1787.

24. *En'âm-ı Şerîf*
Istanbul, 1193/1779
Nesih
Ink, colors, and gold on paper
Binding 16.5 × 11.6 cm (6⅜ × 4½ in.)
(288)

According to the colophon on folio 8or of this *En'âm-ı Şerîf*, Sultan Selim III (r. 1789–1807), the twenty-eighth Ottoman sultan, commissioned the work. It was written by Abdullah Edirnevî in *nesih* script, and dated 1193/1779. It is also noted in the colophon that the illumination was done by one Hâfız Mehmed of the private library in the Topkapı Sarayı.

Beginning in the eighteenth century, it became the custom to add miniatures of Mecca, "the ennobled," and Medina, "the radiant," to the book of prayers for the Prophet called *Delâilü'l-Hayrât* and to the collection of Qur'anic chapters called *En'âm-ı Şerîf*. (See the entry for catalogue number 2 for a description of the contents of the *En'âm-ı Şerîf*.) Such miniatures (folios 78v and 79r) are illustrated here. In the absence of additional signatures, it is assumed that Hâfız Mehmed painted these miniatures.

The work is written on ninety-nine folios, eleven lines per page. The style of illumination is unconventional, as is the vigorous color scheme. The book has no *mıkleb* (flap) on its binding.

HÂFIZ YUSUF EFENDİ

D. 1201/1787

Before coming to Istanbul, Hâfız Yusuf Efendi worked as a towel maker in the eastern part of the Ottoman Empire. In Istanbul, he studied both calligraphy and the Qur'an with the imam of the reed-mat makers' guild, Mustafa Efendi, who was a student of Eğrikapılı Râsim Efendi's (see cat. no. 19). Later, he studied with İbrahim Rodosî (d. 1201/1787), from whom he received his *icâzet*. During this period, Hâfız Yusuf met Eğrikapılı Mehmed Râsim and learned a great deal from him. Hâfız Yusuf taught calligraphy himself, first at the school at the Galata Sarayı and then at the Topkapı Sarayı. He died on Zilhicce 29, 1201/ October 12, 1787. The sources do not say where he was buried.

25. *Kıt'a*
Istanbul, second half of 18th century
Sülüs and *nesih*
Ink, colors, and gold on paper mounted on cardboard
22.6 × 15 cm (8⅞ × 5⅞ in.)
(127)

The harmony of the calligraphy, illumination, and colors in this eighteenth-century *kıt'a* makes it a charming work. Hâfız Yusuf Efendi was one of the third generation of calligraphers to write *sülüs* and *nesih* in the mode of Hâfız Osman (see cat. nos. 14–16). His teacher Eğrikapılı Mehmed Râsim Efendi was trained by Yedikuleli Seyyid Abdullah Efendi (see cat. nos. 17–18), who studied with Hâfız Osman himself.

The illumination of this *kıt'a*, like the writing, belongs to the latter half of the eighteenth century, but the artist is unknown.

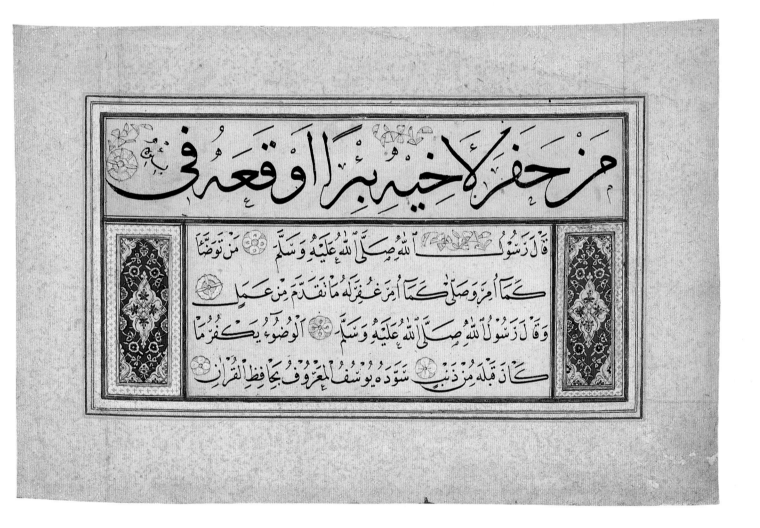

İSMAİL ZÜHDİ

D. 1221/1806

Born in Ünye on the Black Sea, İsmail Zühdi was brought to Istanbul by his father, Mehmed Kaptan. There he learned the six scripts from Ahmed Hıfzı Efendi (d. 1181/1767) and memorized the Qur'an. He also studied with another calligrapher, Mehmed Emin, taking the name Zühdi while earning his *icâzet*. He began to teach calligraphy at the Imperial Palace Service (Enderûn-ı Hümâyun) during Sultan Mustafa III's reign (1757–74) and held that position until the end of his life. İsmail Zühdi was the Ottoman court calligrapher, producing forty *mushaflar* and countless *kıt'alar*, albums, and *hilyeler*. In 1215/1800, he copied the *celî sülüs* inscription for the tomb of Şah Sultan, near the Eyüb and Defterdar districts of Istanbul.

İsmail Zühdi had many calligraphy students, the most prominent of whom was his younger brother, Mustafa Râkım (see cat. no. 27). İsmail Zühdi followed the old method in *celî sülüs;* to spare his feelings, Mustafa Râkım did not reveal his own innovations in that script until his elder brother's death.

İsmail Zühdi died on Şevval 1, 1221/December 12, 1806, and was buried in the Edirnekapı Cemetery, Istanbul, where calligraphers still come to admire the beautiful words Râkım inscribed on the gravestone. According to the late Necmeddin Okyay (see cat. nos. 59–60)—who himself heard the anecdote from Sâmi Efendi (see cat. nos. 49–52)— Mustafa Râkım had a dream the night after he copied the inscription for his brother's gravestone. In the dream, his brother came to him and told him the *elifler* (tall, vertical letters) in the inscription were too thin and that he had better give them kaftans to wear. When he awoke the next morning, Mustafa Râkım looked at the inscription and, sure enough, the letters were too thin, so he rectified the error.

26. ***Kıt'a***
Istanbul, 18th century
Sülüs and *nesih*
Ink, colors, and gold on paper mounted on cardboard
15.6 × 22.7 cm (6⅛ × 8⅞ in.)
(128)

This *kıt'a* has an unusual format: two lines of *nesih*, followed by one line of *sülüs*, ending with four lines of *nesih*. (For a discussion of *kıt'a* formats, see pages 27–29 and figure 15, in the introduction.) Instead of two *koltuk* illuminations, as usual, there are four. The borders are decorated with the *sîm-efşan* (silver-flake) technique. As in the *kıt'a* by Mustafa Kütâhî (cat. no. 23), the *sülüs* line here consists of an Arabic tongue twister, a jingle with little content. Aesthetically, however, İsmail Zühdi's tongue twister is more successful than Mustafa Kütâhî's.

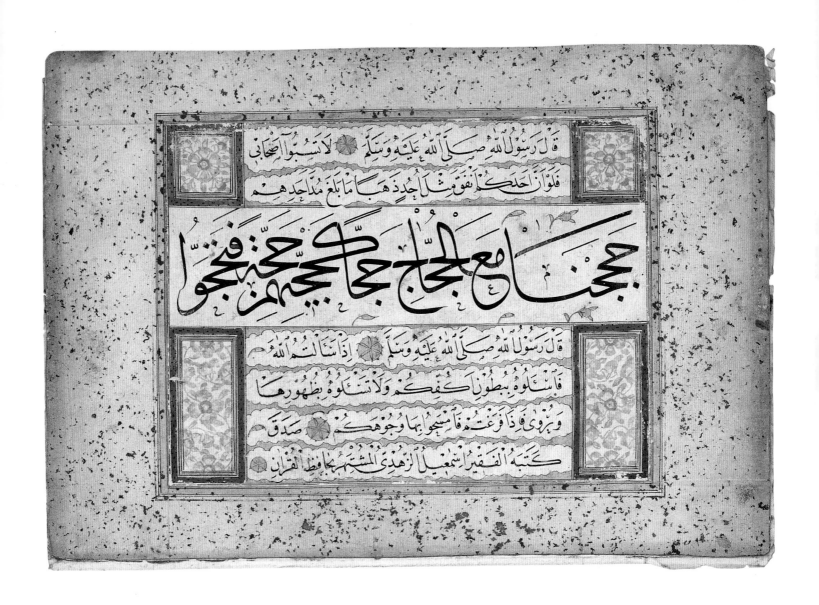

قال رسول الله صلى الله عليه وسلم لا تسبوا اصحابى

فلوان احدكم انفق مثل احد ذهبا ما بلغ مد احدهم

بجحنا مع الحاج حجا يحجه من حجة فنجحوا

قال رسول الله صلى الله عليه وسلم اذا سالتم الله

فاسئلوه ببطون كفكم ولا تسئلوه بظهورها

وبرؤى فاذا فرغتم فامسحوا بها وجوهكم صدق

كتبه الفقير اسمعيل الزهدى المشتهر بحافظ القرآن

MUSTAFA RÂKIM

1171/1758–1241/1826

Mustafa was born in Ünye, on the Black Sea, in 1171/1758. While he was still young, his father, Mehmed Kaptan, brought him to Istanbul to live with his elder brother, İsmail Zühdi (see cat. no. 26). There he began his religious education and was taught the art of calligraphy by his brother and by Üçüncü Derviş Ali (d. 1200/1786). Having received his *icâzet*, Mustafa began to sign his works Râkım (Writer).

Mustafa Râkım was also known as a painter. He presented one painting to Sultan Selim III (r. 1789–1807); the sultan admired it so much that he invited the artist for an audience. During this audience, Mustafa Râkım drew a portrait of the sultan, the whereabouts of which are unknown. He was appointed *müderris* (professor) and given responsibility for making drawings for Ottoman currency and for writing the *tuğra*. When Sultan Mahmud II (r. 1808–39; see cat. no. 34) acceded to the throne, he studied *sülüs* and *celî sülüs* with Râkım, who was later given the titular post of *kâdı* (judge of Islamic law) of Izmir. He occupied several distinguished positions over the years until he became *kâdıasker* (supreme judge) of Anatolia in 1238/1823. He suffered a stroke and died on Şa'ban 15, 1241/March 25, 1826. According to a wish expressed in his will, he was buried in a tomb adjacent to the school named after him in the Karagümrük quarter of Istanbul.

The great innovations introduced by Mustafa Râkım in writing *celî sülüs* script and the *tuğra* are discussed in the introduction to this volume. He also wrote *kıt'alar* in *ta'lîk*, and inscriptions in *celî ta'lîk*, and had some success with them, writing with the same skill he showed in other scripts. Râkım's method in *celî ta'lîk*, however, did not supersede that of Yesârîzâde (d. 1265/1849).

In addition to his various *kıt'alar* and *levhalar*, Râkım produced bands of calligraphy for the interior walls of the mausoleum of Princess Nakşıdil Sultan (the text is from chapter 76 of the Qur'an). He also wrote inscriptions for the gates of the *hazîre* (enclosed burial precinct) in the Fatih quarter of Istanbul, and he copied inscriptions and decorations for gravestones, such as the one for his elder brother. During his final illness, he did the calligraphy for bands inside the Nusretiye Mosque, in the Tophâne quarter (Qur'an 78—*Nebe*, or News—served as the text). Stencils of his calligraphic works in *celî* are now in the collection of the Museum of Turkish and Islamic Art, Istanbul.

In the biographical work *Son hattatlar* (The Last Calligraphers), İbnülemin Mahmud Kemal İnal (1870–1957) draws this verse portrait of Râkım Efendi:

> It is befitting to say of Mustafa Râkım:
> "He is the sultan of the magnificent *celî* style."
> The Almighty Lord created only one like him.
> There never was, nor will be, his peer.

27. *Levha*

Istanbul, after 1225/1809

Celî sülüs

Gold on fabric

45 × 56 cm (17½ × 21¾ in.)

(73)

Though written in two different sizes of *celî sülüs*, this composition achieves great harmony, demonstrating Mustafa Râkım's mastery of the art of calligraphy. This *levha* was produced by the *zer-endûd* method. The signature—the combination of letters written in small script near the lower left—is in the style invented by Râkım Efendi. Formerly, inscriptions in *celî sülüs* and on *tuğralar* were signed in the *tevkî'* script. About 1225/1809, Mustafa Râkım began combining elements of *sülüs* and *tevkî'* in his signature composition, a practice that is still followed today. This format features letters that extend both above and below the base line, and the letters are not dotted. The signature on this piece reads *ketebehû Râkım* (Râkım wrote it). Subsequent calligraphers who wrote the *celî* scripts, as well as *tuğrakeşler* (writers of *tuğralar*), appropriated this style, occasionally using some of the dots.

YESÂRÎ MEHMED ES'AD EFENDI

D. 1213/1798

Yesârî (the Left-Handed) was born in Istanbul, the son of Kara Mahmud Ağa. He was paralyzed on the right side and afflicted with tremors on the left. In spite of his handicap, he was able to usher in a new era in the writing of *ta'lîk*, and because of this achievement, he was what is traditionally called a "marvel of God's might."

Yesârî first sought lessons from the master of *ta'lîk* Şeyhülislâm Veliüddin Efendi (d. 1182/1768), who turned him away because of his seemingly helpless condition. He then began studies with Dedezâde Mehmed Efendi (d. 1173/1759). Young Mehmed Es'ad so surprised his teacher with his talent that he soon won his *icâzetnâme*, in 1167/1754. At the *icâzet* ceremony, Veliüddin is reported to have said, "I would have had the honor, but alas, I let it slip away."

At first, Yesârî Es'ad Efendi followed the method of the great Persian master Mīr ʿImād al-Hasanī (961/1554–1024/1615) in the *nesta'lîk* (*ta'lîk*) script. But after 1190/1776, he began to develop his own style, which led to a new Ottoman method. Yesârî's career reached a peak with this innovative style between 1196/1782 and 1200/1786; and, beginning in the reign of Sultan Mustafa III (1757–74), he served as master of calligraphy in the imperial palace. Sultan Selim III (r. 1789–1807) was favorably inclined toward him and admired the inscriptions Yesârî wrote for architectural monuments the sultan had commissioned. Among Yesârî's students was his son, Yesârîzâde Mustafa İzzet (d. 1265/1849). Other students included Arabzâde Sa'dullah (see cat. no. 29), Mehmed Şehabeddin, and Mîr Emin (1171/1758–1224/1809). It is said that so many students came to Yesârî's house to take lessons that the stationer Kadri Usta was able to make a living selling *âhâr* paper outside Yesârî's front door.

Yesârî was so weak and small that he was carried from room to room in a special basket. In 1206/1792, his son took him on a pilgrimage to Mecca. His illness worsened in his last years, and he died on Recep 11, 1213/December 19, 1798. He was buried in a small cemetery in the Gelenbevî section of the Fatih district of Istanbul. His son was eventually buried beside him. The site has been covered by a road and the gravestones moved to the cemetery of the Fatih Mosque.

Over the course of his career, Yesârî wrote *kıt'alar*, *murakkaalar*, *levhalar*, and some well-known inscriptions. His inscriptions at such sites in Istanbul as Sultan Mehmed II's tomb (where his work appears on the inside of the door), the Hacı Selim Ağa Library in Üsküdar, the Topkapı Sarayı (his work can be found at the barracks of the Black Eunuchs, inside the Harem), the Beylerbeyi Mosque, and the Aynalı Kavak Sarayı are among the finest examples of Ottoman *ta'lîk*.

28. *Murakkaa*
Istanbul, 18th century
Ta'lîk
Ink, colors, and gold on paper mounted on cardboard
Each *kıt'a* 34.7 × 21.4 cm (13½ × 8¼ in.)
(347)

In learning calligraphy, one first practices the letters one by one, then in pairs. These initial lessons are called the *müfredât* exercises. Upon finishing these to the master's satisfaction, the student moves on to the *mürekkebât* exercises, which consist of poetic odes in praise of the Prophet, aphorisms, and such. Writing these sentences teaches the student how to compose the letters into lines.

Shown here, on the right-hand page, are *müfredât* exercises in the *ta'lîk* script, from the letter *mim* (M) through the letter *he* (H). On the left-hand page, also in *ta'lîk*, is a verse in Persian, which translates, "The time for deliverance from the *müfredât* has come. It is now time to practice the *mürekkebât*." There is no doubt that all twelve *kıt'alar* in this undated *meşk* album were written by Yesârî Mehmed Es'ad Efendi, but the line of smaller *ta'lîk* at the bottom of the left-hand page is believed to have been added to the album by another calligrapher.

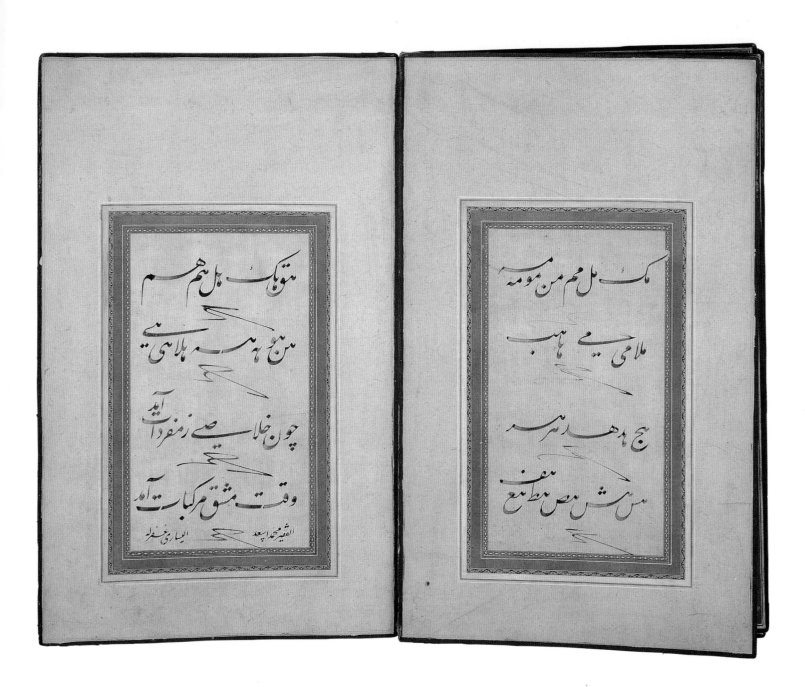

ARABZÂDE MEHMED SA'DULLAH EFENDİ
1180/1767–1259/1843

Born in Istanbul on Şa'ban 12, 1180/January 13, 1767, Arabzâde Mehmed Sa'dullah Efendi was the son of Mehmed Ârif Efendi and the grandson of Arabzâde Atâullah Efendi, an Ottoman *şeyhülislâm*, or supreme religious authority. Like his father and grandfather, he belonged to the *ilmiye* (religious-scholar) class of Ottoman society. He became the *kâdı* (judge of Islamic law) of Istanbul, then *kâdıasker* (supreme judge) of Anatolia and Rumelia, and finally *reisülulemâ* (chief of the *ulemâ*, or Islamic religious establishment). He died on Ramazan 5, 1259/September 29, 1843, and was buried in the family graveyard, on Divanyolu Avenue in the Çarşıkapı quarter of Istanbul.

Sa'dullah Efendi is reported to have had an exemplary character. He studied *ta'lîk* calligraphy with Yesârî Es'ad Efendi (see cat. no. 28) and received his *icâzet* in 1208/1794. *Kıt'alar* and *celî ta'lîk levhalar* by him are still extant. His inscriptions in *celî ta'lîk*, cut in stone, can be seen at the Sütlüce Sa'diye Lodge, the State Press of Istanbul, and the Mevlevî Sufi Lodge (Mevlevîhâne) in Kütahya.

29. *Murakkaa*
Istanbul, late 18th century
Ta'lîk
Ink, colors, and gold on paper mounted on cardboard
Binding 33 × 21.4 cm (12⅞ × 8¼ in.)
(379)

The favored texts for *mürekkebât meşki* exercises were the *kasîde* (ode) in Persian on the *besmele* (cat. no. 53) by ᶜAbd al-Rahmān Mullā Jāmī (817/1414–898/1492) and the *Hilye-i Hâkânî*, an ode by Hâkânî Mehmed Bey (d. 1015/1606) that describes the *besmele* and the Prophet. The opening lines of the latter work are shown here, on the thirteenth and fourteenth *kıt'alar* of this seventeen-*kıt'a* album. The text translates as follows:

> Let us begin the discussion with the *besmele*.
> May it solve even this famous mystery.
> The *besmele* is a mirror showing
> The description of purity—that beautiful face.

> May God be praised, as he is the unique,
> Also all-wise and mighty.
> He does as He wills in all things perfectly.
> There is no distinction with him between the highborn and the lowly.

A device that stands for the Arabic word *saᶜy* (Turkish spelling: *sa'y*), meaning "persevere," can be seen under each line of calligraphy.

The twelve preceding *kıt'alar* are *müfredât* exercises. Following the album's final *kıt'a* is a painting of a vase of flowers. The paper was manufactured especially for *ta'lîk kıt'alar*. On some pages, the stamp of the papermaker Rif'atî Efendi can be seen; it appears in the lower left corner of the right-hand *kıt'a* shown here.

This album was formerly considered to be by Yesârî Es'ad Efendi, but critical examination shows that it is actually by his student Arabzâde Mehmed Sa'dullah Efendi.

The *Hilye-i Hâkânî* is also the text in catalogue number 55.

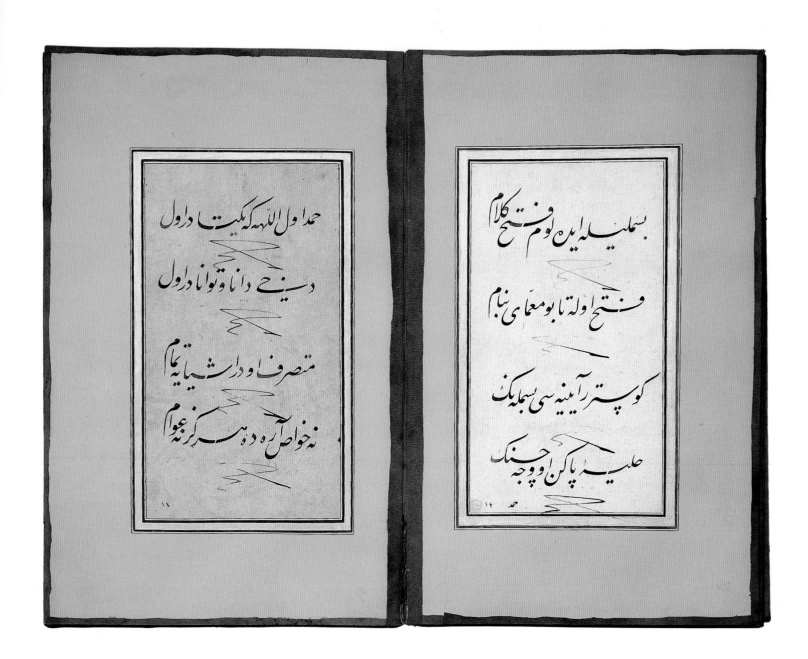

بسم الله این لوم فتح کلام

فتح اوله تا بو معمای نبام

کوپستر آیینه سی سبمله یک

حلیه پاک کن او وجه جنک

حمد اول اللهه که نکیت دراول

دسینج دانا و توانا دراول

متصرف او دراشیایه تمام

نه خواص آره ده هر کز نه عوام

۱۸

۱۴

SEYYİD OSMAN EFENDİ

D. 1220/1805

Son of a man who was also named Osman, Seyyid Osman Efendi studied with a calligrapher called Hacızâde Mustafa Karamânî who lived in Istanbul's Çengelköy neighborhood, on the Anatolian shore of the Bosphorus. Seyyid Osman Efendi's calligraphic pedigree goes directly back to Hâfız Osman (see cat. nos. 14–16), through five generations of calligraphers.

Seyyid Osman Efendi married the daughter of a calligrapher named İbrahim Afif (d. 1181/1767) and for that reason usually added to his signature the words "son-in-law of İbrahim Afif." He was said to have been a large man who, by his occasionally erratic behavior, earned the name Deli Osman, or Crazy Osman. He died on Safer 23, 1220/ May 23, 1805, and was buried near Şeyh Hamdullah (see cat. nos. 1–2).

30. ***Kasîde-i Bürde***
Istanbul, early 19th century
Nesih
Ink, colors, and gold on paper
Binding 13.9 × 10.1 cm (5⅜ × 3⅞ in.)
(329)

This work by Seyyid Osman Efendi contains the text of an ode in praise of the Prophet, the *Kasîde-i Bürde*. Shown here are folios 5v and 6r, from a total of fifteen folios written in a small but elegant *nesih*. (This ode can also be written as an album; see catalogue number 36.) The hemistiches and verses are separated by gilded *duraklar*. The first page of this volume is illuminated, but the illuminator is unknown.

Aware of this calligrapher's predilection for small script, Sultan Selim III (r. 1789–1807) commissioned him to write a *sancak mushafı* (emblem Qur'an). These tiny Qur'ans—approximately two inches high—would be encased in special boxes and affixed to the tops of military standards carried by the Ottoman army. These small volumes were written in a fine version of the *nesih* script called *gubârî* (like dust).

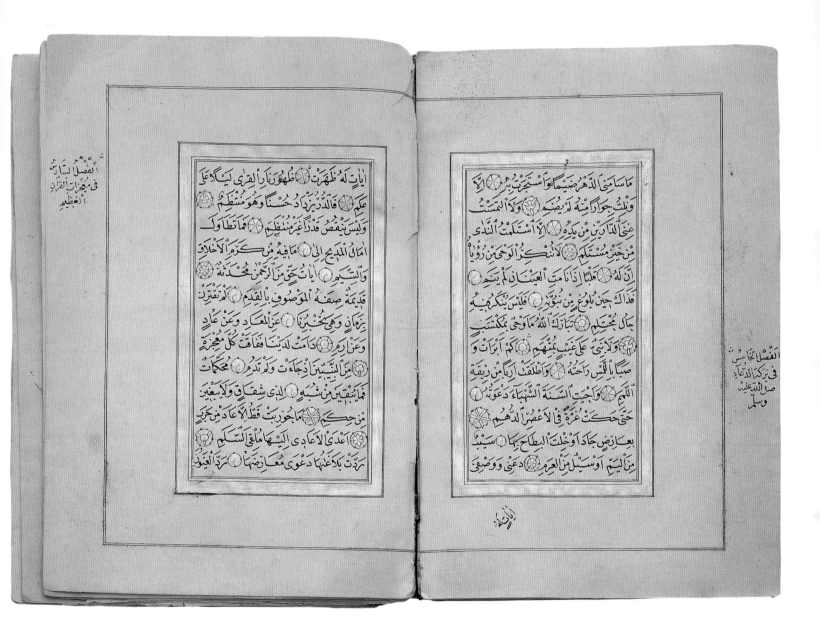

آيَاتٍ لَهُ ظَهَرَتْ ۞ ظُهُورَ نَارِ الْقِرَى لَيْلًا عَلَى
عَلَمِ ۞ فَالدُّرُّ يَزْدَادُ حُسْنًا وَهُوَ مُنْتَظِمٌ ۞
وَلَيْسَ يَنْقُصُ قَدْرًا غَيْرَ مُنْتَظِمٍ ۞ مَا تَطَاوَلَ
آمَالُ الْمَدِيحِ إِلَى ۞ مَا فِيهِ مِنْ كَرَمِ الْأَخْلَاقِ
وَالشِّيَمِ ۞ آيَاتُ حَقٍّ مِنَ الرَّحْمَنِ مُحْدَثَةٌ ۞
قَدِيمَةٌ صِفَةُ الْمَوْصُوفِ بِالْقِدَمِ ۞ لَمْ تَقْتَرِنْ
بِزَمَانٍ وَهِيَ تُخْبِرُنَا ۞ عَنِ الْمَعَادِ وَعَنْ عَادٍ
وَعَنْ إِرَمِ ۞ دَامَتْ لَدَيْنَا فَفَاقَتْ كُلَّ مُعْجِزَةٍ
مِنَ النَّبِيِّينَ إِذْ جَاءَتْ وَلَمْ تَدُمِ ۞ مُحْكَمَاتٌ
فَمَا يُبْقِينَ مِنْ شُبَهٍ ۞ لِذِي شِقَاقٍ وَلَا يَبْغِينَ
مِنْ حَكَمِ ۞ مَا حُورِبَتْ قَطُّ إِلَّا عَادَ مِنْ حَرَبٍ
أَعْدَى الْأَعَادِي إِلَيْهَا مُلْقِيَ السَّلَمِ ۞
رَدَّتْ بَلَاغَتُهَا دَعْوَى مُعَارِضِهَا ۞ رَدَّ الْغَيُورِ

مَا سَامَنِي الدَّهْرُ ضَيْمًا وَاسْتَجَرْتُ بِهِ ۞ إِلَّا
وَنِلْتُ جِوَارًا مِنْهُ لَمْ يُضَمِ ۞ وَلَا الْتَمَسْتُ
غِنَى الدَّارَيْنِ مِنْ يَدِهِ ۞ إِلَّا اسْتَلَمْتُ النَّدَى
مِنْ خَيْرِ مُسْتَلَمِ ۞ لَا تُنْكِرُ الْوَحْيَ مِنْ رُؤْيَاهُ
إِنَّ لَهُ ۞ قَلْبًا إِذَا نَامَتِ الْعَيْنَانِ لَمْ يَنَمِ ۞
فَذَاكَ حِينَ بُلُوغٍ مِنْ نُبُوَّتِهِ ۞ فَلَيْسَ يُنْكَرُ فِيهِ
حَالُ مُحْتَلِمٍ ۞ تَبَارَكَ اللَّهُ مَا وَحْيٌ بِمُكْتَسَبٍ ۞
وَلَا نَبِيٌّ عَلَى غَيْبٍ بِمُتَّهَمِ ۞ كَمْ أَبْرَأَتْ وَ
صِبًا بِلَمْسٍ رَاحَتِهِ ۞ وَأَطْلَقَتْ أَرِبًا مِنْ رِبْقَةِ
اللَّمَمِ ۞ وَأَحْيَتِ السَّنَةَ الشَّهْبَاءَ دَعْوَتُهُ ۞
حَتَّى حَكَتْ غُرَّةً فِي الْأَعْصُرِ الدُّهُمِ ۞
بِعَارِضٍ جَادَ أَوْ خِلْتَ الْبِطَاحَ بِهَا ۞ سَيْبٌ
مِنَ الْيَمِّ أَوْ سَيْلٌ مِنَ الْعَرِمِ ۞ دَعْنِي وَوَصْفِيَ

AHMED NÂİLÎ

D. 1229/1814

Hacı Ahmed Nâilî signed himself both Galatalı and Eyyûbî, indicating that he lived sometimes in the Galata section of Istanbul, sometimes in the Eyüb district. His father, İbrahim Zarîfî, was a boatman. Father and son went together to Mustafa Kütâhî (see cat. no. 23) for calligraphy lessons. Nâilî Efendi taught at the Taşmekteb School in Galata. He wrote mostly in *nesih* and always indicated in the colophon of his *mushaflar* which number the codex was. At his death, he had completed at least 121 copies of the Qur'an.

His surviving works, in addition to *mushaflar*, include such religious texts as the *al-Shifā'* (a biography of the Prophet and collection of *hadîsler*), by al-Qādī ʿIyād (476/1083–544/1149), and the *Delâilü'l-Hayrât*. Ahmed Nâilî died in 1229/1814 and was buried in the Yâvedûd Cemetery, in the Defterdar district of Istanbul, near the Golden Horn. His son, Hâfız İbrahim Efendi (d. 1227/1812), was also a calligrapher and was buried in the same cemetery—the third generation in a family bound together by calligraphy.

31. *Delâilü'l-Hayrât*
Istanbul, 1214/1799
Nesih
Ink, colors, and gold on paper
Binding 16.3 × 11.2 cm (6¼ × 4¼ in.)
(287)

According to the signature on the last page, this *Delâilü'l-Hayrât*, a handbook of prayers for the Prophet, was written by Galatalı Ahmed Nâilî in 1214/1799. The book consists of eighty-five folios, written in *nesih*, thirteen lines per page. As can be seen here on folios 70v and 71r, Nâilî Efendi wrote in a delightful small *nesih* script.

The top, side, and bottom margins, and the notes and commentary written in the margins, are called, collectively, the *hâşiye*. In this book, the marginalia are written in a minuscule *nesih* in diagonal lines (see the upper left margin of folio 71r). The book is bound in the *zilbahar* style, which became popular in the late eighteenth century. In this style, a simple design, usually geometric, is painted directly on the leather in gold ink, then burnished. The illumination of the *unvan sahifesi* (opening page) was painstakingly executed in the *zer-ender-zer* (gold-upon-gold) style, but the illuminator is unknown.

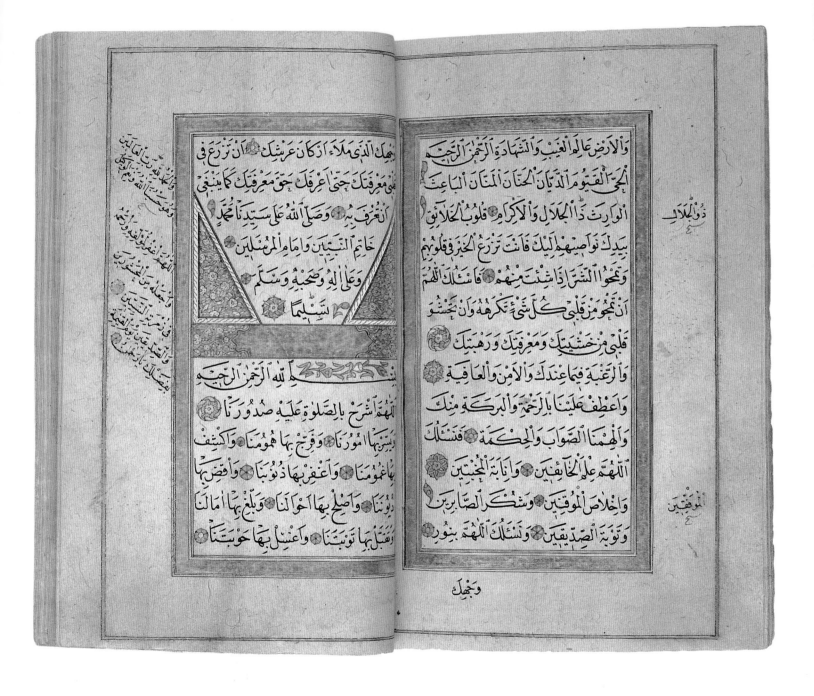

MAHMUD CELÂLEDDİN EFENDİ

1163/1750?–1245/1829

Mahmud Celâleddin was born in the Daghestan region of Caucasia. Although the exact date of his birth is not known, judging from the level of ability in an album he wrote dated 1188/1778, one can surmise that he was born about 1163/1750. He moved with his father to Istanbul, where he studied calligraphy with a number of masters. It is said that because of his obstinacy, he was not amenable to traditional lessons and instead developed his skill by studying the works of Hâfız Osman (see cat. nos. 14–16), becoming a well-known master himself. His early works—for example, two items in the Topkapı Sarayı Museum Library, Istanbul (EH 273 and GY 322-9)—are signed Mahmûdü'l-Mevdûd, or Mahmud the Beloved. Later, he always signed himself Mahmud Celâleddin.

He wrote many excellent Qur'ans, prayer handbooks, *kıt'alar*, *murakkaalar*, *hilyeler*, and *levhalar*. Because of its hard and static qualities, however, his *celî sülüs* did not bear comparison with that of Mustafa Râkım (see cat. no. 27). Nevertheless, Sultan Abdülmecid (r. 1839–61) took calligraphy lessons from Celâleddin's student Mehmed Tahir Efendi (d. 1262/1848), thus giving Celâleddin's method a brief life before it became obsolete. A *celî sülüs* inscription by Celâleddin, dated 1207/1793, can be found on the tomb of Mihrişâh Vâlide Sultan, in the Eyüb district of Istanbul.

Mahmud Celâleddin's stubborn character was said to be reflected in his writing. He spent his life in the İstavroz quarter on the Bosphorus, now the Abdullah Ağa quarter of Beylerbeyi. He died in 1245/1829 and was buried in the cemetery of the Şeyh Murad Lodge, in the Eyüb district. His student Esmâ İbret Hanım (b. 1194/1780), whom he later married, was one of the foremost female calligraphers of her day.

32. *Levha*
Istanbul, late 18th–early 19th century
Sülüs
Ink, colors, and gold on paper mounted on cardboard
54.2 × 42.3 cm (21⅛ × 16½ in.)
(74)

The text of this *levha* is an Ottoman Turkish poem:

O heart! Put aside vanity. Life doesn't end well.

Even if you attain your desires in this world, the outcome is still separation and rejection.

But because the end is bad, must there be gloom and anxiety?

Whether merry and cheerful, or sorrowful and afflicted, the end is one.

So come, O heart, to the corner of divine reliance and celebrate God's unity.

Let us see, whatever God decrees, the end is full of benevolence.

Set free the ship of human affairs to glide in the sea of divine reliance.

Unfurl the sail of aspiration, stand aside, and watch!

The *duraklar* and the *koltuk* tulip illuminations are contemporary with the calligraphy. The *zencerekli* (chain) inner border and the outer border, executed in the *halkârî* style, were done by Rikkat Kunt (1321/1903–1406/1986) in the 1970s, when the *levha* was restored. (Rikkat Kunt sought to rediscover the classic style of the art of illumination. The ceramics teacher Feyzullah Dayıgil [1910–1949] and the calligrapher Necmeddin Okyay [see cat. nos. 59–60] played a part in the stylistic renaissance that Rikkat Kunt initiated. Her style of *halkârî* illumination, in particular, has left its mark.)

This *levha* is in *sülüs* script. Celâleddin's *sülüs* was usually stiff, the exact opposite of that of his contemporary Mustafa Râkım. That stiffness is especially evident in Celâleddin's *celî sülüs levhalar*, but it is not obvious in this piece.

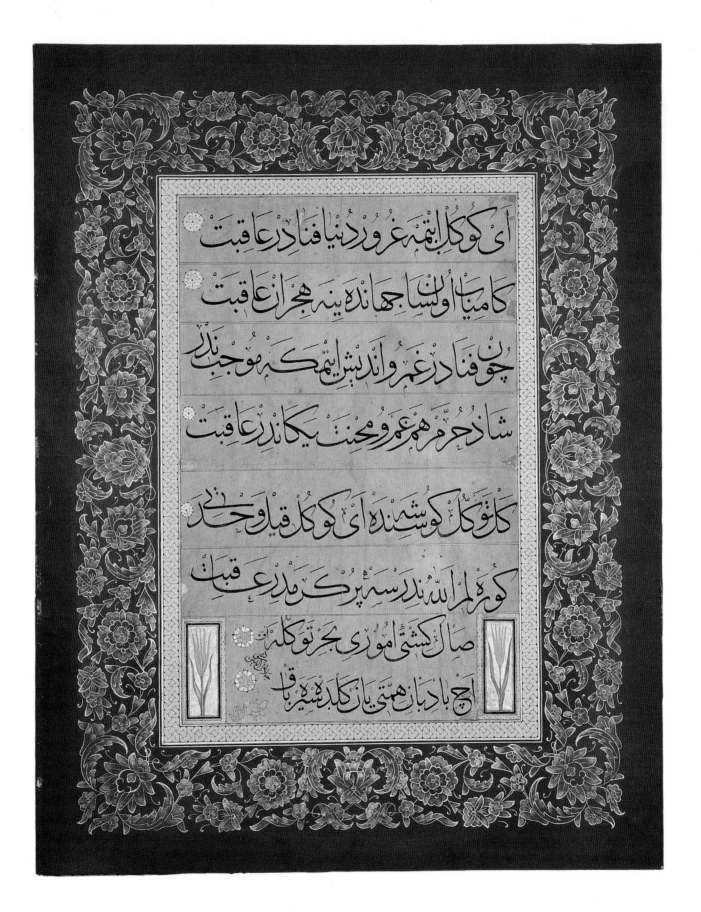

اى كوكل اينقه غرور دنيا فنادر عاقبت

كاميابى الوسآ جهانده بنه هجران عاقبت

چون فنادر غم و انديشى ايتمكه موجب ندر

شاذ حرم هم غم و محنت يكسان در عاقبت

كل توكل كوشنده اى كوكل قيل وحدتى

كوره لمرالله اندر سه پر كر مدرع قبتك

صال كشتى امورى بحر توكله

اچ بادبان هستى يان كلده سيره قا

33. Kıt'a

Istanbul, early 19th century

Sülüs and *nesih*

Ink and gold on paper mounted on
cardboard

18.5 × 24.2 cm (7¼ × 9⅜ in.)

(338,1)

At the end of this *kıt'a*, written in diagonal lines of *nesih* between two lines of *sülüs*, Mahmud Celâleddin signed himself Hâfız Mahmud, adding in the right *koltuk* that he copied the work from one by Hamdullah, "son of the sheikh" (see cat. nos. 1–2). Celâleddin so successfully mimics Şeyh Hamdullah here that, at first glance, his own artistic identity seems to have been submerged.

Imitation is not regarded favorably in other arts, but it is accepted that calligraphy is an imitative (*taklîdî*) art. Traditionally, master calligraphers wrote exactly like their teachers, adopting their styles entirely. In later centuries, however, the concept of *taklîd* (imitation) acquired a new meaning. After being trained and credentialed, calligraphers preferred to develop their own artistic identity. Only then would a calligrapher choose to imitate a work by his teacher or by one of the old masters. It was considered an honor to the original calligrapher to

indicate on a work that it was done in imitation of his style. Moreover, by doing so, the calligrapher prevented the work's being considered a forgery.

The art of *taklîd* is an inestimably difficult art. It requires a thorough study of the master whose work is being copied. What is more difficult, it also requires the calligrapher to engrave a work on his memory, so to speak, and reproduce it with near-photographic fidelity. The result of *taklîd* is as exact as a tracing—although tracing itself is an unacceptable means of copying a work.

On this *kıt'a*, the inner border is composed of *kumlu* (sand-patterned) marbling and the outer border is in the *battal* pattern. (The simplest of all *ebrû* papers, *battal* is made from one or more pigments left exactly as they fell on the tragacanth bath, untouched by a stylus or comb; it is similar to, but not identical with, the stone pattern of Western marbling.) All the parts of the work are surrounded with golden *cedvel* frames.

ضاقت الدنيا على المتبالغضين

العبد حر ان قنع والحر عبد ان طمع

SULTAN MAHMUD II
1199/1785–1255/1839

The son of the twenty-seventh Ottoman sultan, Abdülhamid I (r. 1774–89), Mahmud was born in Istanbul on Ramazan 13, 1199/ July 20, 1785. His father died while he was still a young child, and he was brought up under the patronage of his uncle, Sultan Selim III (r. 1789–1807). On Cemâziyelâhır 4, 1223/July 28, 1808, after a period of political turbulence, he ascended the throne as the thirtieth Ottoman sultan and held the sultanate until his death on Rebiülâhır 18, 1255/ July 1, 1839. The political and administrative details of his life and reign can be found in history books; here, only his connection with calligraphy will be addressed.

As a prince, Mahmud studied *sülüs* and *nesih* with Kebecizâde Mehmed Vasfi (d. 1247/1831); in 1222/1807, he wrote a *hilye* as his *icâzet* piece (Topkapı Sarayı Museum Library, Istanbul, GY 1353). He is known to have written two Qur'ans in *nesih* during this period. Following his ascension to the throne, he began studying calligraphy with Mustafa Râkım (see cat. no. 27). Whenever affairs of state allowed, he devoted time to writing in *celî sülüs*, leaving nearly forty *levhalar* in that script. Enlarged copies of these pieces were made for mosques by the *zer-endûd* process or in *malakârî* (stuccowork), using stencils.

It is common for a master to correct his pupil's work, and it is understood that after Sultan Mahmud wrote a *levha*, Mustafa Râkım corrected the calligraphy. For this reason, the only extant *levhalar* by Sultan Mahmud are those that approach the quality of Râkım's work. Nevertheless, in the *meşkler* that he wrote with his own hand, Sultan Mahmud showed genuine talent and mastery. He was also, incidentally, gifted in musical composition.

34. *Levha*
Istanbul, early 19th century
Celî sülüs
Gold on painted cardboard
54 × 87 cm (21⅛ × 33⅞ in.)
(109)

This *levha* was written by Sultan Mahmud II in the style of his teacher, Mustafa Râkım. The text reads: "I cannot have success except with the help of God" (Qur'an 11:88). The piece was prepared by the *zer-endûd* method: it was painted in gold on a dark blue background, using a stencil. To the left of the text is a magnificent composition designed by Râkım for the sultan. It reads: *ketebehû Mahmud bin Abdülhamid Hân* (Mahmud, son of Abdülhamid, wrote this).

In the early eighteenth century, Turkish illumination began to be influenced by Western decorative principles. The border decoration of this *levha*, drawn on a fez-red background, is in the so-called Turkish Rococo style of the nineteenth century. After 1826, when Sultan Mahmud II conferred on his non-Muslim subjects the right to become illuminators, the Turkish Rococo began to lose its originality, resulting in the kind of lackluster decoration seen on this *levha*.

113

Çömez Mustafa Vâsif

D. 1269/1853

A native of Aksu, near the north-central Anatolian city of Kastamonu, Mustafa Vâsıf went to Istanbul as a young man and studied calligraphy with Kebecizâde Mehmed Vasfi (d. 1247/1831), from whom he received his *icâzet*. He was known by the nickname *çömez*, or apprentice, which was given to him by his teacher. Çömez Mustafa studied as well with Ömer Vasfi (d. 1240/1825), who was also called Lâz Ömer.

Mustafa Vâsıf was the custodian of the mausoleum of Sultan Abdülhamid I (r. 1774–89), in Bahçekapı, Istanbul, and was later appointed director of the Hamid I Philanthropic Foundation (Hamîd-i Evvel Vakfı). As a calligrapher, he wrote *kıt'alar* and *hilyeler* in *sülüs* and *nesih* and surely wrote Qur'ans as well. It was Çömez Mustafa who, on the pilgrimage to Mecca, saw a Muslim from Java write with a palm-thorn pen, and introduced such pens to Ottoman calligraphers. Because of its durability, the *cava kalemi* became the instrument of choice for writing long texts in small scripts. Çömez Mustafa is also known for having a powerful wrist, probably due to his prowess with the slingshot.

Mustafa Vâsıf died in 1269/1853 and was buried on the seaward side of the Eyüb Mosque, Istanbul. His son, Çömezzâde Muhsin (d. 1304/1887), was also a calligrapher.

35. *Hilye*
Istanbul, 1236/1821
Muhakkak, sülüs, and *nesih*
Ink, colors, and gold on paper mounted on painted cardboard
107 × 73 cm (41¾ × 28½ in.)
(383)

In general, this *hilye* conforms to the traditional *hilye* format described in the introduction to this volume (see pages 34–37 and fig. 18). The *besmele* is in *muhakkak* script. The *Rahmet Âyeti* (Mercy Verse; Qur'an 21:107) and the names of the first four caliphs are written in *sülüs*, and the rest of the text is in *nesih*. This *hilye* differs from most, however, in Mustafa Vâsıf's inclusion of a *hadîs* transmitted by ʿAlī about the description of the Prophet. Because of this additional text, the *etek* section is deeper than usual and the *koltuklar* are elongated. The *göbek* and its *hilâl* are flanked by two *takozlar* (chocks), illuminated so as to harmonize with the *koltuklar*. The illumination is contemporary with the calligraphy, with the exception of the border immediately surrounding the *hilye*, which was illuminated by Muhsin Demironat (1325/1907–1403/1983) in pale colors with elegant *halkârî* designs. (At the suggestion of Necmeddin Okyay [see cat. nos. 59–60], Muhsin studied and adopted the classic style of illumination. One of the greatest Turkish illuminators of the twentieth century, he left many fine examples of illumination on *kıt'alar, hilyeler*, and *levhalar*.) The outermost border was illuminated over an ultramarine blue background in the nineteenth century.

115

KÂDIASKER MUSTAFA İZZET EFENDİ

1216/1801–1293/1876

Seyyid Mustafa was born in Tosya, a town south of Kastamonu, which is near the Black Sea, in 1216/1801. Upon the death of his father, Destan (or Bostan) Ağazâde Mustafa Ağa, his mother sent him to Istanbul to study. He began taking lessons in the Fatih *medrese* (Islamic theological school) at an early age and also studied music. When Sultan Mahmud II (r. 1808–39; see cat. no. 34) heard Seyyid Mustafa reciting the Qur'an and singing hymns in the Hidâyet Mosque, in Bahçekapı, Istanbul, he ordered that the young man be sent to the Imperial Palace Service (Enderûn-ı Hümâyun), where he spent three years. He spent three more years in the Galata Sarayı, where he studied science and art and became an accomplished reed-flute player. He also learned *sülüs* and *nesih* from Çömez Mustafa Efendi (see cat. no. 35) and *ta'lîk* and *celî ta'lîk* from Yesârîzâde Mustafa İzzet Efendi (d. 1265/1849). Seyyid Mustafa adopted the pen name İzzet from his master and used it to sign his calligraphy.

Although the sultan came to love and respect him, Seyyid Mustafa found court life too confining and the rules of protocol too uncongenial, and thought of running away. He asked the sultan's permission to perform the pilgrimage and, on his way back from Mecca, stayed in Cairo for some time before finally returning to Istanbul. Once there, instead of going back to the imperial palace, he decided to spend the remainder of his life in piety and worship.

One day in the month of Ramazan 1247/1832, the sultan attended prayers in the Bâyezid Mosque, where he heard the unmistakable voice of Mustafa İzzet Efendi. Offended that Seyyid Mustafa had not returned to the palace, the sultan ordered that he be punished; in the end, however, Seyyid Mustafa was pardoned and went on to occupy distinguished religious and juridical posts during the reign of Sultan Abdülmecid (1839–61).

The following anecdote was reported by the late Necmeddin Okyay (see cat. nos. 59–60). It is worth noting, for it shows that calligraphy, like any other art, suffers if not practiced daily and with dedication. In 1255/1839, Okyay said, Mustafa İzzet Efendi was appointed preacher of the Eyüb Mosque, and he continued in that position for six years. Every Friday, he would stop working on calligraphy to prepare the Friday prayer and to perform his own worship. Later, he would say to his students, "I know which works I wrote on Saturdays, even if I view the calligraphy from the wrong side, even after forty years have elapsed."

Mustafa İzzet Efendi was calligraphy master for the princes of the ruling family and was a member of the Supreme Council of Judicial Ordinances (Meclis-i Vâlâ-yı Ahkâm-ı Adliye). He became *kâdıasker* (supreme judge) of Rumelia, the *reisülulemâ* (chief of the *ulemâ*, the Islamic religious establishment), and supervisor of the affairs of the Prophet's descendants. He died on Şevval 27, 1293/November 15, 1876,

36. *Murakkaa*
Istanbul, 1265/1849
Sülüs and *nesih*
Ink, colors, and gold on paper mounted on cardboard
18.7 × 26.3 cm (7¼ × 10⅜ in.)
(164)

This is the last *kıt'a* of a *körüklü murakkaa* composed of twenty-three *sülüs*-and-*nesih kıt'alar* from the hand of one of the most prominent calligraphers of the nineteenth century (see also fig. 16 on page 28). Kâdıasker Mustafa İzzet Efendi wrote this album at the age of forty-eight or forty-nine. Its text is the *Kasîde-i Bürde*, a well-known ode in praise of the Prophet (see also cat. no. 30). The piece follows the format used for *meşk* exercises: one line of *sülüs*, two shorter lines of *nesih*, and one line of *sülüs*. In the left-hand *koltuk* the calligrapher signed the work, in rhyming prose, *Hâk-pây-ı evliyâ Seyyid İzzet Mustafâ* (Dust of the feet of the saints, Seyyid İzzet Mustafa), and dated it [1]265/1849.

Two of the preceding *kıt'alar*, and three near the end of the album, have stylized flower bouquets in the *koltuklar*. The illumination, contemporary with the calligraphy, is very fine, featuring attractive colors and designs. Unfortunately, the illuminator left no signature.

The *murakkaa* is bound between simple covers, each bearing the *tuğra* of Sultan Abdülmecid.

Meşk albums like this one, which contain a unified text (such as a single work of poetry), read consecutively from top to bottom of each *kıt'a*.

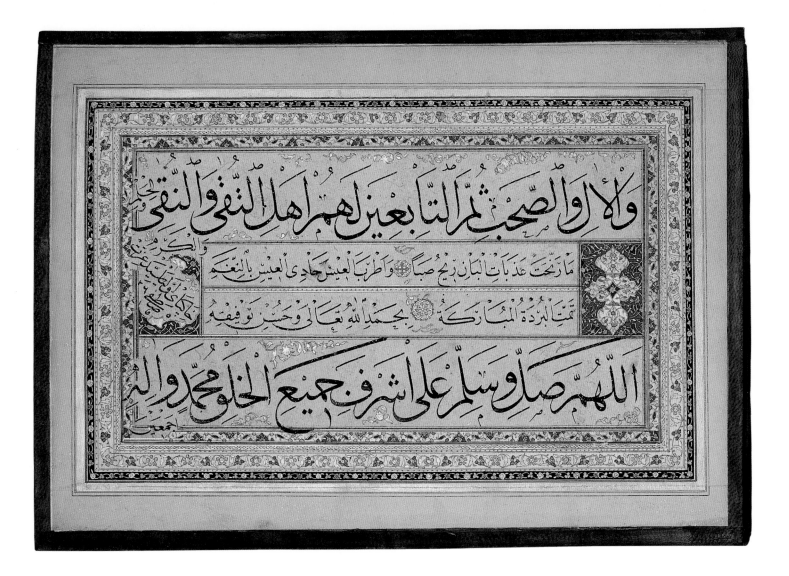

and was buried in the *hazîre* (enclosed cemetery) of the Kâdirî Lodge (Kâdirîhâne) in the Tophâne quarter of Istanbul.

Seyyid Mustafa's most important calligraphy pupils were Şefik Bey (see cat. no. 39), Abdullah Zühdi Efendi (see cat. no. 38), Muhsinzâde Abdullah Bey (see cat. no. 42), and Hasan Rıza Efendi (see cat. no. 56).

Kâdıasker Mustafa İzzet Efendi wrote eleven *mushaflar*, more than two hundred *hilyeler* (a few of them quite large), and numerous *kıt'alar* and *levhalar*. His 1275/1859 round *levhalar* in Ayasofya Mosque are still the largest of their kind in the Islamic world (each is twenty-five feet in diameter). He also produced inscriptions in *celî sülüs* or *celî ta'lîk* for other buildings, including the Hırka-i Şerîf Mosque, the Âli Paşa Mosque, the Dolmabahçe Sarayı, the rear facade of the Ministry of War (now the University of Istanbul), the sultan's loge of the Ayasofya Mosque, and the Nalli Masjid in Bâbıâli—all in Istanbul—and Muhammad ʿAlī Pasha's mausoleum in Cairo. He also wrote part of the famous *Nûr Âyeti* (Verse of Light; Qur'an 24:35) in *celî sülüs* inside the domes of various Istanbul mosques, including the Ayasofya, Hırka-i Şerîf, Büyük Kasımpaşa, Küçük Mecidiye, Sinan Paşa, and Yahya Efendi. These inscriptions were enlarged from Mustafa İzzet's original stencils by means of squaring.

An interesting historical footnote: When the Washington Monument was being erected, the nations of the world were asked to contribute plaques or panels to be set in the walls of the monument's staircase. Naval Commander Emin Bey, who was then the Ottoman representative in the United States, became interested in the project, and Sultan Abdülmecid approved Turkish participation. Kâdıasker Mustafa İzzet wrote the following lines under the sultan's *tuğra*, in *celî ta'lîk*:

In support of eternal friendship, Abdülmecid Hân
wrote his honorable name for the tall stone edifice in Washington.

The text was carved on a marble plaque, which was transported to the United States by sea at a cost of 390 *kuruş* (about $290 today).

In addition to being a calligrapher, Mustafa İzzet was a masterful performer on the *ney* (reed flute) and had a particularly beautiful singing voice. His religious and secular musical compositions are few in number (there are just twenty-six) but highly regarded by musicians. No master musician ever reached the level of Kâdıasker Mustafa İzzet Efendi in calligraphy, and no calligrapher ever reached the *kâdıasker*'s degree of achievement in music.

As Mustafa İzzet was being buried, a wise man standing by the grave said, "Gentlemen, we have just interred here a casket of accomplishments."

37. *Kıt'a*

Istanbul, 1288/1871
Sülüs and *nesih*
Ink, colors, and gold on paper mounted on cardboard
21.5 × 26 cm (8⅜ × 10⅛ in.)
(115)

This *kıt'a* is dated 1288/1871, more than twenty years later than catalogue number 36. In a sense, it shows the effect of the passing years on Mustafa İzzet's work. As Necmeddin Okyay once said, "The *nesih* script that the *kâdıasker* wrote after 1280 [1863] recalls the flight of butterflies."

The *kıt'a* has four lines of *nesih* between two lines of *sülüs*. In the signature, Mustafa İzzet states that, at the time he made this piece, he was the *reisülulemâ*. This title was not official; rather, it was the custom to bestow it on the senior *kâdıasker* of Rumelia, the European territory of the empire. In his earlier works, the calligrapher signed himself *Hâk-pây-ı evliyâ Seyyid İzzet Mustafâ* (Dust of the feet of the saints, Seyyid İzzet Mustafa). In his later years, he preferred to sign himself *Bende-î âl-i Abâ, Seyyid İzzet Mustafâ* (Servant of the family of the cloak [the family of the Prophet], Seyyid İzzet Mustafa). Both these formulas are in rhyme, and both express a dervishlike modesty.

The work is decorated in the *zer-ender-zer* (gold-upon-gold) style by an unknown illuminator.

ABDULLAH ZÜHDİ EFENDİ

D. 1296/1879

In some of the signatures on his works, Abdullah Zühdi claims descent from the venerable Companion of the Prophet Tamīm al-Dārī. Probably born in Damascus, he moved with his family to Istanbul and began studying calligraphy with Eyüblü Râşid Efendi (d. 1292/1875). His true master, however, was Kâdıasker Mustafa İzzet Efendi (see cat. nos. 36–37), and he wrote *sülüs* and *nesih* in Mustafa İzzet's style. Zühdi Efendi taught calligraphy and painting in the *meşkhâne* (scriptorium) in the Nuruosmaniye Mosque and at the Imperial School of Military Engineering (Mühendishâne-i Berrî-i Hümâyun). He had a special talent for *taklîd* (imitative) calligraphy.

It is said that Sultan Abdülmecid (r. 1839–61) admired the sample of *celî sülüs* written by Zühdi Efendi so much more than the samples presented by other calligraphers that he chose him, in 1273/1857, to write the inscriptions for the Prophet's Mosque in Medina. Zühdi Efendi stayed in Medina for about seven years. During that time he wrote Qur'anic verses, *hadîsler*, and odes to the Prophet in *celî sülüs* on the drums of the 140 domes of the Prophet's Mosque and on bands running along its walls. Zühdi Efendi is unsurpassed among calligraphers in the amount of *celî sülüs* he produced for a single building. Zühdi Efendi's *celî sülüs* text in the Prophet's Mosque, including the three bands on the *kıble* wall (the wall facing Mecca), comes to more than 6,500 feet. Most of these elegant inscriptions are still extant.

Zühdi Efendi was assisted in this work by Çömezzâde Muhsin Efendi (d. 1304/1887), the gilder Hacı Hüseyin Efendi (see cat. no. 40), and pupil Hacı Ahmed Efendi. Because Zühdi Efendi was a painter as well as a calligrapher, he paid a great deal of attention to interlacing forms in *celî sülüs* and excelled in creating artistic shapes. But, because he disregarded accepted composition design, it is difficult for someone who does not know the verses by heart to read them correctly.

After his stay in Medina, Abdullah Zühdi settled in Cairo, where he spent the rest of his life practicing calligraphy for the government (writing legends on bank notes, for example); superintending calligraphy lessons in schools; and preparing calligraphic inscriptions for buildings, including the distinguished inscriptions he wrote for the Umm ʿAbbās Public Fountain. Many calligraphers were apprenticed to Abdullah Zühdi, who was instrumental in making calligraphy a popular art in Egypt in the last century and won the title "calligrapher of Egypt." He died in Cairo in 1296/1879 and was buried near the tomb of the founder of the Shāfiʿī school of Islamic jurisprudence, Imam Idrīs al-Shāfiʿī.

38. *Amme cüzü*
Istanbul, 1263/1847
Nesih
Ink, colors, and gold on paper
Binding 21.3 × 14.8 cm (8¼ × 5⅞ in.)
(21)

In earlier times, the Qur'an was bound in thirty individual volumes, one *cüz* (one-thirtieth of the text) per volume, for the purpose of sequential recitation. The thirtieth *cüz*, called the *Amme cüzü* after the first word of the section, was frequently written as a separate work for use in schools. After learning the alphabet, students would be taught the short chapters in this *cüz* as a prelude to learning the rest of the Qur'an by heart.

Shown here are the first two pages (folios 1v and 2r) of an *Amme cüzü* written by the young Abdullah Zühdi in 1263/1847, when he still lived in Istanbul. In complete Qur'ans (*mushaflar*), the first two pages are illuminated symmetrically as a *serlevha*, but in a *cüz* only folio 1v is fully illuminated. This folio is called the *unvan sahifesi*, or opening page.

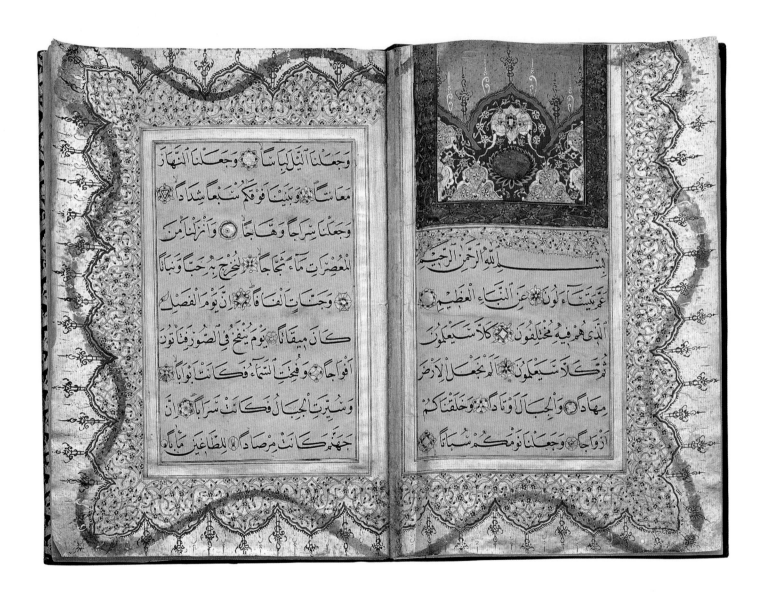

MEHMED ŞEFİK BEY

ca. 1235/1820–1297/1880

Şefik Bey was born about 1235/1820 in Istanbul and learned *sülüs* and *nesih* first from Ali Vasfi Efendi (d. 1253/1837), then from his uncle by marriage, Kâdıasker Mustafa İzzet Efendi (see cat. nos. 36–37). In his youth, he worked as a clerk in the chancery of the Imperial Council of State (Divân-ı Hümâyun), where he learned the *dîvânî* and *celî dîvânî* scripts and how to write the *tuğra*. He also taught calligraphy for thirty-four years—to the First Regiment of the Palace Cavalry, at the Imperial College of Music (Mûsıka-i Hümâyun; a teaching institution for the Imperial Brass Band), and to the officials of the sultan's palace. Aided by Abdülfettah Efendi, he repaired the inscriptions in the Ulu Cami (Great Mosque) in the city of Bursa, which had suffered serious damage in the earthquake of 1855, and added work of his own in *celî* scripts.

It was Şefik Bey who wrote a band of Qur'anic verses for the mausoleum of Sultan Abdülmecid (r. 1839–61). He also copied chapter 36 of the Qur'an (*Yâsîn*) for a band of faience on the Dome of the Rock, Jerusalem, during its restoration in 1292/1875; the band is still extant. His most famous works, however, are inscriptions sculpted in low relief on the gate of what is now the University of Istanbul: the first and third verses of chapter 48 (*Feth*, or Victory) of the Qur'an, and the name of the former Directorate of Military Affairs (Dâire-i Umûr-ı Askeriyye).

There is an interesting story in connection with these inscriptions. When Sultan Abdülaziz (r. 1861–76) ordered the construction of a building for the Ministry of War in the Bâyezid quarter of Istanbul, he wanted it in operation immediately, but the inscription was among the details that remained unfinished. Şefik Bey was retained to do the job for a fee of sixty gold *lira* (about $4,500 today). It took Şefik Bey six hours to prepare the stencil. The captain of the general staff, who had made the agreement with Şefik Bey, reflected that he himself earned only six gold *lira* a month. "Why, then," he asked, "should a calligrapher who worked only six hours earn sixty gold *lira*?"

When Şefik Bey heard this, he said, "Tell the captain: This inscription did not take six hours to write; it took sixty years. Go and tell him that I give him not six days, not six weeks, not six months. I give him a full six years. If, in that time, he can write just one letter like what I have written, I will make him a gift of six times what I have asked." The message was conveyed, and the construction committee intervened in the dispute. Knowing the value of things, the committee paid the calligrapher what his art was worth.

Mehmed Şefik Bey died in Istanbul in 1297/1880 and was buried in the Yahya Efendi Cemetery, in the Beşiktaş quarter. He left two *mushaflar* and countless *kıt'alar*, *levhalar*, and albums. Among his many students were two distinguished calligraphers, Hasan Rıza Efendi (see cat. no. 56) and Haydarlı Ali Efendi (see cat. no. 44).

39. *Levha*

Istanbul, 1275/1859
Celî sülüs and *rıkâ'*
Ink and colors on paper mounted on cardboard
39.2 × 44.5 cm (15¼ × 17⅜ in.)
(70)

Şefik Bey was able to write a piece of calligraphy as easily as one writes a letter, without planning the piece or practicing it in advance. One can sense his easy spontaneity in this *levha*. Here, as on some of his other works, the signature is in the *rıkâ'* (*icâzet*) script and says, in rhyme, *Bende-î âl-i Abâ, Mehmed Şefîk-î pür Hatâ* (Servant of the family of the cloak [the family of the Prophet], Mehmed Şefik full of sins).

The inner and outer borders of this *levha* were decorated at a later time with *ebrû* (marbled paper) made by Necmeddin Okyay (see cat. nos. 59–60), and later still, the lower portions were soiled.

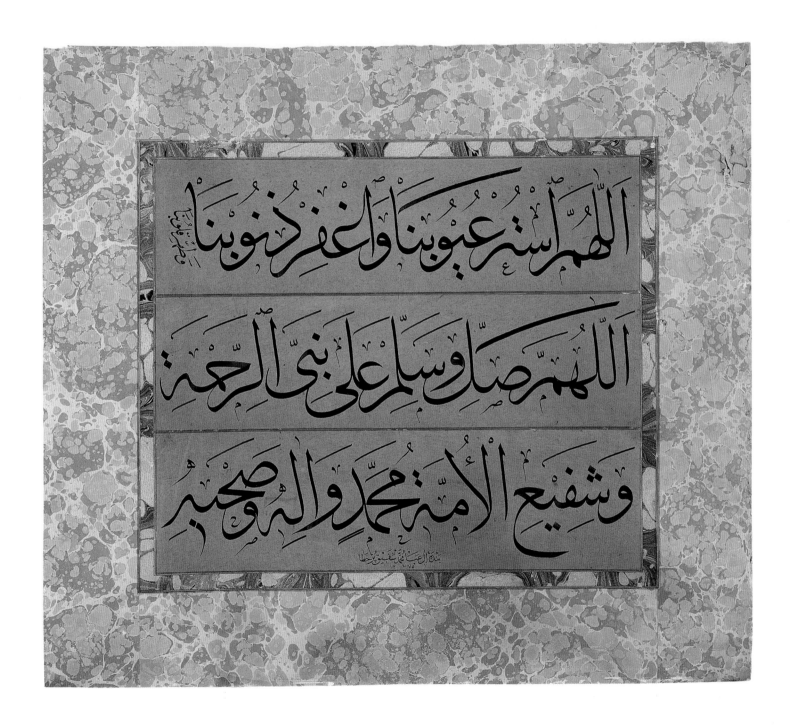

اللهم استر عيوبنا واغفر ذنوبنا

اللهم صل وسلم على بني الرحمة

وشفيع الأمة محمد وآله وصحبه

MEHMED ŞEVKİ EFENDİ
1245/1829–1304/1887

Mehmed Şevki Efendi was born in the village of Kastamonu, just south of the Black Sea, in 1245/1829 and moved to Istanbul while still a boy. In addition to his formal education, he took lessons from his uncle, Mehmed Hulûsi Efendi (d. 1291/1874), in *sülüs, nesih,* and *rıkâ',* obtaining his *icâzet* in 1257/1841.

Hulûsi Efendi was the first librarian of the famous Koca Ragıp Paşa Library in Istanbul. He was also a gifted calligraphy teacher, with a number of pupils in addition to his nephew, and although his own calligraphic works were rather mediocre, he was sincerely devoted to the art. Seeing how talented Şevki was, he said, "This is as far as I can go with you in this art; from now on, I have to take you to Kâdıasker Mustafa İzzet Efendi, and you must stick to his lessons until you have made real progress in the art." In acknowledging the mastery of others, Hulûsi revealed his modesty and noble nature. But Şevki said to him, "I will seek no other teacher but you," whereupon Hulûsi wished his pupil well and prayed that he would meet with success.

Because of that prayer, there emerged a new style of calligraphy, later called Şevki's Manner. Had Şevki Efendi listened to his uncle's advice and apprenticed himself to Kâdıasker Mustafa Efendi (see cat. nos. 36–37), his name would simply have been added to the list of calligraphers belonging to the "Kâdıasker school," such as Şefik Bey (see cat. no. 39), Abdullah Zühdi Efendi (see cat. no. 38), and Hasan Rıza Efendi (see cat. no. 56). Instead, strengthened by his uncle's prayer and inspired by the works of the great calligrapher Hâfız Osman (see cat. nos. 14–16) and other innovators in the art, Şevki was able to develop a style of his own. He is reported to have said, "They taught me calligraphy in the world of dreams." He wrote twenty-five copies of the Qur'an, and a large number of the *Delâilü'l-Hayrât, evrâdlar* (personal prayers), *kıt'alar,* albums, and *hilyeler.* He also created beautiful *levhalar* in *celî sülüs,* but his *celî* works are not up to the level of those by Sâmi Efendi (see cat. nos. 49–52).

Şevki Efendi's works earned him a well-deserved popularity, for they are free of defects and reflect his individuality. His close friend Sâmi Efendi was not far from the truth when he said of Şevki Efendi, "He couldn't write a letter poorly even if he wanted to."

Şevki Efendi put equal care into all his writings, regardless of the status of those who commissioned them. He did the same with the practice sheets he prepared for his pupils. He worked as a *rık'a* teacher in the Menşe-i Küttâb-ı Askerî, which trained military scribes, in the Bâyezid quarter of Istanbul. At the same time, he taught calligraphy to the sons of Sultan Abdülhamid II (r. 1876–1909) for two and a half years. His principal job, however, was in the Secretariat of the Ministry of War (Harbiye Nezâreti Mektubî Kalemi).

A man of virtue and integrity, Şevki Efendi died on Şa'ban 13, 1304/May 7, 1887, and was buried near his uncle's grave in the Merkez

40. Qur'an
Istanbul, 1279/1862
Nesih and *rıkâ'*
Ink, colors, and gold on paper
Binding 19.3 × 12.6 cm (7½ × 4⅞ in.)
(57)

Mehmed Şevki Efendi developed a new method for writing the *sülüs, nesih,* and *rıkâ'* scripts, which is still being used by some calligraphers today. He wrote this Qur'an in the middle of his artistic career, in 1279/1862. The text is written in *nesih* script, fifteen lines per page. Shown here is the illuminated *serlevha* (folios 1v and 2r). The chapter titles are written in white-lead ink in *rıkâ'* script against a gold background. The illumination is by Hacı Hüseyin Efendi (d. 1293/1876). (Müzehhib [the Illuminator] Hüseyin left many works. He learned illumination from Hacı Ahmed Efendi and Tevfik Efendi and worked with Abdullah Zühdi [see cat. no. 38] in Medina.)

Efendi Cemetery, Istanbul. Among the best-known of his many pupils were Hacı Ârif Efendi (see cat. no. 45), Fehmi Efendi (d. 1333/1915), Pazarcıklı Mehmed Hulûsi Efendi (d. 1326/1908), and Zıyâeddin Efendi. The eminent artist, teacher, and physician Dr. Süheyl Ünver (1898–1986) was his grandson.

41. **Murakkaa**
Istanbul, 1280/1863
Sülüs and *nesih*
Ink, colors, and gold on paper mounted on cardboard
Binding 16.8 × 26 cm (6½ × 10⅛ in.)
(216)

This is the first *kıt'a* of an album of *meşkler* by Mehmed Şevki Efendi. In a *meşk*, or exercise, the calligraphy teacher writes the text in the script being studied, first letter by letter and then in pairs of letters. In *meşkler* for the *sülüs* and *nesih* scripts, study begins with the famous prayer *Rabbi yessir, ve lâtuassir, Rabbi, temmim bi'l-hayr* (O Lord, make things easy and do not make them difficult. O Lord, make everything come out well). Here this prayer is the text of the first line of *sülüs* and the first line of *nesih*. Lines of individual letters follow.

Calligraphy lessons proceed as follows: first, the principal letters of the alphabet are written in order, from *elif* (A) to *ye* (Y). The second lesson is the letter *bâ* (B) combined with each letter in turn: *bâ* with *elif*, *bâ* with *bâ*, *bâ* with *cim* (J), and so on through the alphabet. The letters *çe*, *ha*, and *hı* all have the same shape as *cim* and are

distinguished from one another by the addition of dots. Other groups of letters also look alike and are differentiated by dots. In these cases, only one letter of each group is practiced to master its shape. If a letter has alternate forms—such as the *sin* (S) with teeth and the *keşıdeli* (extended) *sin*—all the forms are practiced. This group of exercises is called *müfredât* (lessons on single and double letters). Under each line is a device representing the word *sa'y* (persevere).

Letters are measured by means of dots made by the fine pen used for *sülüs* and *nesih*, or by the thick pen for *ta'lîk*. The teacher may put dots in red ink over the letters to show their proper dimensions, as here and in catalogue number 55, or he may leave these measurements out, as in catalogue numbers 18, 28, 29, and 53.

After finishing each *müfredât meşki*, the student begins a *mürekkebât meşki*: writing Qur'anic verses, poetry, or aphorisms to learn how to combine letters in words and sentences (see cat. nos. 18, 29, 53, and 55).

This album consists of eleven *kıt'alar* of *müfredât* exercises, and two final *kıt'alar* of *mürekkebât* exercises.

Muhsinzâde Seyyid Abdullah Hamdi Bey

1248/1832–1317/1899

Seyyid Abdullah Hamdi Bey belonged to the Muhsinzâde family, which twice produced a grand *vezir* of the Ottoman state. He was born in the Kuruçesme quarter of Istanbul, on the European shore of the Bosphorus, in 1248/1832 and developed an interest in calligraphy while he was in school. His interest became professional after he took lessons from Kâdıasker Mustafa İzzet Efendi (see cat. nos. 36–37). He attended gatherings hosted by his teacher until the latter's death in 1293/1876. Muhsinzâde was one of Mustafa İzzet Efendi's best students.

For a while, Muhsinzâde worked in the Scribal Department (Sadâret Mektubî Kalemi) of the Central Office of the Ottoman imperial government (the Bâbıâli). Upon the death of Şevki Efendi (see cat. nos. 40–41), he was appointed calligraphy teacher at the Menşe-i Küttâb-ı Askerî (a school for training military scribes), in the Bâyezid quarter of Istanbul. At that time, Sultan Abdülhamid II (r. 1876–1909) conferred on him the title of *reisü'l-hattâtîn*, or chief calligrapher. Additionally, he was charged with copying the well-known biography of the Prophet and collection of *hadîsler* titled *al-Shifā'*, by al-Qādī ʿIyād (476/1083–544/1149). He would write one part every day and give lessons at the Menşe-i Küttâb-ı Askerî on Mondays. He spent the rest of his time growing flowers and trees in the garden of his seaside villa. He copied several *mushaflar* and numerous *kıt'alar* and *levhalar*. Abdullah Bey is described as a genuine and noble person with an exceptional temperament.

Muhsinzâde Abdullah Bey maintained a close friendship with the calligrapher Şefik Bey (see cat. no. 39) until the latter's death in 1297/1880. When their teacher Kâdıasker Mustafa İzzet Efendi heard that they frequently met to talk about calligraphy, he advised them, "Those who have nothing to do with calligraphy will get bored with your talk and become hostile to you. In the company of such men, talk about the things they, too, can talk about. Speak of calligraphy only when you are by yourselves."

Abdullah Bey died on Rebiülâhır 12, 1317/August 20, 1899, and was buried in the *hazîre* (enclosed cemetery) in the Eyüb quarter of Istanbul. The fine inscriptions that he wrote for the entrance to the Hacı Köçek Mosque and for its fountain, in the Sultanhamamı quarter, can still be seen today.

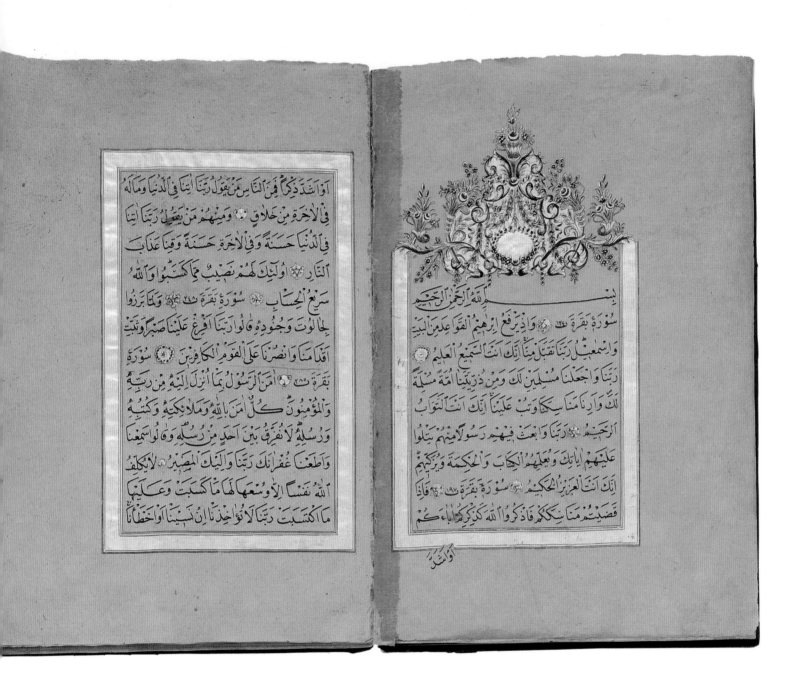

42. Prayer Handbook
Istanbul, 1282/1865
Nesih
Ink, colors, and gold on paper
Binding 21.8 × 15 cm (8½ × 5⅞ in.)
(305)

This prayer handbook consists of selected verses from the Qur'an. It is written in *nesih* script, thirteen lines per page, on sixteen folios. Muhsinzâde Abdullah Bey completed this handbook on Recep 7, 1282/November 26, 1865, in the early part of his artistic career. Shown here are folios 1v and 2r. The *unvan sahifesi* (opening-page)

illumination, on folio 1v, was done by one Ahmed Zihni in a conspicuously Western-influenced style. When compared with earlier works in this catalogue, this piece clearly demonstrates the evolution of Ottoman illumination over the centuries.

The binding is also in a Western-influenced style.

Kayışzâde Hâfız Osman Efendi

D. 1311/1894

Hâfız Osman Nuri Efendi was born in the southwestern Anatolian city of Burdur. He came to Istanbul to acquire a religious education and to learn calligraphy, which he studied with Kâdıasker Mustafa İzzet Efendi (see cat. nos. 36–37). Although the date he received his *icâzet* is not recorded, it is known that, after the death of his teacher, he continued his studies with the *kâdıasker*'s student Muhsinzâde Abdullah Bey (see cat. no. 42). Kayışzâde Hâfız Osman Efendi pledged to employ his perfect *nesih* script only in copies of the Qur'an and the *Delâilü'l-Hayrât*.

Hâfız Osman Nuri Efendi lived mostly in Istanbul but from time to time resided in his hometown of Burdur. Aside from his activities as a calligrapher, he taught at primary schools and served as imam for some of the government ministers during Ramazan. It was when he was leading the night prayers on Ramazan 4, 1311/March 11, 1894, that he began to bow and breathed his final breath. He was buried in the Merkez Efendi Cemetery, in Istanbul. The epitaph for his grave was copied by Muhsinzâde. It includes Qur'an 12:12—"Send him [Joseph] with us tomorrow, so he can enjoy himself and play"—the last verse Hâfız Osman Nuri Efendi had written during his lifetime, in his incomplete 107th *mushaf*.

Of all Kâdıasker Mustafa İzzet Efendi's students, two are remembered for their skill at copying the Qur'an. One is Hasan Rıza (see cat. no. 56), and the other is Hâfız Osman Nuri Efendi. Each wrote (although not exclusively) *âyet-berkenar* Qur'ans, fifteen lines per page, with each page ending at a verse-stop *durak*. Copies of these *mushaflar* were printed in the finest way possible at the time and received wide circulation, especially among students memorizing the Qur'an. Because of the similarity of their names, Kayışzâde Hâfız Osman Nuri is often confused with the great Hâfız Osman (see cat. nos. 14–16), although the earlier calligrapher is not known to have written Qur'ans in the *âyet-berkenar* format.

43. Qur'an

Istanbul, 1290/1873
Nesih and *rıkâ'*
Ink, colors, and gold on paper
Binding 17 × 11.8 cm (6⅝ × 4⅝ in.)
(160)

Shown here are folios 1v and 2r (the *serlevha*) of a *mushaf* written in a delicate *nesih* script, thirteen lines per page, on 381 folios. According to his own note in the colophon, this is the sixtieth Qur'an that Kayışzâde Hâfız Osman Efendi wrote. He was to complete forty-six more in the remaining twenty-one years of his life, which suggests that he could finish a copy in five or six months. In his youth, he is known to have been able to write even more swiftly. This copy was finished near the middle of Rebiülâhır 1290/June 1873. The chapter headings, between plain rosettes, are written in an elegant *rıkâ'* script, in gold ink. This Qur'an was illuminated in the *zer-ender-zer* (gold-upon-gold) method in 1298/1881 by Müzehhib Hasan Efendi. (Hasan Efendi was born in Istanbul, the son of Lâlelili Şâkir Efendi, one of the illuminators [*müzehhibler*] of the period of Sultan Mahmud II [r. 1808–39; see cat. no. 34]. Nothing is known about Hasan Efendi's career except that he learned his art from his father.)

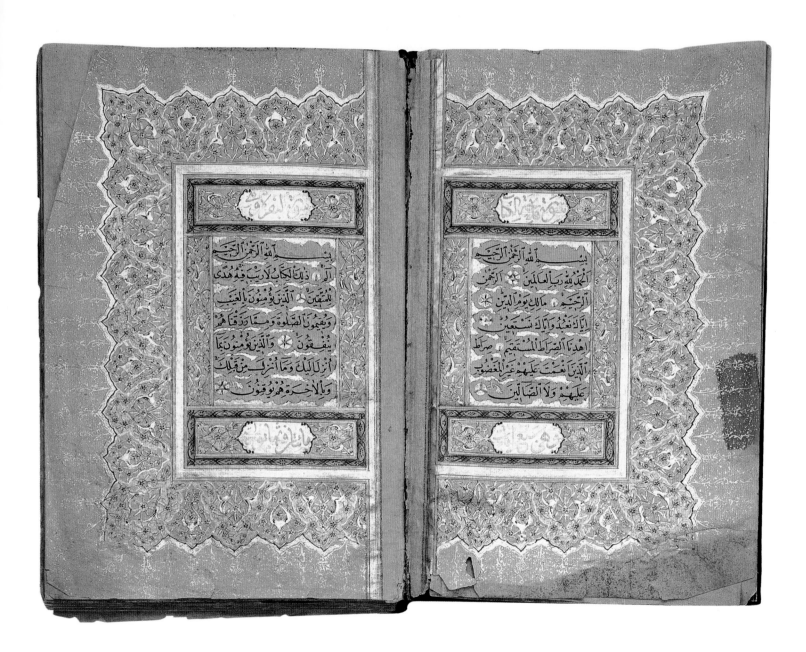

ÇIRÇIRLI ALİ EFENDİ
D. 1320/1902

Mehmed Ali Efendi was born in a quarter of Istanbul known as Cırcır, or Haydar, and is also known as Haydarlı Ali Efendi. Employed as a clerk in the Ministry of Finance, he studied *sülüs*, *nesih*, and *celî sülüs* with Şefik Bey (see cat. no. 39) and won wide admiration with his novel and perfect compositions. He also won the respect of his teacher's teacher, Kâdıasker Mustafa İzzet Efendi (see cat. nos. 36–37).

Few calligraphers have had such a firm hand. With a fine pen and thin paper, Mehmed Ali Efendi used to trace the works of great masters, making his own private record of their writing. These tracings—which were intended as a research tool, and should not be confused with *taklîd* calligraphy—are as sharp and fine as a strand of human hair. Ali Efendi could trace even such tiny scripts as *nesih*, winning no small acclaim.

Another aspect of Ali Efendi's success at *taklîd* is worth noting. He would say to his students one day, "Today, let us be Râkım." And on that day they would follow the method of Mustafa Râkım (see cat. no. 27). On another day he would say, "Today, let us be Celâleddin." And they would write that day in the style of Mahmud Celâleddin (see cat. nos. 32–33). Ali Efendi's ability to write in these two sharply divergent styles is a mark of his great talent.

After living his life with the simplicity of a dervish, Ali Efendi died and was buried in the Karacaahmed Cemetery, in the Üsküdar district of Istanbul, but the site of his grave is no longer known. His epitaph, which has been preserved although it was not cut into stone, gives the date of his death as Rebiülevvel 30, 1320/July 7, 1902.

44. *Levha*
Istanbul, 1297/1880
Celî sülüs
Ink and gold on paper mounted on cardboard
50.3 × 49.7 cm (19⅞ × 19⅝ in.)
(68)

The text of this *levha* is a poem in Ottoman Turkish:

> I held fast to the skirt of purity and God's pleasure forever.
> I embraced the dust of the Prophet's feet forever.
> Perplexed and powerless was my response to the unexpected.
> I found shelter in the court of God's grace forever.

Ali Efendi was the consummate follower of the method of Kâdıasker Mustafa İzzet Efendi and Şefik Bey. In this piece, each line is composed in a harmonious way, giving the whole extraordinary elegance. The *levha* was written in 1297/1880. The decoration of the borders reflects the taste of the age.

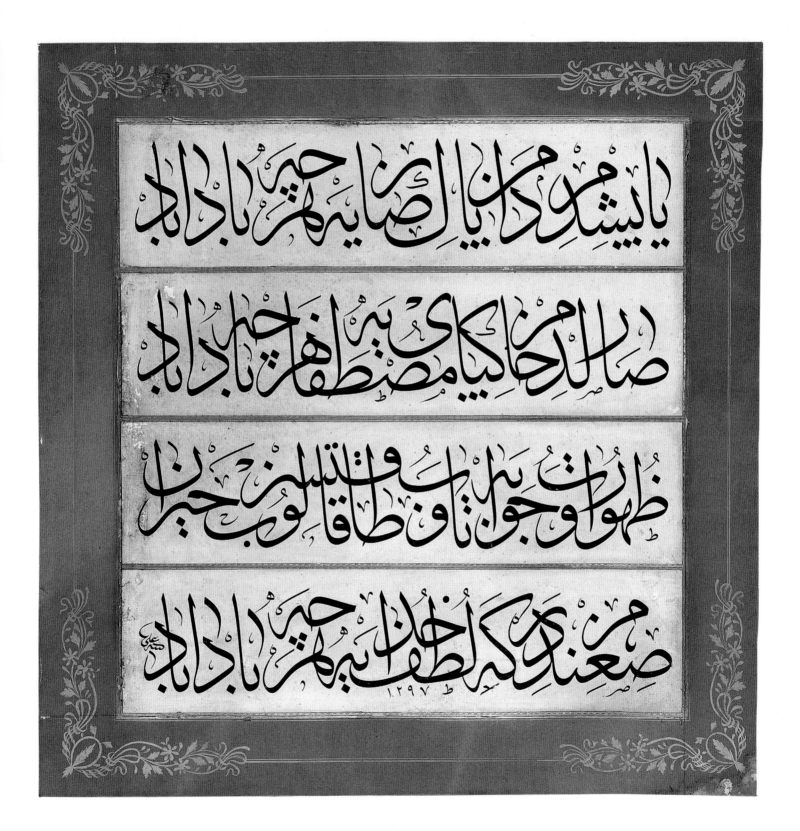

١٢٩٧

133

HACI ÂRİF EFENDİ

1246/1830–1327/1909

Ahmed Ârif Efendi was born in Filibe, the present-day city of Plovdiv, in southern Bulgaria, in 1246/1830. Alongside his religious schooling, he studied *sülüs* and *nesih* with a local calligrapher by the name of İsmail Sâbir, from whom he received his *icâzet*. In 1293/1876, as the Ottomans began to withdraw from Rumelia (the European provinces of the empire), and massacres of Bulgarian Muslims ensued, Ârif Efendi fled to Istanbul and settled there. He opened a grocery store in the Saraçhane quarter, and for that reason is known more commonly as Bakkal (the Grocer) Ârif Efendi than as Filibeli Ârif Efendi.

When Şevki Efendi (see cat. nos. 40–41) saw the calligraphy that Ârif Efendi had written before coming to Istanbul, he encouraged Ârif Efendi to continue with the art. As a student of this exceptional master, Ârif Efendi began the study of calligraphy all over again, from the beginning. He studied with zeal and, with a masterful *hilye*, earned a second *icâzet* in 1301/1883. He abandoned the grocery trade and began teaching calligraphy in the *medrese* (Islamic theological school) of the Nuruosmaniye Mosque and at his home. Among the hundreds of students he taught, the finest was Şeyh Azizü'r Rifâî (1288/1871–1353/1934), who himself taught for ten years in Cairo, thus ensuring the spread of Şevki Efendi's method throughout the Islamic world.

Ârif Efendi suffered a stroke and spent the last five years of his life paralyzed. He died on Ramazan 2, 1327/September 17, 1909, and was buried in the Edirnekapı Cemetery, Istanbul, near the grave of the calligrapher İsmail Zühdi (see cat. no. 26).

Hacı Ârif Efendi left countless examples of his writing in *sülüs* and *nesih: meşkler, kıt'alar, murakkaalar, hilyeler*, many *evrâdlar* (personal prayers), and copies of the *Delâilü'l-Hayrât*. His *levhalar* in *celî sülüs* are also numerous. The *besmele* he wrote for the facade of the left-hand gate of the Şehzâde Mosque is highly regarded. Among his less-familiar works are *celî sülüs* epitaphs written not with a stencil to guide the stonemason but in ink applied directly to the stone.

45. Qur'an

Filibe, before 1293/1876
Nesih
Ink, colors, and gold on paper
Binding 17.7 × 12.2 cm (6⅞ × 4¾ in.)
(272)

Shown here are folios 124v and 125r of an *âyet-berkenar* Qur'an written on 311 folios by Filibeli Hacı Ahmed Ârif Efendi. *Mushaflar* written by Ottoman calligraphers usually have eleven, thirteen, fifteen, or seventeen lines per page, although the most common format is thirteen lines. The *âyet-berkenar* format has fifteen lines per page; each page begins at the beginning of an *âyet* (verse) and ends with the completion of another. When and with whom this format originated is unclear. The arrangement is useful in memorization but presents a problem for the calligrapher. In order to fit the verses on the page exactly, the calligrapher must tightly space the letters on some lines of text and loosely space those on other lines. The *âyet-berkenar* format thus prevents the calligrapher from doing his best work, and for that reason the great masters did not use it. Only two masters of *nesih* script—Kayışzâde Osman Nuri Efendi (see cat. no. 43) and Hasan Rıza Efendi (see cat. no. 56)—successfully wrote the Qur'an this way. The tight and loose spacing characteristic of this format are visible in their Qur'ans.

The date this *mushaf* was copied is not mentioned in the colophon. While the *nesih* script is sharp and clear, it does not meet the standard of this calligrapher's second teacher, Şevki Efendi, which suggests that this *mushaf* was written before Ârif Efendi fled to

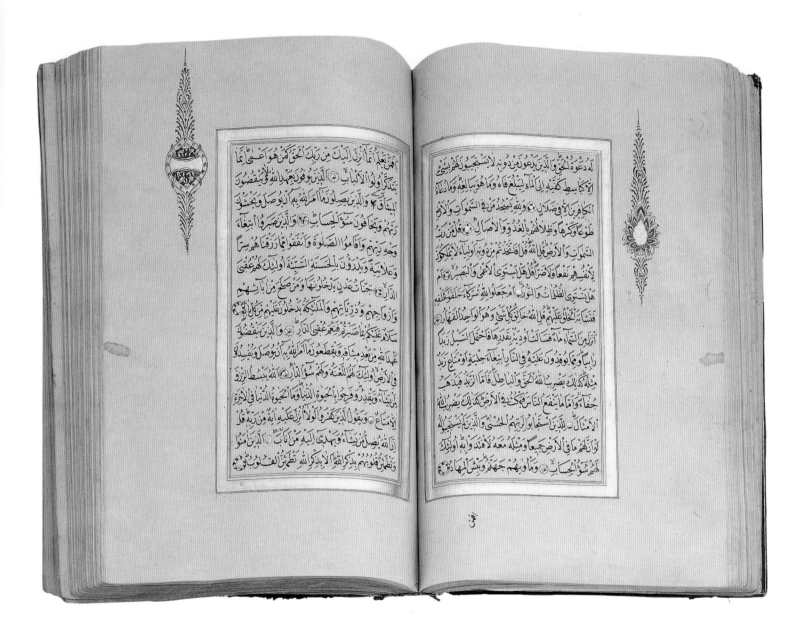

Istanbul in 1293/1876 and began
studying with Şevki Efendi. After he
became a follower of Şevki Efendi's
method, Ârif Efendi's writing
approached perfection.

This volume was illuminated in a
provincial style by a man from Filibe
called Derviş.

Hacı Ârif Bey

D. 1310/1892

Hacı Mehmed Ârif Bey was born in Istanbul, where he lived in the Çarşanba neighborhood, in the Fatih district; he became known as Çarşanbalı Ârif Bey. Despite the similarity of their names, Çarşanbalı Ârif Bey should not be confused with his contemporary Filibeli (or Bakkal) Hacı Ârif Efendi (see cat. no. 45).

Çarşanbalı Ârif Bey studied *sülüs* and *nesih* with Hâşim Efendi (d. 1261/1845), a student of Mustafa Râkım's (see cat. no. 27). He studied *ta'lîk* with Kıbrısîzâde İsmail Hakkı Efendi (1200/1785–1279/1862) and Ali Haydar Bey (1217/1802–1287/1870). Ârif Bey wrote beautiful compositions in *celî sülüs* in Râkım's style, and *ta'lîk* in the style of Yesârîzâde Mustafa İzzet Efendi (d. 1265/1849). He also made elegant mirror-image compositions (*müsennâ*) and was famous for his ability to attribute authorship of unsigned calligraphic works. In *celî sülüs*, *celî ta'lîk*, and the *tuğra*, he achieved the same level of artistic success as his contemporary Sâmi Efendi (see cat. nos. 49–52). Indeed, during their lifetimes, there was no perceptible difference in the quality of their work. But because of Ârif Bey's early death, his work was eclipsed by that of Sâmi Efendi, who was blessed with two more decades of artistically productive life.

Ârif Bey died in 1310/1892 and was buried in the Yâvedûd Cemetery, in Defterdar.

46. *Levha*
Istanbul, 1301/1884
Celî sülüs
Colors on paper mounted on cardboard
53 × 72.2 cm (20⅞ × 28⅛ in.)
(63)

A yellow paint was used in place of gold in this *celî sülüs* composition, which was prepared by an illuminator using a stencil made by Ârif Bey. Many of Ârif Bey's *levhalar* were prepared in this manner. The text reads: "In it [the holy precinct of Mecca] are the clear signs [of God's governance] and the place where Abraham stood to pray" (Qur'an 3:97). The calligraphy takes an elliptical form, the result of the artist's laying out the letters in their most logical and legible positions. This elliptical *istif* (composition) is placed within a rectangular frame and finished with floral bouquets in the European mode. The equilibrium of the composition is emphasized by the strong verticals of the six *elif* letters, which divide the *istif* into seven strips, giving the whole an elegant appearance.

137

YAHYA HİLMİ EFENDİ
1249/1833–1325/1907

Born in the Süleymaniye district of Istanbul in 1249/1833, Yahya Hilmi Efendi learned *sülüs* and *nesih* first from Mehmed Hâşim Efendi (d. 1261/1845), a pupil of Mustafa Râkım's (see cat. no. 27). When his master died, Yahya Hilmi Efendi began studying with Halil Zühdi Efendi, receiving his *icâzet* in 1263/1847. As a young man, he worked in the Memorandum Department (Jurnal Kalemi) of the Office of the Ministry of War (Bâb-ı Seraskerî), and eventually rose to become the department's director. After serving there for nearly sixty years, he was stricken by paralysis, which led to his leaving office and, eventually, to his death. He died on Şevval 17, 1325/November 23, 1907, and was buried in the *hazîre* (enclosed cemetery) of the Süleymaniye Mosque. His granddaughter, the painter Güzin Duran (1898–1981), and her husband, the painter Feyhaman Duran (1886–1970), donated Yahya Hilmi Efendi's wooden house—painted red ocher, a favored color in Ottoman domestic architecture—to the University of Istanbul. The house remains as it was in Yahya's time, with all its historical artifacts, *levhalar*, and paintings intact.

Like the nineteenth-century masters Kâdıasker Mustafa İzzet Efendi (see cat. nos. 36–37) and Şevki Efendi (see cat. nos. 40–41), Yahya Hilmi Efendi is an unforgettable master of the *nesih* script. During his artistic career, he wrote twenty-five *mushaflar* (the last of which he completed only up to the twenty-first *cüz*) and countless other works, including *En'âmlar*, copies of the *Delâilü'l-Hayrât*, *evrâdlar* (personal prayers), thirty-volume Qur'ans, *hilyeler*, and *levhalar*. Hilmi Efendi was famous for his speed of execution and delicacy of touch.

The following anecdote illustrates his swiftness: in his youth, Yahya Hilmi Efendi was preparing to go on the pilgrimage to Mecca, and his mother asked to accompany him. He did not have enough money to pay for two, so, beginning on the first day of Ramazan, he began to write a *mushaf*. He worked night and day, completing half a *cüz* by daylight and another half after dark. By the time of the Şeker Bayramı festival at the end of Ramazan, he had finished all thirty *cüzler*. His mother sold the *mushaf* to a wealthy man for 7,500 *kuruş* (about $5,500, approximately what it costs one person traveling first-class from Istanbul to make the pilgrimage today—over fifteen days rather than the three to four months customary in Yahya Hilmi Efendi's time). With this money, mother and son were able to go on the pilgrimage together. In his last years, however, Yahya Hilmi Efendi would write one or two pages of a *mushaf* a day, taking about a year and a half to finish the volume.

47. Qur'an
Istanbul, 1306/1889
Nesih
Ink, colors, and gold on paper
Binding 22.2 × 14.2 cm (8⅞ × 5½ in.)
(316)

This *mushaf* was written in 1306/1889, thirteen lines per page, in *nesih* script. It is written on 406 folios. A detail of folio 404v is shown here; the text runs from the end of the second verse of chapter 108 through most of chapter 110. Like Mustafa İzzet and Mehmed Şevki, Yahya Hilmi Efendi wrote *nesih* with an élan for which he became famous. One cannot help admiring the flow of these lines.

The illuminator was Bahaddin Tokatlıoğlu (1283/1866–1358/1939). Born in Istanbul, Mehmed Bahaddin Efendi was the son of a professional illuminator and bookbinder who had studied with Lâleli Şâkir Efendi, one of the master illuminators of the nineteenth century. During the course of his artistic career, Bahaddin Efendi trained many students and illuminated nearly twenty Qur'ans and *En'âm-ı Şerîfler*, as well as numerous *hilyeler* and *levhalar*. He was an excellent gilder of *zer-endûd levhalar*. "In the old days, I considered myself an illuminator and walked around full of pride," he once remarked. "When I became familiar with the works in the palace of my predecessors, I learned my true place."

Bahaddin Efendi added to the *mushaf*'s effect with his application of gleaming gold in the border frames—adding material rays of light to the spiritual light of the Qur'an. Bahaddin Efendi also bound the volume.

Opposite: Detail, folio 404v

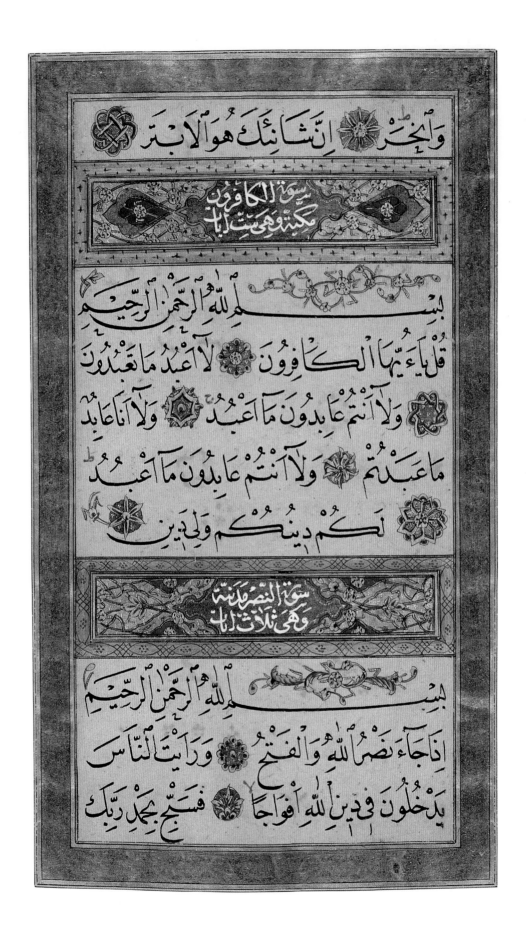

وَٱنْحَرْ ۞ اِنَّ شَانِئَكَ هُوَ ٱلْأَبْتَرُ

سُورَةُ ٱلْكَافِرُونَ
مَكِّيَّةٌ وَهِيَ سِتُّ آيَاتٍ

بِسْمِ ٱللَّهِ ٱلرَّحْمَٰنِ ٱلرَّحِيمِ
قُلْ يَا أَيُّهَا ٱلْكَافِرُونَ ۞ لَا أَعْبُدُ مَا تَعْبُدُونَ
وَلَا أَنْتُمْ عَابِدُونَ مَا أَعْبُدُ ۞ وَلَا أَنَا عَابِدٌ
مَا عَبَدْتُمْ ۞ وَلَا أَنْتُمْ عَابِدُونَ مَا أَعْبُدُ
لَكُمْ دِينُكُمْ وَلِيَ دِينِ

سُورَةُ ٱلنَّصْرِ مَدَنِيَّةٌ
وَهِيَ ثَلَاثُ آيَاتٍ

بِسْمِ ٱللَّهِ ٱلرَّحْمَٰنِ ٱلرَّحِيمِ
اِذَا جَاءَ نَصْرُ ٱللَّهِ وَٱلْفَتْحُ ۞ وَرَأَيْتَ ٱلنَّاسَ
يَدْخُلُونَ فِي دِينِ ٱللَّهِ أَفْوَاجًا ۞ فَسَبِّحْ بِحَمْدِ رَبِّكَ

HÂFIZ TAHSİN EFENDİ

1267/1851–1334/1915

The full name of this calligrapher was Elhac Hâfız Hasan Tahsin Efendi. He was born in 1267/1851 in the north-central Anatolian city of Tokat, where he began his study of calligraphy. He moved to Istanbul in 1284/1867 and studied *sülüs* and *nesih* with the current *reisü'l-hattâtîn*, Muhsinzâde Abdullah Bey (see cat. no. 42), from whom he received his *icâzet*. He also studied with his teacher's teacher, Kâdıasker Mustafa İzzet Efendi (see cat. nos. 36–37).

When construction of the Ali Paşa Mosque in the Bâyezid quarter was finished in 1286/1869, Hâfız Tahsin Efendi was appointed imam and *hatib* (preacher). He continued in this function for forty-five years, during which time he also taught in various schools. In addition, he was appointed deputy director of the Bâyezid Public Library when it opened in 1301/1884. He served there for twenty-nine years, eventually becoming director and preparing a catalogue of the library's fifteen thousand volumes.

A person of high moral character, Tahsin Efendi was familiar with music and had a personal collection of valuable manuscripts, calligraphic works, and calligrapher's tools. He wrote some 120 Qur'ans and other works during the course of his life. He died on Safer 5, 1334/December 13, 1915, and was buried in the cemetery of the Kaşgârî Sufi Lodge in the Eyüb district of Istanbul.

48. Qur'an

Istanbul, 1312/1894
Nesih
Ink, colors, and gold on paper
Binding 35.6 × 24.4 cm (13⅞ × 9½ in.)
(352)

In reading the Qur'an to oneself, it is customary to use a single volume, but when handwritten Qur'ans were in use, it was not economical to have a complete Qur'an for each reader. Instead, the Qur'an was often separated into thirty *cüzler* (sections), each approximately twenty pages in length, allowing thirty people to read the Qur'an simultaneously.

The large Qur'an shown here was originally written as a thirty-volume Qur'an, in 1312/1894. After it was illuminated, in 1322/1904, it was, for whatever reason, bound as a single volume. The format is thirteen lines per page, on 362 folios. It is written in a pleasant and readable *nesih*.

Osman Yümni Efendi illuminated the work, using rather garish nineteenth-century design elements. (Osman Yümni was born in the eastern Black Sea city of Trabzon. He worked as an illuminator in Istanbul, where he produced much work of less than top quality. He died in 1337/1919.) The pages shown here, folios 1v and 2r, are the *serlevha* of the volume. The remaining twenty-nine *cüzler* begin with the usual *unvan sahifesi* (single illuminated opening page), and the chapter headings are in white-lead ink over a gold background.

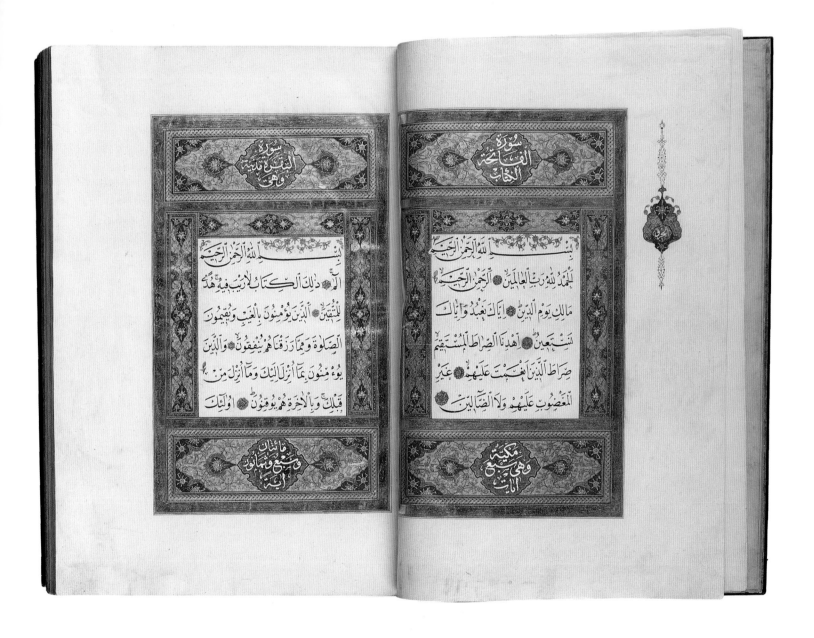

SÂMİ EFENDİ

1253/1838–1330/1912

Mehmed Sâmi Efendi was born in Istanbul on Zilhicce 16, 1253/ March 13, 1838. His father was Hacı Mahmud Efendi, known as Yorgancılar Kethüdası, or steward of the quilt-makers' guild. Mehmed Sâmi received his schooling at the Sıbyan Mektebi (elementary school) and, at the age of sixteen, was employed as a clerk in the Finance Department. Later, he worked as a writer of correspondence in the Imperial Council of State (Dîvân-ı Hümâyun) and as a junior clerk in the Department of Imperial Medals and Medallions. He ultimately became chief clerk in that office, a position he retained until his retirement in 1327/1909, shortly after the 1908 restoration of the constitution.

Sâmi Efendi learned *sülüs* and *nesih* from a local teacher named Boşnak Osman Efendi and *celî sülüs* from Recâi Efendi (1218/1804– 1291/1874), a pupil of Mustafa Râkım's (see cat. no. 27). The *dîvânî* and *celî dîvânî* scripts and *tuğra* writing he learned from Nâsıh Efendi (see cat. no. 70); *ta'lîk* from Kıbrısîzâde İsmail Hakkı Efendi (1200/1785–1279/1862); *celî ta'lîk* from Ali Haydar Bey (1217/1802– 1287/1870); and *rık'a* from Mümtaz Efendi (1225/1810–1287/1871). With his native talent, he mastered all these scripts.

Sâmi's artistic individuality was in particular evidence in his *celî* works. Indeed, he was so proficient in the *celî* scripts that he could write them with a lead pencil rather than a reed pen. Meticulous by nature, he kept working on some pieces for years, correcting and improving them until they emerged as masterpieces, eliciting the wonder of all. He followed the style of Râkım in *celî sülüs* and the *tuğra*, and the style of Yesârîzâde (d. 1265/1849) in *celî ta'lîk*—and excelled at both. After 1310/1893, the influence of İsmail Zühdi (see cat. no. 26) begins to show in Sâmi Efendi's works in *celî sülüs*.

There are few works by Sâmi Efendi in lampblack ink. Most of his works were done first on black paper, using ink made from orpiment. He corrected the pieces later, when opportunity arose, and then made stencils from them. The top illuminators of the day vied for the chance to gild the works produced with these stencils. Indeed, Sâmi's greatest achievements—those that account for his dominance and influence— are his works in gold, which show off most admirably the magnificence of his art. Foremost among these are the *levhalar* in *celî* that can be seen in Istanbul in the Cihangir and Altunîzâde mosques, as well as in other mosques and museums. Among his inscriptions in stone are those on the *sebil* (public fountain) of the Yeni Cami (New Mosque). His twelve lines of *celî sülüs* there have become a model for other calligraphers. Also worth seeing are Sâmi's works in the Şehzâde Mosque, the Nalli Masjid in Bâbıâli, the gates of the Covered Bazaar, the Zihni Paşa Mosque, and the Galip Paşa Mosque in Erenköy. (The inscriptions in the last three buildings are in *celî ta'lîk*.) Sâmi also left many inscriptions on gravestones.

49. *Levha*

Istanbul, 1297/1880

Celî sülüs

Gold on painted cardboard

49 × 73 cm (19⅛ × 28½ in.)

(120)

Sâmi Efendi is considered to have reached the highest degree of mastery ever in the scripts of *celî sülüs*, *celî ta'lîk*, *dîvânî*, and *celî dîvânî*, and in the *tuğra*. He wrote this *levha*, dated 1297/1880, in *celî sülüs*. Its text is the famous *Nazar Âyeti* (Verse of the Stare): "It is almost as if those who reject [God] would stab you [Muhammad] with their stares when they hear the Remembrance [the Qur'an] and say, 'Truly, he [Muhammad] is insane'" (Qur'an 68:51). The chapter of the Qur'an from which the verse is taken is called *Kalem*, or The Pen.

Sâmi Efendi had a rare innate grasp of aesthetic principles and constantly progressed in the art. Although others considered him extraordinarily successful, Sâmi Efendi was never satisfied. He was always improving, so that his work in any one year was superior to his work the year before.

This *levha* was produced from a stencil by Sâmi Efendi, using the *zerendûd* process. In both content and quality, it is an exquisite example of his artistry during the middle of his career. The illumination is contemporary with the calligraphy.

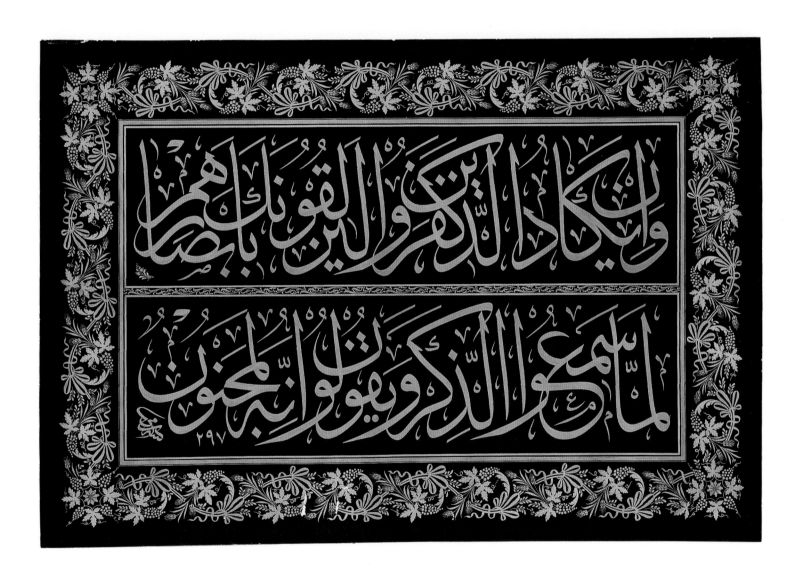

143

Among Sâmi Efendi's students are the following calligraphers, who demonstrate his success as a teacher: Hulûsi Efendi (see cat. no. 53); Nazif Bey (see cat. nos. 54–55); Hasan Rıza Efendi (see cat. no. 56); Kâmil Efendi (see cat. no. 57); Tuğrakeş Hakkı Bey (see cat. no. 58); Aziz Efendi (1288/1871–1353/1934); Ömer Vasfi Efendi (1297/1880–1347/1928); Necmeddin Efendi (see cat. nos. 59–60); and Emin Efendi (1300/1883–1364/1945).

While Sâmi Efendi taught calligraphy at the Imperial Council and at the Imperial Palace Service (Enderûn-ı Hümâyun), he would also hold calligraphy lessons at his home each Tuesday. Among friends, he was known for his easy manners and witticisms. Late in life, he was stricken with paralysis. He died on Recep 16, 1330/July 1, 1912, and was buried in the *hazîre* (enclosed cemetery) of the Fatih Mosque, Istanbul. The calligraphy for his gravestone was written by his pupil Kâmil Efendi.

50. *Tuğra*
Istanbul, 1298/1881
Gold on painted cardboard
73.5 × 90.5 cm (28⅝ × 35¼ in.)
(114)

Sâmi Efendi wrote this perfect example of the imperial *tuğra* of Sultan Abdülhamid II (r. 1876–1909). It reads: *Abdülhamid Hân bin Abdülmecid* (Sultan Abdülhamid, son of Abdülmecid), followed by the customary phrase *el-muzaffer dâimâ* (the ever-victorious). The *tuğra* bears the date 1298/1881.

The components of the *tuğra* are shown in figure 20 on page 37 of this volume. Using the width of the *kürsü* as a unit, one can measure the rest of the *tuğra*. The outer oval is one unit wide; the *kürsü* is one unit high; and, from the bend, the *kol* is one unit long. The complete *tuğra* is two units high and three units wide. The *tuğra* shown

here exemplifies these aesthetic and mathematical proportions.

Sâmi Efendi lived through the reigns of six sultans, from that of Sultan Mahmud II (r. 1808–39; see cat. no. 34) to that of Sultan Mehmed V (Reşad; r. 1909–18). He designed the *tuğralar* for Sultan Abdülaziz (r. 1861–76), Sultan Abdülhamid II, and Sultan Reşad. Because the reign of Sultan Abdülhamid II lasted thirty-three years, the *tuğralar* Sâmi Efendi wrote for him reached aesthetic perfection. The *tuğra* shown here was prepared by a *müzehhib* (illuminator) from a stencil by Sâmi Efendi, using the *zer-endûd* process. Its narrow outer border is decorated with motifs popular at the time. In the upper right quadrant is a small bouquet, in the place where the title of the sultan usually appeared. Later *tuğralar* of Abdülhamid II have the title *el-Gâzi* (champion of Islam) written, in *celî sülüs*, in this quadrant.

145

51. *Levha*
Istanbul, 1318/1900
Celî sülüs
Gold and color on painted cardboard
60.8 × 127.3 cm (23¾ × 49⅝ in.)
(47)

In figure 17 on page 30 is a *kalıp* (stencil) of a *celî sülüs levha*, written in orpiment ink on brown paper, with tiny holes tracing the outlines of the letters. The *levha* here, which shows Sâmi Efendi's art at its apex, was produced from that same stencil, using the *zer-endûd* process. It was written in 1318/1900 and painted by the illuminator Bahaddin Efendi (see cat. no. 47). An attractive secondary composition in the center—a roundish area of smaller *celî sülüs*—completes the text, which is a popular saying of unknown origin: "God is the bestower of success, the best Patron, and the best Companion." In this *levha*, it is not only the beautifully composed letters but also the finely rendered vowels, reading and other signs, date, and signature (*ketebehû Sâmi*, or Sâmi wrote it) that give the piece distinction. This magnificent *levha*, written at the dawn of the twentieth century, is just as new and fresh as we approach the twenty-first.

Sâmi Efendi, whose art was highly regarded during his lifetime, used to tell his students this anecdote from his youth: "One day I had brought home some large chunks of wood to heat my house and left them in the garden. I needed someone to split them into pieces small enough for the stove, but whom could I find? At that very moment, who should pass by but an old hunchbacked man, carrying an ax over his shoulder. I thought to myself, Such an elderly man could hardly manage to cut such big pieces of wood. But there was no one else around, so I called to him to offer him the job. 'Father,' I called, 'can you split this wood?' 'Very well, son,' said the old man, coming into the garden. Curious how he was going to handle the job, I went to the window and watched. The old fellow carefully studied the first piece, selected a certain spot on it, struck the spot with his ax, and split the wood into many usable small pieces. He then proceeded to do the same with each log. Amazed, I called him inside to pay him and offer him a cup of coffee for refreshment. I confessed that I had not really believed he could do the job, but, seeing such fine results, I wanted to know his secret. 'Son, what do you mean?' the old man asked. 'I dream every night until morning about splitting firewood.' That one sentence slaked my curiosity, for I remembered that, in my early years as a calligrapher, I would sometimes have difficulty fitting a certain letter into a composition and become anxious. But whenever that happened, my late teacher would appear in my dreams that night and explain the solution to my problem. I would immediately awaken, light my candle, and write down the solution on the paper I always kept at my bedside. In the morning, thanks to this explanation, every letter would find its proper place in the composition." When he told his students this story, Sâmi Efendi would add, "Know that if you do not practice your art, your profession, even in your dreams, you will not make progress."

52. *Levha*
Istanbul, 1319/1901
Celî ta'lîk
Gold on painted cardboard
49.5 × 116.9 cm (19¼ × 45⅝ in.)
(62)

This exceptional example of Ottoman *celî ta'lîk* was written in 1319/1901. Bahaddin Efendi (see cat. no. 47) produced this *zer-endûd levha* using Sâmi Efendi's stencil of the piece. The *levha* was decorated according to the tastes of the time. The text is a *hadîs* of arguable authenticity: "The one who works and profits is loved by God." A larger version of this work was written by Sâmi Efendi and produced as an inscription cut in stone above the gate of the Covered Market, Istanbul. It can still be seen, as can his *tuğra*—similar to the *tuğra* in catalogue number 50—on another gate of the same market.

Sâmi Efendi received his *icâzet* in *ta'lîk* calligraphy from Kıbrısîzâde İsmail Hakkı Efendi in 1274/1857. But Hakkı Efendi's artistry lagged behind that of Ali Haydar Bey. Seeing the young Sâmi Efendi's work, Ali Haydar Bey sent him a message saying, "Like your teacher, I studied with Yesârîzâde Mustafa İzzet Efendi—and I was an abler student. I have seen your writing here and there. You have, thanks to God, a great ability. Come, let us discuss calligraphy together."

In fairness to his teacher, Sâmi Efendi did not feel he could respond to this invitation. But when İsmail Hakkı Efendi died, Sâmi Efendi went to Ali Haydar's house after the funeral and knocked on the door. "My son," said Ali Haydar Bey, "for some time I have been sending messages to you. Where have you been?" Sâmi Efendi replied, "If my teacher İsmail Hakkı Efendi heard that I was augmenting my studies with you, he might have been hurt, so I could not come. But today we committed him to God's mercy, and I ran straight to you. At last you are my master."

Years later, Sâmi Efendi related this story to his own students, saying, "Only death can separate a teacher from his student. If I had abandoned my teachers, their spiritual power could not have enlightened my work."

149

Mehmed Hulûsi Yazgan
1286/1869–1358/1940

The son of Hâfız Mustafa Efendi, who was a public lecturer at the Fatih Mosque and a teacher at the Dârüşşafaka School (a boarding school established for orphans), Mehmed Hulûsi was born on Muharrem 15, 1286/April 27, 1869, in the Çarşanba quarter of Istanbul. In the course of his primary education, he committed the entire Qur'an to memory. He also attended lessons at the mosque until he was appointed muezzin at the Sultan Selim I Mosque, a position he held until his death.

Hulûsi Efendi learned the *sülüs* and *nesih* scripts from Muhsinzâde Abdullah (see cat. no. 42). He began studying *ta'lîk* with Hasan Hüsnü Efendi (d. 1333/1914) and completed his studies with Çarşanbalı Hacı Ârif Bey (see cat. no. 46). His real master in the art, however, was Sâmi Efendi (see cat. nos. 49–52). He was appointed calligraphy teacher at the Dârüşşafaka School and began teaching *ta'lîk* and *celî ta'lîk* at the Calligraphers College (Medresetülhattâtîn) as soon as it opened, in 1332/1914. When the Arabic alphabet was replaced with the Latin one in 1347/1928, and the school was closed, Hulûsi Efendi was appointed chief custodian of mausoleums. He died on Zilkade 27, 1358/January 8, 1940, and was buried in the Edirnekapı Cemetery in an unmarked grave.

Apart from Hulûsi Efendi's mastery of the *sülüs, nesih,* and *celî sülüs* scripts, he was among the best calligraphers in *ta'lîk* and *celî ta'lîk*. His *kıt'alar* in *nesta'lîk* in the Iranian style, and his *kıt'alar, hilyeler,* and *celî ta'lîk levhalar* in the Turkish style, are still worthy of recognition. The years between 1320/1902 and 1345/1927 were the most brilliant in his career, but his late works, produced when he was suffering from illness and poverty, do not do justice to his genius. A fine example of his *celî ta'lîk* is the *levha* shown in figure 12 on page 17.

Masterpieces by Hulûsi Efendi are in museums and private collections. His works can also be found at the Sultan Selim I and Sultan Ahmed mosques, Sultan Selim I's tomb, and the Vakıf Gurabâ Hospital, Istanbul, and in the First Parliament Building, Ankara. In Cairo, he wrote the frieze containing the *Ezân-ı Muhammedî* (call to prayer) that adorns the Mosque of Prince Muhammad ʿAlī Pasha, in the Manyal Palace.

Hulûsi Efendi was a man of saintly and exemplary character. Foremost among his students in *ta'lîk* were Mustafa Halim Özyazıcı (1315/1898–1384/1964); Mâcid Ayral (1308/1891–1380/1961); Hâmid Aytaç (1309/1891–1402/1982); and Kemal Batanay (1309/1891–1401/1981).

53. *Murakkaa*
Istanbul, 1322/1904
Ta'lîk
Ink and gold on paper mounted on cardboard
Binding 25.5 × 17.4 cm (9⅞ × 6¾ in.)
(322)

Ottoman *meşkler* (teaching exercises) in the *ta'lîk* script were, like exercises in other scripts, divided into two phases: first came the individual letters and alphabetically arranged combinations of two letters, called the *müfredât*. The advanced exercises were called the *mürekkebât*. In these exercises, the novice would learn to compose words and arrange them properly along a horizontal line.

This *meşk* album was written in 1322/1904. The text in this advanced *ta'lîk* lesson is an ode on the *besmele* written by the great Persian Sufi poet ʿAbd al-Rahmān Mullā Jāmī (817/1414–898/1492), which was frequently used for *mürekkebât* exercises. (Like all calligraphy teachers, Mehmed Hulûsi Yazgan wrote the same text repeatedly for his students.) The first two *kıt'alar* of this *körüklü murakkaa* (bellows album), shown here, contain the first four lines of the ode. The device for the exhortation *sa'y* (persevere) is written under each line of text. Hulûsi Efendi liked to use a thin, watery ink, as in this example, allowing the viewer to follow the flow of ink from the reed pen and emphasizing the beauty of the pen strokes.

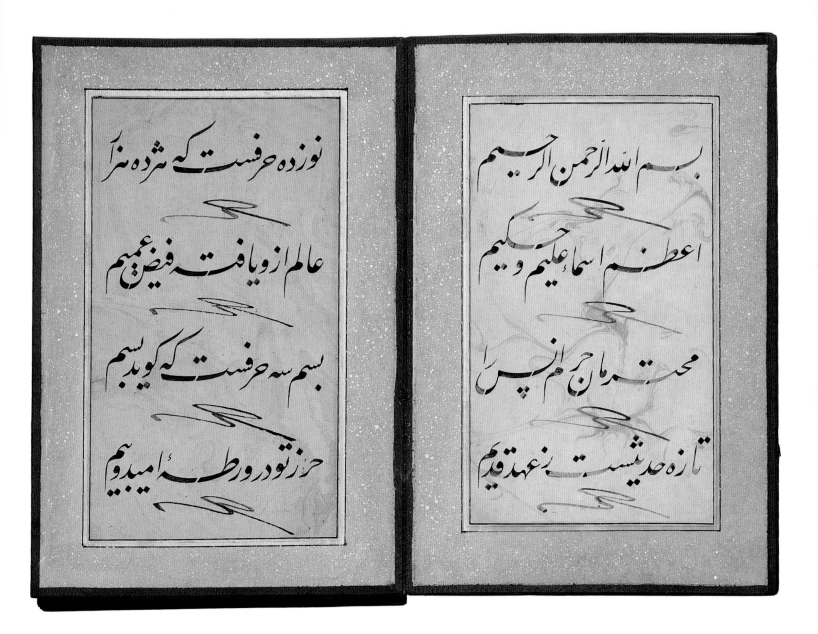

بسم الله الرحمن الرحیم

اعظم اسماء علیم و حکیم

محمد ماجر ام پرا

تازه حدیثیست بعهد قدیم

نوزده حرفست که نهزده هنرآ

عالم ازو یافت فیض عمیم

بسم سه حرفست که گویدیسم

حرز تو در ورطه امیدویم

151

Hacı Nazif Bey

1262/1846–1331/1913

Crimean in origin, Nazif was born in 1262/1846 in the city of Rusçuk (now Ruse, Bulgaria). His father, Mustafa Efendi, brought him to Istanbul, where he was trained in the Imperial Palace Service (Enderûn-ı Hümâyun) of the Ottoman court. He studied *sülüs* and *nesih* first with Şefik Bey (see cat. no. 39) and then with Abdülahad Vahdetî Efendi (1248/1832–1313/1895), a student of Abdullah Zühdi's (see cat. no. 38). He studied *ta'lîk, celî dîvânî,* the *tuğra,* and *celî sülüs* with Sâmi Efendi (see cat. nos. 49–52). It is said that while Sâmi Efendi was grieving over the death of his friend Çarşanbalı Ârif Bey (see cat. no. 46), he saw the work of Nazif Bey and consoled himself, saying, "God has taken Ârif and put Nazif in his place." For his part, Nazif Bey used to say, "Only after meeting Sâmi Efendi did I begin to untangle the secrets of calligraphy."

In his youth, Nazif Bey engaged in the sport of wrestling. To keep up the strength in his hands and arms, he would chop wood at every opportunity. (Calligraphers employed various methods to protect their hands from fatigue. Şevki Efendi [see cat. nos. 40–41] used to put his writing hand inside his jacket, in the gap between buttons, to cushion his hand when he was out walking.)

Nazif Bey worked as a calligrapher in the General Staff Department (Erkân-ı Harbiye Dâiresi), where he was noted for his ability to stretch short place names to fill large spaces on lithographed maps. One of the great calligraphers, he spent his life producing superb works in all the scripts, from the smallest and most delicate to the largest *celî.* Although he wrote an elegant *nesih,* he unfortunately never found time or opportunity to write a Qur'an. His work is most frequently seen in *celî sülüs* and *celî ta'lîk levhalar,* or in inscriptions cut in stone. Examples of the latter include inscriptions on the Orhaniye barracks, the Yıldız clock tower, and the Harbiye dining hall, all in Istanbul. He was also skilled at making camel-hide puppets for the famous Karagöz shadow plays.

Nazif Bey died from a heart ailment on Rebiülevvel 29, 1331/ March 8, 1913, and was buried in the Yahya Efendi Cemetery, in the Beşiktaş quarter of Istanbul.

54. *İstif*

Istanbul, 1323/1905

Celî sülüs

Ink and colors on paper mounted on cardboard

39 × 48 cm (15¼ × 18¾ in.)

(78)

Nazif Bey was one of the two masters of *celî* writing who lived into the twentieth century. The other was Sâmi Efendi, who said of Nazif Bey, "God created Nazif to write calligraphy." Nazif Bey wrote this elliptical composition in the style of Sâmi Efendi, putting his own style aside. The work is an excellent demonstration of Nazif Bey's powerful control of the pen.

153

55. *Murakkaa*

Istanbul, late 19th–early 20th century

Ta'lîk

Ink, colors, and gold on paper mounted
on cardboard

Binding 31.6 × 23.2 cm (12⅜ × 9 in.)

(226)

For the text of *mürekkebât* exercises in
Ottoman *ta'lîk*, some calligraphers used
the ode *Hilye-i Hâkânî*, a description
of the Prophet by Hâkânî Mehmed
Bey (d. 1015/1606), in place of the
Persian ode in catalogue number 53.
In this work, Hacı Nazif Bey wrote the
Hilye-i Hâkânî as a twenty-four-*kıt'a
ta'lîk mürekkebât meşki* album. The
nineteenth and twentieth *kıt'alar* are
shown here.

Nazif Bey wrote this album as a
taklîd (imitation; see cat. no. 33) based
on an original by Yesârîzâde Mustafa
İzzet Efendi (d. 1265/1849). While Nazif
Bey used red ink for the measurement
dots (Yesârîzâde used the same ink as
for the text), Nazif Bey's *meşk* exactly
reflects the method of Yesârîzâde,
who perfected the rules for Ottoman
ta'lîk that had been formulated by his
father, Yesârî Mehmed Es'ad Efendi
(see cat. no. 28).

The verses on these two *kıt'alar*
describe the Prophet's eyebrows:

His moonlike forehead brings to
mind the Qur'an chapter of victory,
   His long eyebrows like its *besmele.*
   With however much subtlety,
   Critics cannot convey

How the eyebrows of the Prophet
are like the indicator of God's unity.
   They look like two drawn swords.
   God the Transcendent has created
his beauty.
   The crescent is the ultimate of the
moon's beauty.

The device for the exhortation
sa'y (persevere) is written under each
line of calligraphy.

155

HASAN RIZA EFENDİ

1265/1849–1338/1920

When one thinks of Ottoman calligraphers of *nesih* in the last century, Hasan Rıza's name is the first that comes to mind. He was especially known for his *mushaflar*, which were reprinted again and again and made him famous throughout the Islamic world.

Hasan Rıza was born in 1265/1849 in the Üsküdar quarter of Istanbul. He studied calligraphy with Yahya Hilmi Efendi (see cat. no. 47) but left to accompany his father, Nazif Efendi, and the rest of the family to Tırnova (now Veliko Tŭrnovo, Bulgaria) when his father was appointed post-office director in that city. When the family returned to Istanbul in 1282/1865, Hasan Rıza enrolled in the Imperial College of Music (Mûsıka-i Hümâyun), a teaching institution for the Imperial Brass Band, and began studying *sülüs* and *nesih* with Şefik Bey (see cat. no. 39), the calligraphy teacher there. He obtained his *icâzet* from Şefik Bey but also benefited from associations with Kâdıasker Mustafa İzzet Efendi (see cat. nos. 36–37), Şefik Bey's teacher, and with Sâmi Efendi (see cat. nos. 49–52), from whom Hasan Rıza learned *ta'lîk*.

In 1288/1871, Hasan Rıza was appointed imam of the Imperial College of Music, and when Şefik Bey retired in 1296/1879, he replaced him as calligraphy master at the college. When the Calligraphers College (Medresetülhattâtîn) was opened on Receb 6, 1332/May 31, 1914, he was appointed its master of *sülüs* and *nesih* but had to give up the job when his eyesight began to fail. He died on Cemâziyelâhır 10, 1338/March 2, 1920, and was buried in the Rumelihisarı Cemetery, in Istanbul.

Hasan Rıza Efendi did his best work between 1300/1883 and 1330/1912, creating a number of exquisite large *hilyeler*. He was particularly adept in *sülüs*. He also produced works in *ta'lîk* and *celî sülüs*, but his greatest achievement was in *nesih* (he left nineteen *mushaflar* in that script).

56. *Hilye*
Istanbul, 1323/1905
Celî sülüs and *nesih*
Ink, colors, and gold on paper mounted on cardboard
107 × 73 cm (41¾ × 28½ in.)
(113)

The nineteenth century was the heyday of the *hilye* in Ottoman art, with masters such as Hasan Rıza Efendi producing fine examples. Hasan Rıza Efendi was the last to follow Kâdıasker Mustafa İzzet Efendi's custom of writing large-size *hilyeler*. In order to extend his *hilyeler*, Hasan Rıza often added a lower line in *celî sülüs*: "If it were not for you, if it were not for you [Muhammad], I [God] would not have created the heavens." This text is considered a *hadîs kudsî*, or holy *hadîs*, in which God speaks in the Prophet's words. (In the Qur'an, by contrast, the words come directly from God, with Muhammad as the vehicle of transmission; a regular *hadîs* consists entirely of the words and opinions of the Prophet.) This *hilye* includes this extra line of *celî sülüs* as its bottom line.

The work was written in Şa'ban 1323/October 1905, at the height of Hasan Rıza Efendi's artistic powers. The illumination, unfortunately, is in the questionable taste of the time.

The *duraklar* (stops) between the sentences have an unusual feature. Here, and on some other large *hilyeler* by Hasan Rıza, each *durak* consists of a small lithographic print of a calligraphic composition of the Muslim profession of faith—"There is no divinity except God, and Muhammad is His Prophet"—surrounded by the sentence "O Muhammad, your name is Victorious, so look wherever you will, you will be victorious and succeed." (This text is associated with Muhammad's being the "Seal of Prophets"—the last prophet.) These small circular compositions were cut out and pasted onto the *levha* and then illuminated around the edges.

Ahmed Kâmil Akdik

1278/1861–1360/1941

Ahmed Kâmil Efendi was born on Cemâziyelevvel 26, 1278/November 29, 1861, in the Fındıklı quarter of Istanbul. In elementary school, he began studying with the calligraphy teacher Süleyman Efendi. When he graduated from high school, he was appointed to the accounts office of the Ministry of Home Affairs. Meanwhile, he had begun learning the *sülüs* and *nesih* scripts from Sâmi Efendi (see cat. nos. 49–52). Four years later, in 1301/1884, at Sâmi Efendi's request, he wrote a *hilye* that became his *icâzetnâme*. When he was transferred to the clerical office of the chancery of the Imperial Council of State (Dîvân-ı Hümâyun), his calligraphy master suggested that he change his pen name from Kâmil to Hâşim—which would make for an easier and more attractive signature. For a few years thereafter, his works are signed Ahmed Hâşim, but he later returned to his original name.

While at the Imperial Council of State, he learned from Sâmi Efendi to write *dîvânî* and *celî dîvânî* and to design the *tuğra*, and was appointed writer of correspondence. When his master retired, Kâmil Efendi took his place and became chief clerk in the Department of Imperial Medals and Medallions at the Imperial Council of State, where he taught the *hutût-ı mütenevvia*—all the scripts then in use. After the Calligraphers College (Medresetülhattâtîn) was opened in 1332/1914, he worked there as a professor of *sülüs* and *nesih*. He also taught *rık'a* at the Galata Sarayı Sultanîsi School, starting in 1337/1918. In 1341/1922, the Central Office (Bâbıâli) of the imperial government was abolished, as was his position at the Imperial Council of State. He continued to work at the Calligraphers College until that, too, was abolished with the change from the Arabic to the Latin alphabet. In 1355/1936, he became professor of calligraphy at the Academy of Fine Arts (now Mimar Sinan University), where he remained until his death, producing a rich body of work. He was invited to visit Egypt twice—first in 1351/1933 and again in 1358/1940—and during both stays produced many works, including several calligraphic pieces that can be seen in Cairo's Mosque of Prince Muhammad ʿAlī Pasha, in the Manyal Palace, and in the palace's calligraphy exhibition room.

Hacı Kâmil Akdik died on the evening of Cemâziyelâhir 29, 1360/July 23, 1941, at his home in the Gelenbevî section of the Fatih quarter of Istanbul and was buried in the Gümüşsuyu Cemetery, in Eyüb. He was the last man to win the title of *reisü'l-hattâtîn*, or chief calligrapher, a title given to the senior and most knowledgeable calligrapher in the Ottoman state. He earned this honor on Şevval 10, 1333/August 21, 1915.

Hacı Kâmil continued to work until the last days of his life, retaining his sureness of touch and power of vision to the end. He left a substantial body of unrivaled works. In his official capacity at the Imperial Council of State, he wrote in *dîvânî, celî dîvânî,* or *rık'a* many *menşûrlar, beratlar, muâhedenâmeler* (treaties), and *tasdiknâmeler*

57. *Kıt'a*

Istanbul, late 19th–first half of 20th century

Sülüs and *nesih*

Ink, colors, and gold on paper mounted on cardboard

17.5 × 27.3 cm (6⅞ × 10¾ in.)

(130)

Kâmil Efendi always wrote beautiful *sülüs* and *nesih*, as he did in this work. Nevertheless, as he lay dying, he said, "I do not grieve at my death. I am only sorry that I could not really learn calligraphy."

The text of this *kıt'a* is a *hadîs*: "The learned ones of my community resemble the prophets of the children of Israel." The *ebrû* used to decorate the *kıt'a* is by Necmeddin Okyay (see cat. nos. 59–60).

(certificates), as well as many *meşk* collections for teaching calligraphy. But it was his works in *sülüs* and *nesih*, in *murakkaalar*, *levhalar*, *kıt'alar*, *hilyeler*, and *cüzler* from the Qur'an, that won the greatest admiration and were most sought after. He made only one *mushaf*.

Although Kâmil Efendi gained great depth from his study of *sülüs* and *nesih* with Sâmi Efendi, in *celî sülüs* he was never able to rise to the level of Nazif Bey (see cat. nos. 54–55). Shortcomings that are insignificant in the small scripts are jarring in *celî*. Sâmi Efendi, the great master of the *celî* style, had this to say about the *celî* scripts, which did not reach artistic maturity until the early nineteenth century: "Not to write *celî* is to be unaware of the secrets of calligraphy."

İSMAİL HAKKI ALTUNBEZER

1289/1873–1365/1946

İsmail Hakkı was born on Zilhicce 10, 1289/February 9, 1873, in the Kuruçeşme quarter of Istanbul. His birth coincided with the Kurban Bayramı prayers for the Festival of the Sacrifice at the end of that year's pilgrimage to Mecca. On his father's side, his ancestors had been calligraphers for five generations, and the young İsmail Hakkı studied *sülüs* and *nesih* with his father, Mehmed İlmi Efendi (1255/1839–1342/1924), who himself had studied with Kâdıasker Mustafa İzzet Efendi (see cat. nos. 36–37). He graduated from the painting division of the Ottoman School of Fine Arts in 1315/1897, but continued to study in the engraving division.

İsmail Hakkı worked in the chancery of the Imperial Council of State (Dîvân-ı Hümâyun), where he learned *dîvânî, celî dîvânî, celî sülüs,* and the *tuğra* from Sâmi Efendi (see cat. nos. 49–52). He was soon appointed to the post of second, then first, *tuğrakeş,* or writer of *tuğralar.* He taught *rık'a* at various schools and taught the *tuğra* and *celî sülüs* at the Calligraphers College (Medresetülhattâtîn). Among the outstanding calligraphers he taught were Mâcid Ayral (1308/1891–1380/1961) and Mustafa Halim Özyazıcı (1315/1898–1384/1964).

When the Arabic alphabet was replaced by the Latin alphabet in 1347/1928, İsmail Hakkı began to teach the art of illumination at the Eastern Decorative Arts School. After 1355/1936, he taught illumination at the Academy of Fine Arts (now Mimar Sinan University), but he did not teach the new classicism of Muhsin Demironat (see cat. no. 35) and Rikkat Kunt (see cat. no. 32). He assumed the surname Altunbezer—*altunbezer* means "gilder" or "illuminator"—because of this work.

İsmail Hakkı fell ill in 1364/1945 and had to give up his job. He died on Şa'ban 20, 1365/July 19, 1946, and was buried next to his father's grave in the Karacaahmed Cemetery, in Istanbul. In accordance with a provision in İsmail Hakkı's will, Necmeddin Okyay (see cat. nos. 59–60) copied the inscription for İsmail Hakkı's gravestone.

İsmail Hakkı's many compositions attest to a highly productive artistic career. His works in *celî sülüs,* which he executed with ease and swiftness, are particularly notable, as are his *tuğralar* and his writing in *dîvânî* and *celî dîvânî* on *fermanlar, beratlar,* and *menşûrlar.* He is also remembered for his works in mosques and domes in Istanbul (in the Selimiye, Lâleli, Edirnekapı, Zeynep Sultan, and Şemsi Paşa mosques, among others) and in Anatolia (in Afyon and Eskişehir). He also left lovely oil paintings, done with academic precision.

Hakkı Bey is also famous as a grower of roses.

58. *Levha*

Istanbul, first half of 20th century
Celî sülüs
Gold and color on painted cardboard
70.5 × 70.8 cm (27¾ × 27⅞ in.)
(246)

The type of *istif* called a *müsennâ* is created by writing a *celî sülüs* composition (the *müsennâ* form was used only rarely for works in *celî ta'lîk*) both normally and in reverse, so that the two halves appear to meet face to face, with some letters intersecting along the central vertical axis. Each half is the mirror image of the other. It is possible to compose any text in this manner, but short quotations work best. The text here—"And He [God] is the knower of every thing"—appears in three places in the Qur'an (2:29, 6:101, 57:3). If a text containing the word *Allah* is chosen for a *müsennâ,* the word is preferably written only once, as a symbolic reference to the singularity of God. If the composition does not allow that, however, *Allah* can be written on both sides of the *müsennâ* and in both directions, as is the case in the *besmele* that appears at the center top of this piece. The signature composition, at the center bottom on this *levha,* is also written as a *müsennâ.*

In this *levha,* İsmail Hakkı Altunbezer showed his skill by making three separate *müsennâ* compositions: the *besmele,* the Qur'anic verse, and the signature. Like other calligraphers who were trained in figurative art, İsmail Hakkı sometimes allowed that training to influence his calligraphy, and a hint of that influence is evident here. This work was prepared by the artist himself with the *zer-endûd*

process, using his own stencil. He decorated the margin area with a design of his own devising, alternating between gold and a yellow gouache. Tuğrakeş Hakkı Bey invented this style, and it disappeared with his death.

NECMEDDİN OKYAY
1300/1883–1396/1976

Born in Üsküdar, in Istanbul, on Rebiülevvel 19, 1300/January 29, 1883, Mehmed Necmeddin Okyay was the son of Mehmed Abdünnebi Efendi, head clerk in the religious court and one of the imams of the Yeni Vâlide Mosque, in Üsküdar. He began committing the Qur'an to memory while still a schoolboy and had learned it by heart by the time he finished his education at the Garden of Progress High School (Ravza-i Terakkî Rüşdiyesi), where he studied the variant recitations of the Qur'an. The calligraphy teacher at the school, Hasan Tal'at Bey, taught him *rik'a*, *dîvânî*, and *celî dîvânî* and granted him the *icâzet*. Aware of the young man's talent, the teacher took him to Filibeli Hacı Ârif Efendi (see cat. no. 45), but the Üsküdar Preparatory School where Necmeddin was then enrolled allowed him to attend the Hacı's calligraphy classes no more than once a week, and the young Necmeddin left the school after a year.

Meanwhile, having developed an interest in *ebrû* paper, he began visiting İbrahim Edhem Efendi (1245/1829–1321/1904), the *şeyh* of the Özbekler order of dervishes, to learn this craft. He also learned to make the glossy calligraphy paper known as *âhâr* paper. At the same time, Necmeddin was learning *ta'lîk* and *celî ta'lîk* from Sâmi Efendi (see cat. nos. 49–52), from whom he obtained the *icâzet* in *ta'lîk* in 1323/1905. He earned the *icâzet* in *nesih* and *sülüs* from Hacı Ârif Efendi in 1324/1906. Moreover, Vehbi Efendi taught him how to make ink in the traditional manner, and Seyfeddin Bey, who was chief archer at the Ottoman court in the time of Sultan Abdülaziz (r. 1861–76), taught him the sport of classic Ottoman archery. All the while, Necmeddin continued to attend lessons given in the mosque until he obtained a certificate known as an *ilmiye icâzetnâmesi*, granting him the rank of *âlim*, or Islamic scholar. After his father died in 1325/1907, Necmeddin was appointed imam and later *hatib* (preacher) in the same mosque, a position he held for forty years.

When the Calligraphers College (Medresetülhattâtîn) opened in Istanbul in 1332/1914, he enrolled in order to learn *celî sülüs* and the *tuğra* from Tuğrakeş Hakkı Bey (see cat. no. 58); in two years' time, he received an appointment at the school to teach the making of *ebrû* and *âhâr* paper. It was Necmeddin who invented the process for making marbled floral pictures (*çiçekli ebrû*) and the resist process for producing marbled calligraphy (*yazılı ebrû*), an extremely difficult art.

With the encouragement of Tuğrakeş Hakkı Bey, he began to cultivate roses in the one-acre garden of his house, in the Toygartepesi neighborhood of Üsküdar. Necmeddin raised four hundred different species of roses. One of his students, Dr. Süheyl Ünver (1898–1986), jokingly used to call him the "Rose Reprobate."

A man of many talents, Necmeddin became interested in bookbinding when, in 1344/1925, he came across some old stamps used to tool designs in leather. With the help of the bookbinder Bahaddin

59. *Levha*
Istanbul, 1351/1932
Celî ta'lik
Ink on paper mounted on cardboard
85 × 119 cm (33⅛ × 46⅜ in.)
(102)

Necmeddin Okyay was the last great practitioner of the style of Ottoman *celî ta'lîk* brought to perfection by Sâmi Efendi.

Celî ta'lîk is usually written in a straight line, but here the calligrapher has used the script to compose an *istif*—a difficult feat. The text is *şefâat ya Nebiyallah* (your intercession, O Prophet of God). Both the *te* (T) of *şefâat* and the *ye* (Y) of *Nebi* (*y*) are written in their *keşıdeli* (extended) forms, parallel to each other. Above them is written the name of God, *Allah*.

An interesting anecdote about this *levha* was told by both Necmeddin Efendi and Fuad Şemsi İnan (1886–1974), who commissioned the work. In 1932, Fuad Şemsi Bey acquired an empty picture frame that had been made by Leduc, the chief framer in the service of Sultan Abdülhamid II (r. 1876–1909). The frame—gessoed and gilded, and 119 centimeters wide—was damaged but still magnificent.

One day, Fuad Şemsi Bey met Necmeddin Efendi and, hoping to pique his interest, asked, "Does any calligrapher nowadays come to mind who could be trusted to write a work worthy of this frame?" In fact, it is extremely difficult to compose a work of calligraphy to fit given dimensions. Only a very experienced artist can do it well, as Fuad Şemsi Bey was certainly aware.

Necmeddin Efendi responded that if he was told the dimensions of the frame, he himself would see whether anything could be done. He wrote the *levha* and decorated it with his own *battal ebrûsu* (a simple marbled paper) and gave it to Fuad Şemsi Bey as a gift. (The frame, however, will not accompany this *levha* in the exhibition.)

163

Efendi (see cat. no. 47), he was able to make splendid book covers using the classic design known as *şemse*. He also spent years restoring precious bindings in the Topkapı Sarayı Museum Library. His teaching activities, begun at the Calligraphers College, continued in 1355/1936 at the Academy of Fine Arts (now Mimar Sinan University), where he taught until retiring in 1367/1948. He gave lessons in his own home until his eyesight began to fail.

Throughout his career as a calligrapher, Necmeddin gave particular attention to the *ta'lîk* and *celî ta'lîk* scripts, at the encouragement of Sâmi Efendi. More than 140 of Necmeddin's *levhalar* and *kıt'alar* are preserved at Mimar Sinan University. His works are also in museums and private collections. In addition, thanks to the efforts of his students in *ebrû* and classic bookbinding, these two arts have been saved from oblivion.

Because Necmeddin was skilled at so many arts, he was also known as *hezarfen*, or he who practices a thousand arts. When a law mandating the use of surnames was passed in Turkey, in 1934, Necmeddin chose as his family name Okyay, from *ok* (arrow) and *yay* (bow), because of his interest in archery. He died on Muharrem 23, 1396/January 5, 1976, and was buried in the Karacaahmed Cemetery, in Üsküdar.

This great artist wasted hardly a moment of his ninety-three years of life. One of his greatest skills was his ability to attribute authorship of unsigned Ottoman calligraphic works and to determine the dates when they were produced. From his youth on, he painstakingly collected calligraphic works; a large part of his collection was presented to the Topkapı Sarayı Museum Library in 1961; the rest was moved to the Museum of Turkish and Islamic Art and to the Türkpetrol Foundation, in Istanbul, following his death.

The author of this book is pleased to acknowledge that he is indebted to Necmeddin Okyay for much of the firsthand information presented in these pages, which he obtained from the master in personal communications during more than twenty years of study and friendship.

60. *Murakkaa*
Istanbul, 19th century; binding
20th century
Ink and colors on paper
Binding 27.6 × 21.1 cm (10¾ × 8¼ in.)
(381)

In 1917–18, Necmeddin Okyay originated two *ebrû* techniques. *Ebrû*, the Ottoman method of marbling paper, differs from its offspring, European marbling, in both materials and technique. In Turkish marbling, the finely ground colors, mixed with ox gall, are floated on a bath of gum tragacanth. The pattern formed on the surface of the bath is lifted off on a sheet of paper, which retains the pattern in reverse. The Europeans first encountered marbling during the sixteenth and seventeenth centuries, on the *ebrû* papers used to wrap Turkish tulip bulbs for export to Europe. Adapting the technique, European marblers usually use a bath of carrageenan (Irish moss) and treat their paper with alum. This process produces sharp-edged patterns, in contrast to the Turkish method, which results in a softer look.

Necmeddin Okyay's new techniques were *çiçekli ebrû*, or flower-picture marbling, and *yazılı ebrû*, a resist process that reproduces calligraphy in marbling. Necmeddin Efendi recounted his invention of *çiçekli ebrû* this way: "One day, a man I did not know came to the Calligraphers College and asked me to do a picture of a flower in *ebrû*. I said to him, 'Sir, in this art it is impossible to draw pictures. Masters of *ebrû* have tried to draw flowers, but the results did not resemble flowers.' The stranger replied, 'Why not try to do it?' So I went home, set up an *ebrû* trough, and began to experiment. While I was trying to produce a tulip design, along came my dear friend [the calligrapher] Mâcid Ayral, who asked, 'Why don't you pull the tips of the petals upward?' Now, over the course of my life, I have

learned a great deal about some things from people who knew nothing about those things, and that was the case here. I dipped a single hair from a horse's tail into the floating pigment and pulled one, and then the other, tip toward the far end of the trough. Sure enough, it looked just like a tulip.

"Because that day was a Friday, I left to do my duty as imam at the Yeni Vâlide Mosque, in Üsküdar. On my way home after the prayer service, I bought some tulips, hyacinths, and carnations. Studying each of them, I began to draw these flowers on the surface of the *ebrû* bath, using a single horse hair. Thanks to Mâcid, and the grace and beneficence of God, I was able to achieve the new design."

Two tulip-pattern *ebrû* works by Necmeddin Okyay, bordered with his *battal ebrûsu* (a simple marbled paper), were used in binding this *sülüs*-and-*nesih murakkaa* by another calligrapher (the writing dates from the nineteenth century). When Necmeddin produced these *ebrû* pieces is not known, but they have the beauty of a painting.

BERAT

61. **Berat** of Bâyezid II
Istanbul, 914/1508
Tuğra and *celî dîvânî*
Ink on paper
77.9 × 23.2 cm (30⅞ × 9 in.)
(35)

This *berat* (document granting an imperial title, privilege, or property) dates from the reign of the eighth Ottoman emperor, Sultan Bâyezid II (1481–1512). It was issued from Istanbul on the last day of Rebiülahır 914/late August 1508. The *tuğra*, written in lampblack ink, reads: *Bâyezid bin Mehemmed Hân [el-]muzaffer dâimâ* (Bâyezid, son of Mehemmed Hân, the ever-victorious). The *berat* opening (or *nişan-ı şerîf*), as well as the text following, is written in the *celî dîvânî* script using lampblack ink. An interesting feature here is the early form of the *celî dîvânî* script, with the letter shapes undeveloped. At this point, the script did not use vowel signs and other markers to fill the spaces in the channel-shaped lines—as it did in examples written since the age of Süleyman I, the Magnificent (or the Lawgiver; r. 1520–66), when the script acquired a new personality.

This type of *berat* is called a *sınırnâme beratı* (statement-of-boundaries *berat*). Addressed to Mustafa Bey, the governor of the *sancak* (division of a province) of Ohri (present-day Ohrid, Macedonia), it defines the boundaries of a zone in the district of Timûrhisar (now Demirhisar) and says no one may interfere in the affairs of this area.

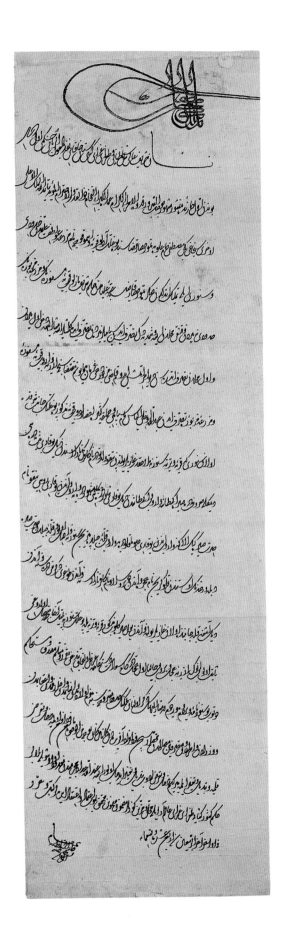

HÜKÜM

62. *Hüküm* of Selim I
Istanbul, 919/1513
Tuğra, muhakkak, and *rıkâ'*
Ink and gold on paper
194 × 24 cm (75⅝ × 9⅜ in.)
(369)

This *hüküm* (decree) dates from the
reign of the ninth Ottoman emperor,
Sultan Selim I, the Grim (1512–20). It
was issued from Istanbul during the
last ten days of Muharrem 919/early
April 1513. The *besmele* is written at
the top of the document in *muhakkak*
script, using gold ink. Under it, also in
gold ink, is the *tuğra: Selimşah bin
Bâyezid Hân el-muzaffer dâimâ* (Shah
Selim, son of Bâyezid Hân, the ever-
victorious). The long text is written in
the *rıkâ'* script. It begins by confirming
the grant of villages and agricultural
property in the area of Üsküb (now
Skopje, Macedonia) to Mustafa Paşa,
then establishes the boundaries for
these properties, place by place, and
ends by saying that the grant is to go
into effect within three days after the
arrival of the document. At the bottom
are written the signatures of thirty-four
persons who witnessed the document.
This is a rare example of a *sınırnâme
hücceti* (statement of boundaries and
title). Such documents were not made
much later than this period.

BERAT

63. **Berat** of Selim II
Edirne, 975/1567
Tuğra and *celî dîvânî*
Ink, colors, and gold on paper
111 × 30.5 cm (43¼ × 11⅞ in.)
(34)

This *berat* dates from the reign of the eleventh Ottoman emperor, Sultan Selim II (1566–74). It was issued from Edirne in the month of Cemâdelûlâ 975/November 1567. At the top is the sultan's *tuğra*, written in lapis lazuli blue and outlined with gold. It reads: *Selim Şah bin Süleyman Şah Hân el-muzaffer dâimâ* (Selim Shah, son of Süleyman Shah Hân, the ever-victorious). The open areas within the *tuğra* are decorated with various eye-catching motifs.

The first line of writing is a formula that begins *nişan-ı şerîf* (this noble sign). This formula, which is not used on *fermanlar*, is written in *celî dîvânî* in gold ink; the rest of the text is in the same script, but written in lampblack ink. The text is in the style preferred during the reign of the previous Ottoman emperor, Sultan Süleyman I, the Magnificent (or the Lawgiver; 1520–66). *Zer-nişanlar* (gold spots) are placed in a calculated pattern over the lines of writing, emphasizing both the shape of the line and the wealth of the Ottoman Empire in the sixteenth century.

This type of *berat* is known as a *mülknâme* (property grant). The text says that the *kâdı* (judge) of Istanbul, Muhiddin Efendi, has prepared the legal measures in accord with Islamic law for Sultan Selim II to grant certain properties in the district of Timûrhisar (now Demirhisar), in the Paşa *sancak*, to the Grand Vezir Sokullu Mehmed Paşa (1505–1579).

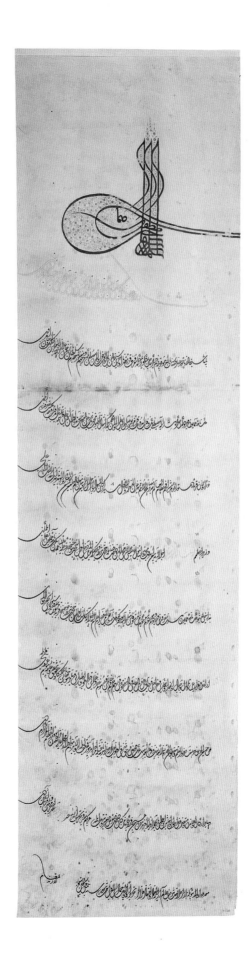

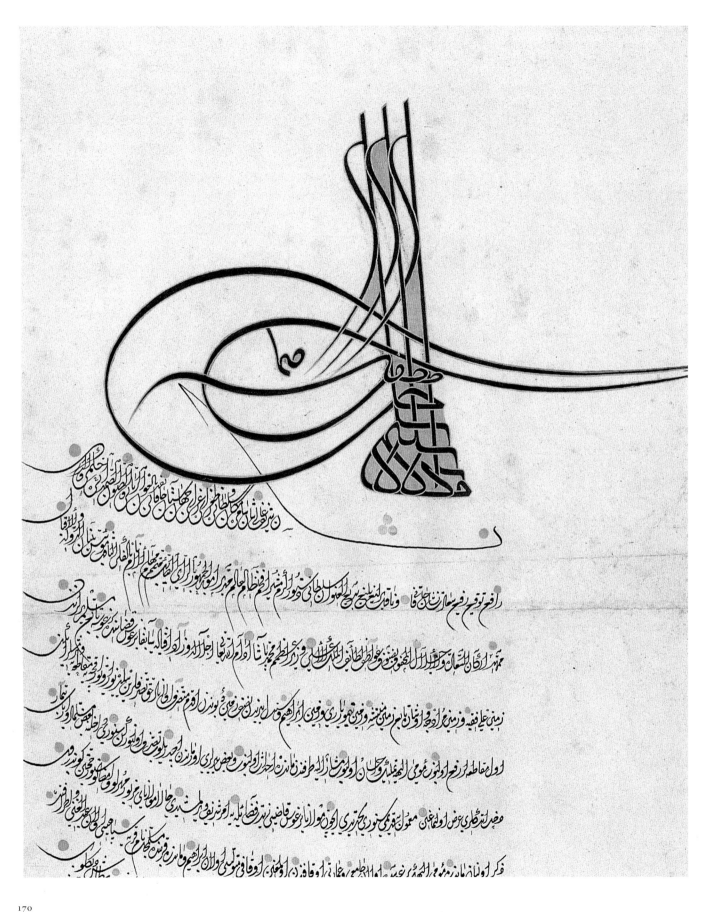

BERAT

64. **Berat** of Murad III
Istanbul, 983/1575
Tuğra and *celî dîvânî*
Ink and gold on paper
139.5 × 34.7 cm (54⅜ × 13½ in.)
(28)

This *berat* dates from the reign of the
twelfth Ottoman emperor, Sultan
Murad III (1574–95). It was issued
from Istanbul during the last ten days
of the month of Safer 983/early June
1575. A short invocation is written at
the top of the document in a small
script. Underneath is the sultan's *tuğra*,
written in lampblack ink and outlined
in gold ink. Some areas between the
letters of the *kürsü* are completely
filled in with gold ink. The *tuğra*
reads: *Şah Murad bin Selim Şah Hân
el-muzaffer dâimâ* (Shah Murad, son of
Shah Selim Hân, the ever-victorious).
The entire text is written in *celî dîvânî*
script, using lampblack ink. The *zer-
nişanlar* (gold spots) above the lines of
text are closely spaced.

   This document defines the
boundaries of real property in the
Bergos district granted by Sultan
Murad III to Grand Vezir Sokullu
Mehmed Paşa (1505–1579).

Opposite: Detail, cat. no. 64

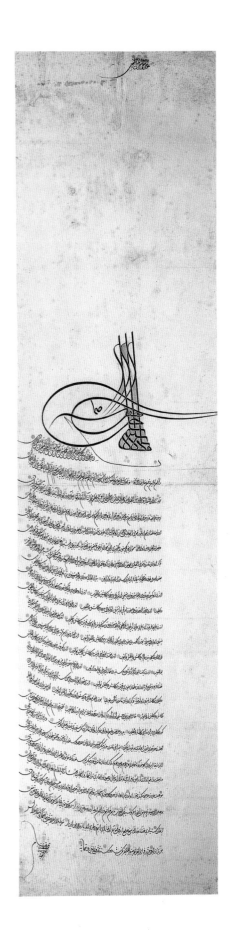

BERAT

65. **Berat** of Murad III
Istanbul, 983/1575
Tuğra and *celî dîvânî*
Ink, colors, and gold on paper
128 × 32.5 cm (49⅞ × 12⅝ in.)
(29)

This *berat* dates from the reign of the twelfth Ottoman emperor, Sultan Murad III (1574–95). It was issued from Istanbul during the last ten days of the month of Receb 983/late October 1575. The *tuğra* was drawn in lapis lazuli blue and outlined in gold ink; it is similar to the *tuğra* in catalogue number 63 but of a superior quality. The illuminated details within the *tuğra*, as well as the curtain of graceful illumination that hangs above it, reflect the brilliant elegance of the sixteenth century. The *tuğra* reads: *Şah Murad bin Selim Şah Hân el-muzaffer*

dâimâ (Shah Murad, son of Shah Selim Hân, the ever-victorious).

This *berat* renews a previous *berat* from Sultan Selim II, which gave the tax revenue of the Cirmen *sancak* to Grand Vezir Sokullu Mehmed Paşa (1505–1579). Therefore, it is called a *mülknâme tecdid beratı*—a *berat* that renews a *mülknâme*. (Grants made during a sultan's lifetime were abrogated after his death, and it was necessary for the succeeding sultan to renew them on documents written under his own *tuğra*.)

The text of this *berat* is written in *celî dîvânî* script. The first line—the *nişan-ı şerîf*—is in gold ink, and the main text is in lampblack ink. As an attractive contrast, references within the text to God and to Mehmed Paşa are written in gold ink.

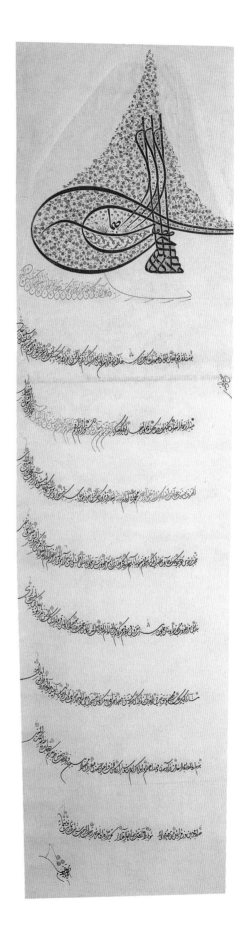

Opposite: Detail, cat. no. 65

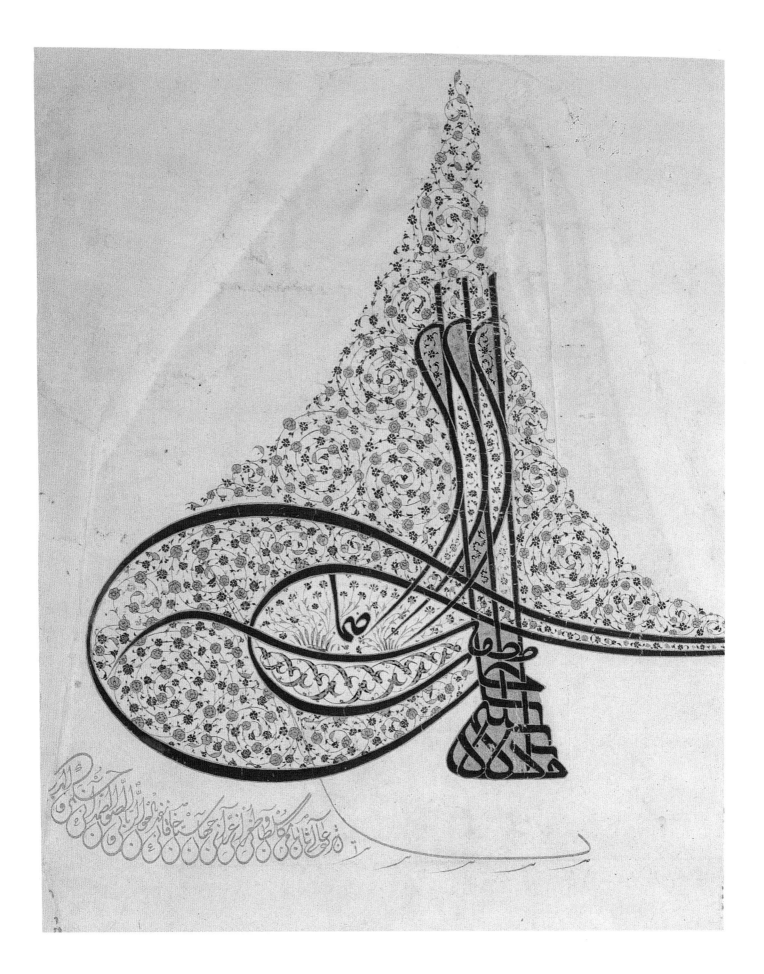

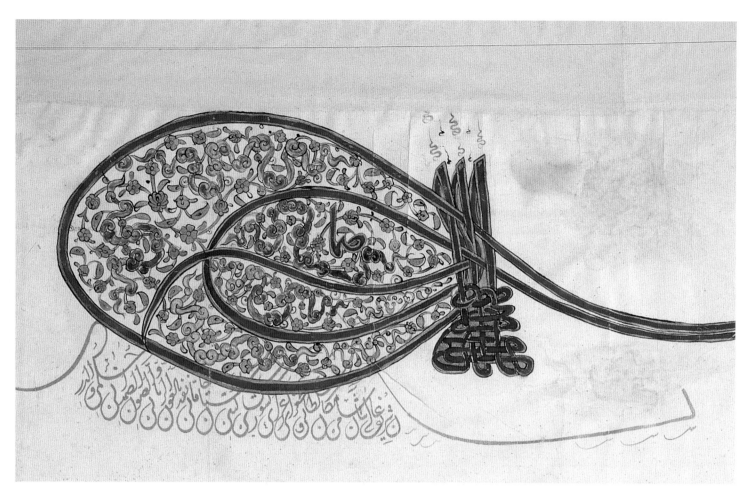

Detail, cat. no. 66

BERAT

66. Berat of Mehmed III
Istanbul, 1004/1596
Tuğra and *celî dîvânî*
Ink, colors, and gold on paper
250 × 41 cm (97½ × 15⅞ in.)
(26)

This *berat* dates from the reign of the thirteenth Ottoman emperor, Sultan Mehmed III (1595–1603). It was issued from Istanbul during the first ten days of Ramazan 1004/early May 1596. The *tuğra* is crudely drawn in lapis lazuli blue and outlined in gold, with some interior illumination. It reads: *Mehemmed bin Murad Hân el-muzaffer dâimâ* (Mehemmed, son of Murad Hân, the ever-victorious). The text is written in a beautiful, flowing *celî dîvânî* that compensates for the flawed *tuğra*. The first line (beginning

with the *nişan-ı şerîf*) is in gold ink, and the rest in lampblack ink.

The document concerns a mosque, school, and caravansaray, in the Canat district of Erdel province, that were constructed by order of Grand Vezir Sokullu Mehmed Paşa (1505–1579). The document is a *temliknâme tecdid beratı*, renewing the contract with the previous sultan. Notable here is the long-drawn-out name of Mehmed Paşa, piled with honorifics and patronymics, which seems to be competing for length with the work itself.

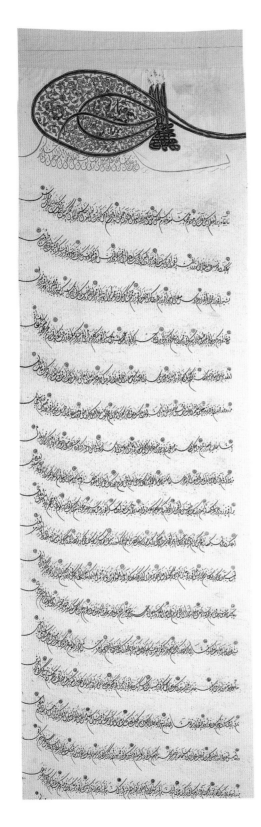

FERMAN

67. **Ferman** of Mehmed IV
Istanbul, 1070/1659
Tuğra and *kırma dîvânî*
Ink, colors, and gold on paper
56.7 × 27.9 cm (22⅛ × 10⅞ in.)
(32)

This *ferman* dates from the reign of the nineteenth Ottoman emperor, Sultan Mehmed IV (1648–87). It was decreed from Istanbul on Rebiülevvel 20, 1070/December 5, 1659. The *tuğra* of the sultan is drawn in gold ink, and the spaces between the letters of the *kürsü* are painted with lapis lazuli blue. It reads: *Şah Mehemmed bin İbrahim Hân el-muzaffer dâimâ* (Shah Mehemmed, son of İbrahim Hân, the ever-victorious). The style of decoration that envelops the *tuğra* is less complex than that of the sixteenth century. It consists of scrolls and *rûmî* motifs—that is, stylized vegetable pods (sometimes baselessly called arabesques).

The *hatt-ı hümâyun* (order of the sultan) is written in his own hand in an *unvan* (as in the *unvan sahifesi*) that is topped by a dome shape and crescent finial. It reads: *Fermân-ı âlîşânim mûcebince amel oluna—hılâfından hazer oluna* (Let my illustrious decree be put into effect; beware of opposing it). The text of the *ferman* is written in a sort of shorthand version of *dîvânî* known as *kırma dîvânî*.

The document decrees that no one except the sheikh of the Aziz Mahmud Hüdâyî Sufi Lodge in Üsküdar and its chapel may interfere with the income of the lodge and chapel.

BERAT

68. **Berat** of Süleyman II
Istanbul, 1099/1688
Tuğra and *celî dîvânî*
Ink, colors, and gold on paper
189 × 43 cm (73¾ × 16¾ in.)
(27)

This *berat* dates from the reign of the
twentieth Ottoman emperor, Sultan
Süleyman II (1687–91). It was issued
from Istanbul during the last ten days
of Rebiülevvel 1099/late January and
early February 1688. The *tuğra* is
written in gold ink, with some color
between the letters of the *kürsü*, and is
finished with simple ornamentation. It
reads: *Şah Süleyman bin İbrahim Hân
el-muzaffer dâimâ* (Shah Süleyman, son
of İbrahim Hân, the ever-victorious).
Written above the *tuğra* is a brief
invocation. The first sentence (with the
nişan-ı şerîf) is written in gold ink,
the rest in lampblack ink, and all in the
celî dîvânî script.

This *berat* renews the tax-
collecting rights—established in the
time of Sultan Selim II (r. 1566–74)
by his daughter İsmihân Sultan
(d. 1585)—in some townships in
the *sancak* of Avlonya.

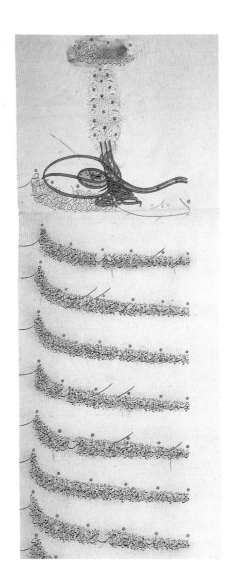

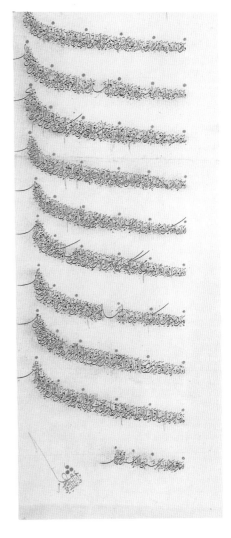

Opposite: Detail, cat. no. 68

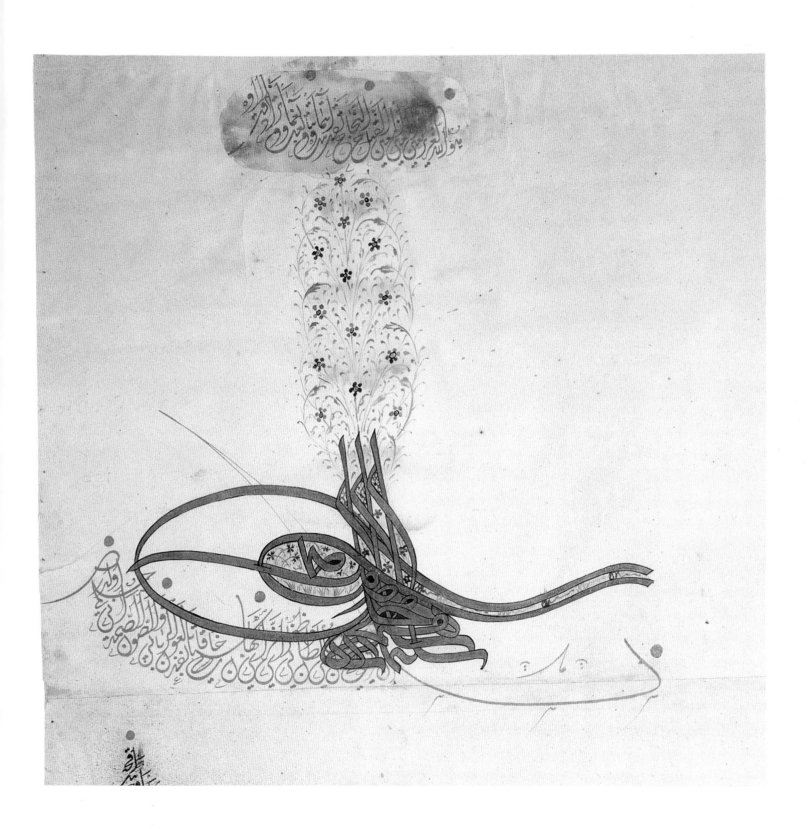

BERAT

69. **Berat** of Ahmed II
Edirne, 1105/1694
Tuğra and *celî dîvânî*
Ink, color, and gold on paper
119.3 × 43.8 cm (46½ × 17⅛ in.)
(38)

This *berat* dates from the reign of the twenty-first Ottoman emperor, Sultan Ahmed II (1691–95). It was issued from Edirne during the last ten days of Receb 1105/late March 1694. The *tuğra* is written in red ink. It reads: *Şah Ahmed bin İbrahim Hân el-muzaffer dâimâ* (Shah Ahmed, son of İbrahim Hân, the ever-victorious). The first sentence (*nişan-ı şerîf*) is written in *celî dîvânî* in gold ink; the rest of the text is in the same script in lampblack ink.

This document is a renewal of an earlier *berat* concerning some properties in the estate of İsmihân Sultan (d. 1585) acquired during the reign of her brother, Sultan Murad III (1574–95).

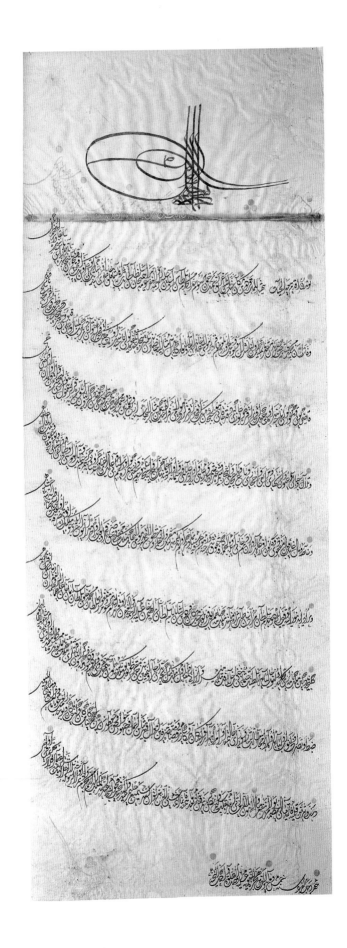

181

NÂSIH EFENDI

1229/1814–1303/1885

Hoca Bekir Nâsıh Efendi was born in Istanbul in 1229/1814. In 1245/1830, after receiving his primary education, he entered service in the chancery of the Imperial Council of State (Dîvân-ı Hümâyun), where he received the name Nâsıh, or Copyist. He learned *dîvânî*, *celî dîvânî*, and *bâbıâli rık'ası* from Mümtaz Efendi (1225/1810–1287/1871). (It is not known with whom he studied *sülüs* and *nesih* writing.) In 1250/1834, he became a teacher of the *hutût-ı mütenevvia* (all the scripts in use) in the chancery, and in 1258/1842, he was transferred to the Bureau of Urgent Affairs, where he was commissioned to copy the sultan's annual address to the pilgrims in Mecca. He continued to rise in rank until his death on Rebiülevvel 13, 1303/December 20, 1885. He was interred in the *hazîre* (enclosed cemetery) of the Ramazan Efendi Mosque, in the Koca Mustafa Paşa quarter of Istanbul.

Nâsıh Efendi wrote the inscriptions on the tomb of Grand Vezir Koca Reşid Paşa, adjacent to the Bâyezid Mosque, Istanbul. His son, Hacı Rif'at Efendi (b. 1259/1876), was also a calligrapher at the Imperial Council of State.

70. *Menşûr* of Abdülhamid II
Istanbul, 1300/1883
Tuğra and *celî dîvânî*
Ink, colors, and gold on paper
156 × 79 cm (60⅝ × 30¾ in.)
(14)

This *menşûr* dates from the reign of the thirty-fourth Ottoman emperor, Sultan Abdülhamid II (1876–1909). It was issued from Istanbul on Rebiülâhır 1, 1300/Febuary 7, 1883. The author is certain that Sâmi Efendi (see cat. nos. 49–52) drew the *tuğra*, executed in the *zer-endûd* process and without outlining. It reads: *Abdülhamid Hân bin Abdülmecid el-muzaffer dâimâ* (Abdülhamid Hân, son of Abdülmecid, the ever-victorious). It was further illuminated in 1970 by Rikkat Kunt (see cat. no. 32), who enclosed the *tuğra* within an elegant teardrop shape that extends to the invocation at the top of the document.

The text concerns the appointment of Abd-i İlah Paşa, who held the rank of governor of Rumelia, as a member of the Imperial Council of State. It is written in *celî dîvânî*, with lines in black alternating with lines in gold. This script reached its most mature form in the nineteenth century. It is written in a channel-shaped line with complex interlacing and composition of the letters and words. From the style of the writing on this piece, it is clear that the *celî dîvânî* is by Hoca Bekir Nâsıh Efendi.

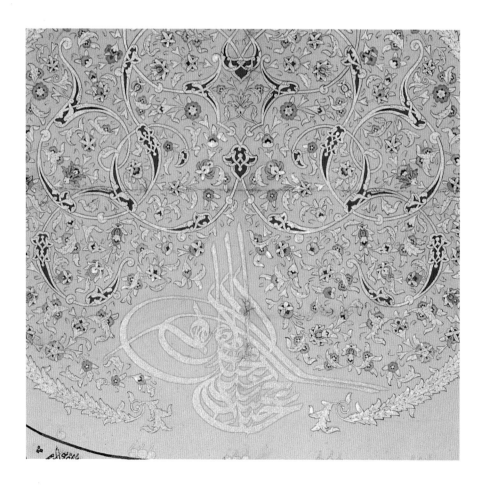

Detail, cat. no. 70

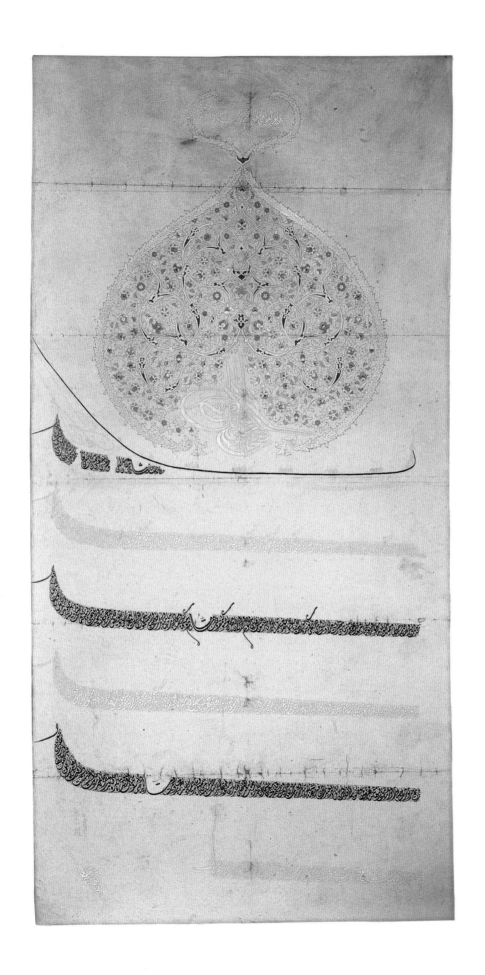

MENŞÛR

71. **Menşûr** of Abdülhamid II
Istanbul, 1316/1898
Tuğra, tevkî', and muhakkak
Ink and gold on paper
141 × 80.5 cm (54⅞ × 31⅜ in.)
(397)

This *menşûr* dates from the reign of
the thirty-fourth Ottoman emperor,
Sultan Abdülhamid II (1876–1909). It
was issued from Istanbul on Şa'ban 15,
1316/December 29, 1898, and was sent
to the emir of Mecca, Vezir Şerif
Avnürrefik Paşa. It concerns various
real properties and their incomes,
which were transferred to a foundation
to support the poor and others living
near the holy shrines in Mecca and
Medina. Because this document was
being sent to the Hijaz, it was written
in Arabic rather than Ottoman
Turkish.

It is most likely that Sâmi Efendi
(see cat. nos. 49–52) wrote the *tuğra*,
which is executed in gold ink with no
outlining. It reads: *Abdülhamid Hân
bin Abdülmecid el-muzaffer dâimâ*
(Abdülhamid Hân, son of Abdülmecid,
the ever-victorious). The text above
and below the *tuğra* is written in a
beautiful nineteenth-century version of
the long-since-abandoned *tevkî'* script.
The author believes this text was
written by Hacı Kâmil Efendi (see cat.
no. 57). At the very top of the *menşûr*
is a *besmele* written in *muhakkak*
script, using gold ink.

The Genealogy of
Ottoman Calligraphers

A major factor in the development of the art of calligraphy among the Ottoman Turks was the strong and continuous master-and-student system. To clarify this tradition, two genealogical trees have been prepared. The first is of calligraphers in the *aklâm-ı sitte* (six scripts), from Şeyh Hamdullah (833/1429–926/1520; see cat. nos. 1–2) to our era. The tree is limited, however, almost exclusively to calligraphers represented in the catalogue. (Indeed, if all the calligraphers who lived and worked within the time frame covered were included, the genealogical tree would become as huge as one of California's world-famous giant sequoias!) With Necmeddin Okyay (1300/1883–1396/1976; see cat. nos. 59–60), the great artists Mustafa Halim Özyazıcı (1315/1898–1384/1964) and Hâmid Aytaç (1309/1891–1402/1982) form the final links in a genealogy unbroken for five hundred years. (Examples of work by Halim Bey and Hâmid Bey can be seen, respectively, in figure 1, on page 2, and figure 19, on page 35, in the introduction to this volume.) Three calligraphers whose education took place outside the system sketched here are not included: Ahmed Karahisârî (875/1470?–963/1556; see cat. no. 6), Mustafa bin İbrahim (active 16th century; see cat. no. 7), and Mahmud Celâleddin (1163/1750?–1245/1829; see cat. nos. 32–33).

A second genealogical tree has been prepared for Ottoman *ta'lîk* calligraphers, some of whom are represented in the catalogue, beginning with the founder of the style, Yesârî Mehmed Es'ad Efendi (d. 1213/1798; see cat. no. 28).

Where applicable, calligraphers' names are accompanied by catalogue numbers in brackets. The names of calligraphers who are not represented in the catalogue yet who need to be mentioned are followed by the calligrapher's date of death, when it is known.

THE SIX SCRIPTS

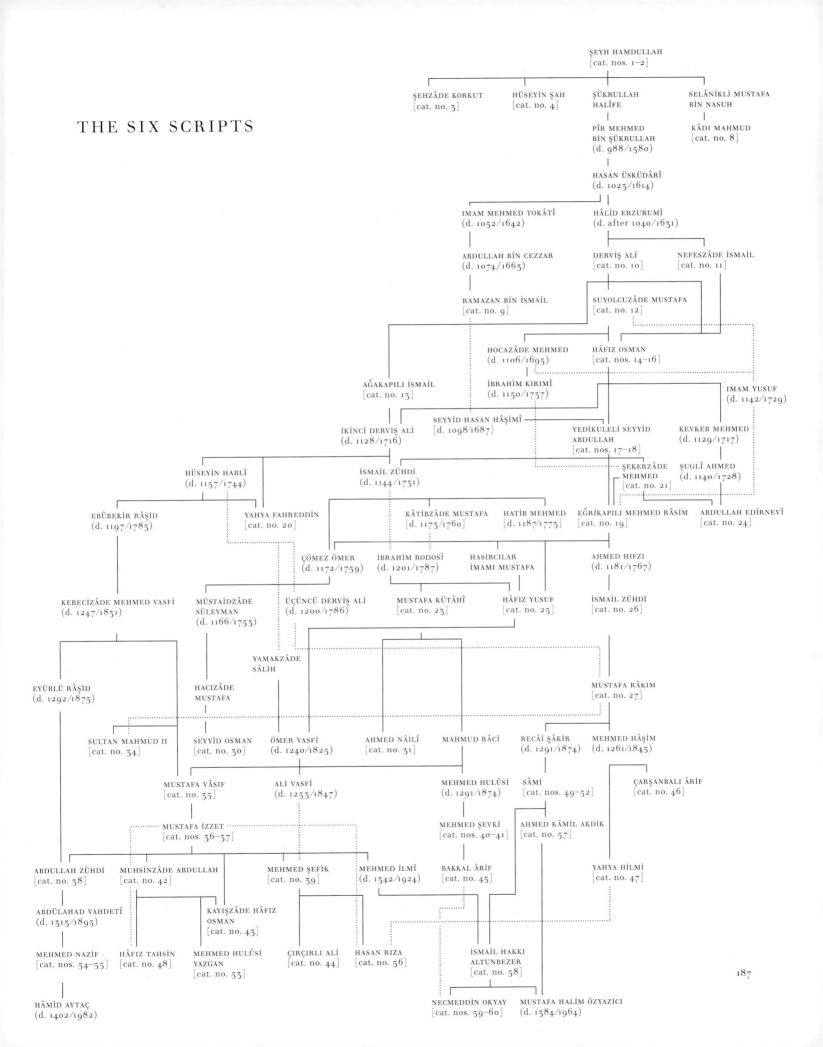

ŞEYH HAMDULLAH
[cat. nos. 1–2]

ŞEHZÂDE KORKUT
[cat. no. 3]

HÜSEYİN ŞAH
[cat. no. 4]

ŞÜKRULLAH
HALÎFE

SELÂNİKLİ MUSTAFA
BİN NASUH

PÎR MEHMED
BİN ŞÜKRULLAH
(d. 988/1580)

KÂDI MAHMUD
[cat. no. 8]

HASAN ÜSKÜDÂRÎ
(d. 1023/1614)

IMAM MEHMED TOKÂTÎ
(d. 1052/1642)

HÂLİD ERZURUMÎ
(d. after 1040/1631)

ABDULLAH BİN CEZZAR
(d. 1074/1663)

DERVİŞ ALİ
[cat. no. 10]

NEFESZÂDE İSMAİL
[cat. no. 11]

RAMAZAN BİN İSMAİL
[cat. no. 9]

SUYOLCUZÂDE MUSTAFA
[cat. no. 12]

HOCAZÂDE MEHMED
(d. 1106/1695)

HÂFIZ OSMAN
[cat. nos. 14–16]

AĞAKAPILI İSMAİL
[cat. no. 13]

İBRAHİM KIRIMÎ
(d. 1150/1737)

IMAM YUSUF
(d. 1142/1729)

SEYYİD HASAN HÂŞİMÎ
[d. 1098/1687]

YEDİKULELİ SEYYİD
ABDULLAH
[cat. nos. 17–18]

KEVKEB MEHMED
(d. 1129/1717)

İKİNCİ DERVİŞ ALİ
(d. 1128/1716)

İSMAİL ZÜHDİ
(d. 1144/1731)

ŞEKERZÂDE
MEHMED
[cat. no. 21]

ŞUGLÎ AHMED
(d. 1140/1728)

HÜSEYİN HABLÎ
(d. 1157/1744)

YAHYA FAHREDDİN
[cat. no. 20]

KÂTİBZÂDE MUSTAFA
[cat. no. 19]

HATİB MEHMED
(d. 1187/1773)

EĞRİKAPILI MEHMED RÂSİM
[cat. no. 19]

ABDULLAH EDİRNEVÎ
[cat. no. 24]

EBÛBEKİR RÂŞİD
(d. 1197/1783)

ÇÖMEZ ÖMER
(d. 1172/1759)

İBRAHİM RODOSÎ
(d. 1201/1787)

HASIRCILAR
İMAMI MUSTAFA

AHMED HIFZI
(d. 1181/1767)

KEBECİZÂDE MEHMED VASFİ
(d. 1247/1831)

MÜSTAİDZÂDE
SÜLEYMAN
(d. 1166/1753)

ÜÇÜNCÜ DERVİŞ ALİ
(d. 1200/1786)

MUSTAFA KÜTÂHÎ
[cat. no. 23]

HÂFIZ YUSUF
[cat. no. 25]

İSMAİL ZÜHDİ
[cat. no. 26]

YAMAKZÂDE
SÂLİH

EYÜBLÜ RÂŞİD
(d. 1292/1875)

HACIZÂDE
MUSTAFA

MUSTAFA RÂKIM
[cat. no. 27]

SULTAN MAHMUD II
[cat. no. 34]

SEYYİD OSMAN
[cat. no. 30]

ÖMER VASFİ
(d. 1240/1825)

AHMED NÂİLÎ
[cat. no. 31]

MAHMUD RÂCİ

RECÂİ ŞÂKİR
(d. 1291/1874)

MEHMED HÂŞİM
(d. 1261/1845)

MUSTAFA VÂSIF
[cat. no. 35]

ALİ VASFİ
(d. 1253/1847)

MEHMED HULÛSİ
(d. 1291/1874)

SÂMİ
[cat. nos. 49–52]

ÇARŞANBALI ÂRİF
[cat. no. 46]

MUSTAFA İZZET
[cat. nos. 36–37]

MEHMED ŞEVKİ
[cat. nos. 40–41]

AHMED KÂMİL AKDİK
[cat. no. 57]

ABDULLAH ZÜHDİ
[cat. no. 38]

MUHSİNZÂDE ABDULLAH
[cat. no. 42]

MEHMED ŞEFİK
[cat. no. 39]

MEHMED İLMÎ
(d. 1342/1924)

BAKKAL ÂRİF
[cat. no. 45]

YAHYA HİLMİ
[cat. no. 47]

ABDÜLAHAD VAHDETÎ
(d. 1313/1895)

KAYIŞZÂDE HÂFIZ
OSMAN
[cat. no. 43]

MEHMED NAZİF
[cat. nos. 54–55]

HÂFIZ TAHSİN
[cat. no. 48]

MEHMED HULÛSİ
YAZGAN
[cat. no. 53]

ÇIRÇIRLI ALİ
[cat. no. 44]

HASAN RIZA
[cat. no. 56]

İSMAİL HAKKI
ALTUNBEZER
[cat. no. 58]

HÂMİD AYTAÇ
(d. 1402/1982)

NECMEDDİN OKYAY
[cat. nos. 59–60]

MUSTAFA HALİM ÖZYAZICI
(d. 1384/1964)

TA'LÎK SCRIPT

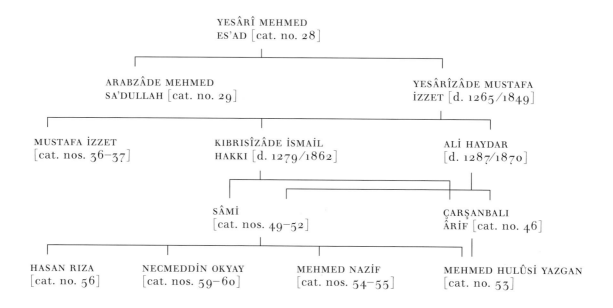

YESÂRÎ MEHMED
ES'AD [cat. no. 28]

ARABZÂDE MEHMED
SA'DULLAH [cat. no. 29]

YESÂRÎZÂDE MUSTAFA
İZZET [d. 1265/1849]

MUSTAFA İZZET
[cat. nos. 36–37]

KIBRISÎZÂDE İSMAİL
HAKKI [d. 1279/1862]

ALİ HAYDAR
[d. 1287/1870]

SÂMİ
[cat. nos. 49–52]

ÇARŞANBALI
ÂRİF [cat. no. 46]

HASAN RIZA
[cat. no. 56]

NECMEDDİN OKYAY
[cat. nos. 59–60]

MEHMED NAZİF
[cat. nos. 54–55]

MEHMED HULÛSİ YAZGAN
[cat. no. 53]

Glossary

âhâr: size applied to calligraphic paper

akkâse: calligraphic paper whose writing area and margins are dyed different colors

aklâm-ı sitte: the *sülüs, nesih, muhakkak, reyhânî, tevkî',* and *rıkâ'* scripts, together known as the six scripts

aşere gülü: rosette that appears after every ten verses of the Qur'an

bâbıâlî rık'ası: method used in Ottoman government offices for writing the *rık'a* script

berat (pl. *beratlar*): document granting an imperial title, privilege, or property

besmele: "In the name of God, the Compassionate, the Merciful"; the first sentence in the Qur'an, and the invocation that occurs at the beginning of all but one of its chapters

çakmak mühre: paper burnisher

cedvel (pl. *cedveller*): ruled gold frame surrounding the text of a calligraphic work; also a gilded line separating poetic verses or elements in a *kıt'a*

celî: scripts (with the exception of *celî dîvânî*) written larger than their normal size, with a broad-nibbed pen, or enlarged by means of squaring

celî dîvânî: version of the *dîvânî* script written with vowels, reading signs, and decorative features, and used only for the most significant documents and proclamations of the Ottoman state

çiharyâr: the first four caliphs (successors of the Prophet) Abū Bakr, ʿUmar, ʿUthmān, and ʿAlī, also called the Four Friends, whose names often appear on *hilyeler*

cüz (pl. *cüzler*): one of thirty sections of the Qur'an, generally twenty pages long

Delâilü'l-Hayrat: handbook of prayers for the Prophet

dîvânî: script that evolved from old Persian *ta'lîk;* in Ottoman Turkey, its use was restricted to the Imperial Council of State

divit: portable inkwell and penholder

durak (pl. *duraklar*): rosette-style decoration occurring between each verse of the Qur'an, as well as between the sentences of the *hilye* text; also used to punctuate *hadîsler*

ebrû: Turkish marbled paper

elif (pl. *elifler*): first letter of the Arabic alphabet, tall and vertical in shape (Arabic spelling: *alif*)

En'âm: The Cattle; chapter 6 of the Qur'an, frequently written as a separate volume

En'âm-ı Şerîf: collection of chapters from the Qur'an

etek: bottom portion of a *hilye* containing the second part of the *hilye* text, a prayer for the Prophet, and the calligrapher's signature

Fâtiha: opening chapter of the Qur'an

ferman (pl. *fermanlar*): imperial edict

Four Friends: see *çiharyâr*

göbek: central cartouche in which the first part of the *hilye* text is written

hacı: title conferred on one who has made the pilgrimage to Mecca

hadîs (pl. *hadîsler*): sayings and deeds of the Prophet recorded by his companions

hâfız: one who has memorized the Qur'an

halkârî: type of illumination in which the motifs are painted in a wash of gold ink and outlined in full-strength gold ink

hareke: vowel signs used in writing the Arabic script

hâtime: colophon

hilâl: crescent that often surrounds the *göbek* on a *hilye*

hilye (pl. *hilyeler*): *levha* composed of a text describing the Prophet Muhammad

hilye-i saadet: "the felicitous *hilye*"; term describing the complete *hilye* text

hızib gülü: rosette that occurs after every five pages of the Qur'an

hokka: inkwell

hurde (or *hafî*) *ta'lîk:* small version of the Ottoman *ta'lîk* script, used for literary works and collections of poetry, and for *fetvâlar* (opinions on Islamic canon law) and *vakfiyeler* (endowment deeds)

icâzet: calligraphy teacher's authorization for the student to sign his own name to his work; also the script (see *rıkâ'*) in which the teacher notes his approval on the permission document

icâzet **ceremony** (*icâzet cemiyeti*): assembly, usually in a mosque, at which a student who has earned the *icâzet* is presented to a jury of master calligraphers

icâzet kıt'ası: *kıt'a* written by a calligraphy student to obtain his *icâzet*

icâzetnâme (pl. *icâzetnâmeler*): document, most often in the form of an *icâzet kıt'ası*, certifying the holder to practice as a professional

iç pervaz: inner border of a *kıt'a* or *levha*

istif (pl. *istifler*): calligraphic composition

kâdı (pl. *kâdılar*): judge of Islamic law

kâdıasker*:* supreme judge

kalıp (pl. *kalıplar*): stencil used in the production of large-scale calligraphic works and inscriptions

karalama (pl. *karalamalar*): calligrapher's practice piece

kırma dîvânî*:* shorthand version of *dîvânî* script

kıt'a (pl. *kıt'alar*): small calligraphic work, usually rectangular, and generally using two scripts (one large and one small) or *ta'lîk* script alone

kol (pl. *kollar*): tail-like projection growing out of, and to the right of, the ovals of the *tuğra;* also called the *hançer*

koltuk (pl. *koltuklar*): rectangular or triangular space in *kıt'alar, hilyeler,* and *levhalar* that allows for the arrangement of longer lines of a larger script with shorter lines of a smaller script; often decorated

körüklü murakkaa*:* accordion album

kubur*:* cylindrical penholder

kürsü*:* monogram proper in the *tuğra;* also called the *sere*

kuruş*:* piaster; unit of Ottoman currency

levha (pl. *levhalar*): large-scale calligraphic composition, most commonly in the *celî sülüs* and *celî ta'lîk* scripts, that can be framed and hung in mosques, offices, and homes

lika*:* wad of raw silk used in an inkwell to absorb ink

mâil kıt'a*: kıt'a* in which the writing slants upward, from the lower right to the upper left

makta (pl. *maktalar*): pen-cutting slab

menşûr (pl. *menşûrlar*): imperial appointment

meşk (pl. *meşkler*): lesson, practice work, or sample for study

meşk kıt'ası (pl. *meşk kıt'aları*): calligraphic-exercise *kıt'a*

mıkleb*:* envelope flap attached to the back of an Islamic binding that protects the edge of the book and can be tucked between the pages to serve as a bookmark

müfredât **exercises**: elementary calligraphy exercises consisting of single and paired letters

müfredât kıt'ası (pl. *müfredât kıt'aları*): *kıt'a* consisting of *müfredât* exercises

müfredât meşki*:* lesson in writing single and paired letters

muhakkak*:* one of the group of six scripts, written with a pen whose nib is approximately 2 millimeters (^{3} 32 inch) wide; used for copying large-format Qur'ans (until the sixteenth century) and for writing the *besmele*

murakkaa (pl. *murakkaalar*): calligraphic album

mürekkebât **exercises**: advanced calligraphic exercises consisting of combinations of letters

mürekkebât kıt'ası*: kıt'a* consisting of *mürekkebât* exercises

mürekkebât meşki*:* lesson in combining letters in words and sentences

mushaf (pl. *mushaflar*): the Qur'an in a single volume or codex

nesih*:* one of the group of six scripts, written with a pen whose nib is approximately 1 millimeter (^{3} 64 inch) wide; favored in Ottoman calligraphy for copying the Qur'an; also used in writing *vakfiyeler* (endowment deeds)

nesta'lîk*:* Persian name for the Ottoman *ta'lîk* script

reisü'l-hattâtîn*:* chief of the calligraphers

reisülulemà*:* chief of the Islamic religious establishment

reyhânî*:* one of the group of six scripts, written with a pen whose nib is approximately 1 millimeter (^{3} 64 inch) wide; a smaller-scale version of the *muhakkak* script; used until the sixteenth century for copying small-format Qur'ans

rıh (or *rîk*): fine, colored sand sprinkled over writing to dry it

rıhdan*:* container for *rıh* powder

rık'a*:* script for daily use not considered worthy of artistic treatment

rıkâ'*:* one of the group of six scripts, written with a pen whose nib is approximately 1 millimeter (^{3} 64 inch) wide; a smaller-scale version of the *tevkî'* script; mainly used for official purposes and rarely for copying manuscripts; also called *icâzet* script

Rumelia: European territory of the Ottoman Empire

sancak*:* banner or standard; also a division of a province in the Ottoman Empire *sa'y:* "persevere"; a device representing this exhortation appears between the lines of writing in calligraphic exercises

secavend: symbols, in red ink, added by the calligrapher to indicate stops, pauses, and other elements in the recitation of the Qur'an

secde gülü: rosette in the border of a page of the Qur'an marking where the reader is required to prostrate himself

şemse: sunburst design stamped into a leather binding

şemse kap: classic Ottoman bookbinding using the *şemse* design, alone or in combination with other motifs, on embossed leather decorated with gold

serlevha: symmetrical double-page illumination opening a Qur'an

şeyh: sheikh

şeyhülislâm: highest Islamic authority in the Ottoman state

seyyid: descendant of the Prophet

six scripts: see *aklâm-ı sitte*

sülüs: one of the group of six scripts, written with a pen whose nib is approximately 2 millimeters (^{3}/$_{32}$ inch) wide; with *nesih*, particularly favored by Ottoman calligraphers

sûre başı (pl. *sûre başları*): chapter heading

taklîd: imitation of the work of other calligraphers as a method of education, to receive the *icâzet*, or as a token of homage

takoz (pl. *takozlar*): "chock"; extra strip of paper, illumination, or *ebrû* added to a calligraphic work, "propping up" the work in the manner of a chock

tal'îk: delicate script (unrelated to the old Persian script of the same name) written with a pen whose nib is 2 millimeters (^{3}/$_{32}$ inch) wide; largely used for writing *kıt'alar*

tashih kalemtıraşı: correction knife

tevkî': one of the group of six scripts, written with a pen whose nib is approximately 2 millimeters (^{3}/$_{32}$ inch) wide; mainly used for official purposes and rarely for copying manuscripts

tomar (pl. *tomarlar*): scroll; also the very large script and pen for writing on a scroll

tuğra (pl. *tuğralar*): sultan's calligraphic emblem

tuğrakeş (pl. *tuğrakeşler*): writer of *tuğralar*

unvan sahifesi: single illuminated opening page

vezir: one of the sultan's ministers; the grand *vezir* was the sultan's chief minister

zahriye (pl. *zahriyeler*): frontispiece

zer-endûd: method using a stencil to produce *levhalar* in gold ink or gold leaf

Selected Bibliography

Abbott, Nabia. *The Rise of the North Arabic Script and Its Kur'anic Development.* Chicago, 1939. An early attempt to uncover the origins of Arabic writing. Of historical interest but unreliable in matters related to calligraphic technique and terminology.

Abdurrahman Şeref. *Tarih musâhabeleri.* Istanbul, 1339 [1921].

Ahmed Cevdet Paşa. *Tarih-i Cevdet.* 12 vols. Istanbul, 1309 [1893].

Akimushkin, Oleg. "The Calligraphy of the St. Petersburg Album." In *The St. Petersburg Muraqqa*', pp. 39–46. Exh. cat. Milan, 1996.

Atıl, Esin. "The Nakkaşhane." In *The Age of Sultan Süleyman the Magnificent*, pp. 29–111. Exh. cat., National Gallery of Art, Washington, D.C. New York, 1987.

Ayverdi, Ekrem Hakkı. *Fatih devri hattatları ve hat san'atı.* Istanbul, 1953.

Baltacıoğlu, İsmayil Hakkı. *Türklerde yazı san'atı.* Ankara, 1958.

————. "Türk yazılarının tedkîkine medhal." *Darülfünun İlâhiyat Fakültesi mecmuası* 5–6 (1927), pp. 78–110.

Birol, İnci A., and Çiçek Derman. *Motifs in Turkish Decorative Arts.* Istanbul, 1991. In English and Turkish.

Croisier, Jean-Paul, et al. *Islamic Calligraphy: Sacred and Secular Writings.* Text of catalogue by David Lewis James. Exh. cat. Geneva: Musée d'Art et d'Histoire, 1988. In English and French. Catalogue of a traveling exhibition that was seen in Europe and Jordan, May 26, 1988, to November 11, 1989. Excellent illustrations; introductory text.

Dânişmend, İsmail Hâmi. *İzahlı Osmanlı tarihi kronolojisi.* 4 vols. Istanbul, 1947–55.

Derman, M. Uğur. "The Art of Calligraphy in Islam." *Arts: The Islamic World* 4, no. 3 (1987), pp. 81–87. A brief introductory article. Two related articles appear in the same issue.

————. *The Art of Calligraphy in the Islamic Heritage.* Translated by Mohamed Zakariya and Mohamed Asfour. Istanbul, 1998. Features 192 color illustrations of calligraphy from all periods, and the most extensive bibliography published to date on Islamic and Ottoman calligraphy. Includes a superlative essay by Nihad M. Çetin on the history of the art of calligraphy through the Yāqūt era.

————. "Calligraphy." In *The Sabancı Collection*, translated by Priscilla Mary Işın and Adair Mill, pp. 12–179. Akbank Culture and Art Publication, no. 60. Istanbul, 1995.

————. *Türk hat sanatının şâheserleri.* Istanbul, 1982. An album containing sixty-seven colorplates, with a critical description of each work and a brief biography of each calligrapher.

————."The Turks and the Art of Calligraphy." In *The Turkish Contribution to Islamic Arts*, pp. 58–84. Istanbul, 1976. In Turkish, English, and Arabic.

————. *Türk sanatında ebrû.* Istanbul, 1977. A history of Turkish paper marbling, with black-and-white illustrations. Contains valuable information on technical matters. Summary in English.

The Encyclopaedia of Islam, s.v. "Arabic writing."

The Encyclopaedia of Islam. New ed., s.v. "khatt."

Habîb. *Hatt u hattâtân.* Istanbul, 1305 [1888].

Huart, Clément. *Les Calligraphes et les miniaturistes de l'Orient musulman.* Paris, 1908.

İnal, İbnülemin Mahmud Kemal. *Son hattatlar.* Istanbul, 1955. The most important and detailed biographical volume on Ottoman and Turkish calligraphers working between the eighteenth century and 1955. With illustrations in black and white.

İnalcık, Halil. *The Ottoman Empire: The Classical Age, 1300–1600.* Translated by Norman Itzkowitz and Colin Imber. London, 1973.

James, David Lewis. *Qur'ans of the Mamlukes.* New York, 1988. Interesting, readable text but unreliable on technical matters. Excellent illustrations of superior artworks.

Khatibi, Abdelkebir, and Mohammed Sijelmassi. *The Splendor of Islamic Calligraphy.* Translation by James Hughes of *L'Art calligraphique arabe.* New York, 1976. Some illustrations of important, rarely seen Moroccan work, but they are poorly reproduced and displayed. Text is unreliable in matters of history and technique.

Kütükoğlu, Mübahat S. *Osmanlı belgelerinin dili: diplomatik.* Kubbealtı neşriyatı, no. 35. Istanbul, 1994.

Levey, Martin. *Medieval Arabic Bookmaking and Its Relation to Early Chemistry and Pharmacology.* Philadelphia, 1962. An extremely rare and valuable work that delivers everything its title promises.

Lings, Martin. *The Quranic Art of Calligraphy and Illumination.* London, 1976. Interesting text from the standpoint of Islamic mysticism. Unreliable on technique. Excellent illustrations from early Qur'ans.

Lowry, Heath. "Calligraphy—Hüsn-i Hatt." In *Tulips, Arabesques and Turbans: Decorative Arts from the Ottoman Empire*, edited by Yanni Petsopoulos, pp. 169–92. New York, 1982. Excellent short essay accompanied by illustrations of very fine Ottoman works.

Mehmed Süreyya. *Sicill-i Osmanî.* 4 vols. Istanbul, 1308–15 [1890–97].

Minorsky, T. *Calligraphers and Painters: A Treatise by Qadi Ahmad, Son of Mir-Munshi, circa A.H. 1015/A.D. 1606.*

Translated from the Persian by V. Minorsky; translated from the Russian by T. Minorsky. Smithsonian Institution, Freer Gallery of Art, Occasional Papers, vol. 3, no. 2. Washington, D.C., 1959. A valuable insight into the worldview of Persian artists and calligraphers working before A.D. 1600.

Mustafa Âli. *Menâkıb-ı hünerverân*. Edited by İbnülemin Mahmud Kemal. Istanbul, 1926.

Müstakîmzâde Süleyman Sadeddin. *Tuhfe-i hattâtîn*. Edited by İbnülemin Mahmud Kemal. Istanbul, 1928.

Nadir, Ayşegül, ed. *Imperial Ottoman Fermans*. Exh. cat. Istanbul: Türk ve İslam Eserleri Müzesi. London, 1986. In English and Turkish. Comprehensive, beautifully illustrated catalogue of an exhibition at the Museum of Turkish and Islamic Art, Istanbul, 1986–87. Reliable and useful text.

Nefeszâde İbrahim. *Gülzâr-ı savab*. Edited by Kilisli Muallim Rifat. Istanbul, 1939. A very important Ottoman source, which contains some biographies of calligraphers but whose chief value resides in its collection of formulas for inks, *âhâr* size, colors, and dyes. This is an annotated edition in modern Turkish.

Okyay, Necmeddin. Unpublished memoirs. Derman Collection, Istanbul.

Ottoman Fermans. Istanbul, 1992.

Pakalın, Mehmed Zeki. *Osmanlı tarih deyimleri ve terimleri sözlüğü*. 3 vols. Istanbul, 1971.

Rado, Şevket. *Türk hattatları*. Istanbul, [1984]. A useful overview of Ottoman and Turkish calligraphy from the origins of the art to the early 1980s. Numerous illustrations in black and white, with some colorplates.

Safadi, Yasin Hamid. *Islamic Calligraphy*. Boulder, Colo., 1979. A short, generally useful introductory work, but unreliable on technical matters. Profusely illustrated in black and white.

Safwat, Nabil F. *The Art of the Pen: Calligraphy of the 14th to 20th Centuries*. Vol. 5 of *The Nasser D. Kahlili Collection of Islamic Art*. London, 1996. Excellent, beautifully written art criticism. Knowledgeable about technical matters. An extremely valuable reference work, although some of the artworks it catalogues are of dubious quality.

———. *The Harmony of Letters: Islamic Calligraphy from the Tareq Rajab Museum*. Exh. cat. Singapore: Asian Civilization Museum, 1997. A well-written and reliable reference work.

Schimmel, Annemarie. *Calligraphy and Islamic Culture*. Hagop Kevorkian Series on Near Eastern Art and Civilization. New York, 1981. A detailed and readable personal account.

———. *Islamic Calligraphy*. Iconography of Religions, Section 22: Islam. Leiden, 1970. A short introductory work with some good illustrations.

Serin, Muhiddin. *Calligraphist Sheih Hamdullah*. Istanbul, 1998. The definitive work on Şeyh Hamdullah, beautifully illustrated. The author is both a calligrapher and a scholar of the art.

Shaw, Stanford J. *Empire of the Gazis: The Rise and Decline of the Ottoman Empire, 1280–1808*. Vol. 1 of *History of the Ottoman Empire and Modern Turkey*. Cambridge, 1976. Shaw's *History* contains perhaps the most useful and detailed outline of the history of the Ottoman state.

Sijelmassi, Mohamed. *Enluminures des manuscrits royaux au Maroc*. Courbevoie,

1987. Useful text in French, Arabic, and English. Profusely illustrated, in color, with rarely seen works in the Moroccan style. An excellent work.

Soucek, Priscilla P. "The Arts of Calligraphy." In *The Arts of the Book in Central Asia, 14th–16th Centuries*, pp. 7–34. London, 1979.

Suyolcuzâde Mehmed Necib. *Devhatülküttâb*. Edited by Kilisli Muallim Rifat. Güzel San'atlar Akademisi neşriyatından, no. 16. Istanbul, 1942.

Umur, Suha. *Osmanlı padişah tuğraları*. Istanbul, 1980. An extremely reliable and detailed reference work on the *tuğra*.

Ünver, A. Süheyl. *Türk yazı çeşitleri ve faideli bazi bilgiler*. Istanbul, 1953.

Uzunçarşılı, İsmail Hakkı. *Osmanlı tarihi*. 4 vols. Ankara, 1982–83.

Welch, Anthony. *Calligraphy in the Arts of the Muslim World*. Exh. cat. New York: Asia House Gallery. Austin, Tex., 1979. A scholarly text that uses obsolete terminology. Good illustrations, especially of calligraphy on objects.

Yazır, Mahmud Bedreddin. *Medeniyet âleminde yazı ve İslâm medeniyetinde kalem güzeli*. Edited by Uğur Derman. 3 vols. Ankara, 1972–74, 1989. A comprehensive and indispensable work on Ottoman calligraphy and related arts. This is an annotated edition in modern Turkish, with illustrations of important works.

Zakariya, Mohamed. "Islamic Calligraphy: A Technical Overview." In *Brocade of the Pen: The Art of Islamic Writing*, edited by Carol Garrett Fisher, pp. 1–17. East Lansing, Mich., 1991. A very short outline of calligraphy from the perspective of a practitioner, with examples of fifteen scripts.

Index